CONSUMER KIDS

HOW BIG BUSINESS IS GROOMING
OUR CHILDREN FOR PROFIT

Ed Mayo and Agnes Nairn

CONSTABLE • LONDON

Constable & Robinson Ltd
3 The Lanchesters
162 Fulham Palace Road
London W6 9ER
www.constablerobinson.com

First published in the UK by Constable,
an imprint of Constable & Robinson Ltd

A copy of the British Library Cataloguing in
Publication Data is available from the British Library

ISBN: 978-1-84529-880-7

Printed and bound in the EU

1 3 5 7 9 10 8 6 4 2

Ed Mayo is a leading campaigner and commentator on social and economic issues and is Chief Executive of Consumer Focus. Ed has written widely, including research on children as consumers, described by Jonathan Freedland in the *Guardian* as 'a groundbreaking study'. Ed helped to found the Fairtrade brand and was the strategist behind the world's most successful anti-poverty campaign, Jubilee 2000. The *Guardian* nominated him as one of the top 100 most influential social innovators and he is a World Economics Forum 'Young Global Leader'. Ed is married with three children and lives in South East London.

Dr Agnes Nairn is an academic researcher, writer, speaker and consultant. She is Professor of Marketing at two of Europe's leading business schools, EM-Lyon Business School in France and RSM Erasmus University in the Netherlands. Agnes's academic research has been published in a wide range of international journals and her policy-related work includes the first study of the links between media exposure, materialism and self-esteem in UK children. She has also written on Barbie torture, how children use David Beckham to understand moral values, covert marketing techniques on the internet and how neuroscience throws new light on how children relate to advertising. She is on the government panel convened by the Department of Children, Schools and Families to assess the impact of the commercial world on children. Agnes is married with two daughters and lives in Bath.

To the children in both our families:
Joe, Siân, Tom, Frankie and Mollie.

Contents

Acknowledgements

This book is above all a work of investigation, bringing together research we have completed over recent years and, as such, we owe a huge debt of thanks to everyone who opened up a window for us on their experience of today's consumer kids. The data we have gathered first hand comes from almost 3,000 children and over 300 parents and, while we can't thank them all individually, we gratefully acknowledge that, without their insight, ideas and support, *Consumer Kids* would not exist. We have met many wonderful people of every age in the preparation of this book and met them again as we worked through thousands of pages of conversation transcripts, calculated streams of statistics from the quantitative research, read scrapbooks and watched again and again the many hours of video footage that captured the thoughts and feelings of the families that gave us their time. We want to thank those who collaborated with us on this research, including Paul Bottomley, Anna Fielder, Cordelia Fine, Will Gardner, Christine Griffin, Stephanie

O'Donohoe, Jo Ormrod, Jillian Pitt, Graeme Traynor and Patricia Gaya Wicks.

Alongside this contact with children and parents, we have delved into the practices of the companies that generate returns to shareholders through the profits they make by selling to kids. We talked to marketers and market researchers who were generous with their time. Many are passionate advocates for children, aware that marketing to them is a sensitive issue and aware, too, that all is not right. When we asked a number of marketing leaders to share non-confidential information, we were given a warm and generous response, including from Marita Carballo (TNS), Vanessa Edwards (WPP), Jez Frampton (Interbrand), Adam Hildreth (Crisp Thinking), Robert Lerwill (Aegis), Kieran O'Neill (Holy Lemon), Ben Page (Ipsos MORI) and Mark Read (WPP).

The subject of this book has been one of wide interest and we have learned a lot from contact and suggestions from Baroness Susan Greenfield and Jonathan Sharples of Centre for the Future of the Mind, Oxford University (on marketing and the development of children's brains), Sue Palmer (whose book *Toxic Childhood* has stirred new debate), Juliet Schor (who prompted and inspired us to look further), Chris Pole and Sharon Boden (for their research on children and clothing), Andy Croft (whose poetry produced with children you will read in later chapters), Mary and Liam Caulfield, Sharon McLaughlin (for her work on video-games), Mary MacLeod and Lucy Lloyd (at the Family and Parenting Institute), Sylvie Collins-Mayo (Kingston University), Geoff

Mulgan (Young Foundation), Barbara Crowther and Harriet Lamb (at the Fairtrade Foundation), colleagues at University of Bath, EM-Lyon Business School and at Consumer Focus, and its predecessor, the National Consumer Council, including Gilles Marion, Christiane Prange, Florence Thizy, Philip Cullum, Martyn Evans, Rhys Evans, Jeff French, Diane Gaston, Chris Holmes, Jill Johnstone, Rowena Merritt, Dawn Muspratt, Jennifer Wallace and Larry Whitty.

Just as children's experiences vary across age, place, class and community, so families come in different forms with different ideas of how to be true to being a good parent in today's world. So, with the support of the charity, Care for the Family, we set up a 'Pester-power' online survey to see what survival tips parents would have. Altogether, we collected over 1,183 tips, summarized in the pamphlet *Pester-power: families surviving the consumer society*, published by Care for the Family in Parents' Week 2007. We are grateful for the open arms of Dr Samantha Callan, Rob Parsons and Jon Matthias, who could see immediately what an issue this was for families today.

Mistakes, as they say, are ours, but a number of people were kind enough to minimize them by looking over drafts of the book, including Professor Philip Graham (Emeritus Professor of Child Psychiatry at the Institute of Child Health and member of the Children's Society Good Childhood Inquiry), Andrew Simms (Policy Director at the New Economics Foundation and author of *Tescopoly*), Sue Davies (Policy Officer at Which?), Katy Evans-Bush (poet and National Consumer Council), Philip Monaghan, Jill Chapman (secondary school teacher and environment group leader) and Jennifer Renney (lawyer). In particular, author of children's and parenting books, Caroline Young gave us invaluable advice and help on our first full draft.

We'd both like to thank our parents David and Effie Nairn and Susan Mayo for their love and support over the past decades, not least when we were children ourselves. We owe our partners, Courtney and John, very special thanks as they gave us time and space to research and write. Alongside these family members there were five people that ceded space on the computer and looked through chapters as they emerged, propping them up to read in bed and putting away, for a short moment, their GCSE texts, Malorie Blackman, Philip Pullman or JK Rowling. The five, of course, are our respective children. Thank you all.

Introduction

Who's your child working for?

Sarah is a bright and bubbly girl. She enjoys Brownies on Mondays, modern dance on Tuesdays and she's just got a place in the elite gymnastics squad at the local Eagles club, which means training three times a week and travelling to competitions around the country. She has an easy-going nature, making her a little 'people magnet' – always the centre of fun and laughter at school. She goes on the computer a lot and has just started using the internet to play games and chat.

Sarah also has a secret. Because she's a busy little girl with lots of contacts in lots of places, she has been recruited through a children's chat room site to work as a sales agent for the Barbie Girls MP3 player. It's quite a tough job. OK, the job provided her with a brand new, shiny, pink Barbie Girls MP3 player but she must be sure that it accompanies her wherever she goes: to school, to gym, to Brownies, to training sessions, to dance – everywhere. And she can't just leave it in the locker room: she has been instructed to extol the many and various virtues of the Barbie

Girl MP3 player to everyone she meets and urge them to buy one too. What's more, she has been briefed to take copious photos of each and every one of these sales missions and mail them back to the chat room for Mattel.

Her demanding job description also includes constructing and designing her own fan site for the MP3 player and conscripting her extended network of friends into membership. And it doesn't stop there. Sarah has to log on to her favourite websites and blog madly about Barbie Girl and then persuade all of her mates to meet her on the Barbie Girl website so she can pepper their conversations with product recommendations. Because this is a serious contemporary employment contract she is on a payment-by-results scheme too. There are points to be collected for leaving Barbie endorsements on other sites and bonuses for producing truly convincing photographic evidence that she is selling hard, hard, hard.

Sarah, by the way, is 7 years old.

Hard to believe? Well, in 2007, 7 to 11-year-old girls up and down the UK were recruited by Dubit on behalf of Mattel to market the Barbie Girl MP3 player, while primary school boys of the same age were signed up to sell their Hot Wheels brand.[1] Every weekend, a range of children from seven and up report back what is in and what is out to companies. The truth, widely known in the marketing world, is that children are wonderful salespeople and conduits to other children. Young people know this too. Liam, who is 16, told us quite clearly: 'The most effective marketing to young people is by other young people.' Whether they are paid to do so or whether they advertise for free, they are like walking billboards for the brands they like, from the bag over their shoulder to the shoes on their feet or the phone in their hand.

Commercial cocoon

Children today are cogs in a great, spinning commercial wheel. Whilst children actually working for brands in the way Sarah is are still in a minority, all children are encouraged to want, to buy, to drink, to snack, to collect, to grow up fast and get spending. Children are consumers and by and large they enjoy it, but some of what is on offer is problematic. The marketing that surrounds them is full of sexual promise yet they are supposed to be passive onlookers, to remain sexually naïve. Touched-up, choreographed images, adverts and celebrities fill their world with offers of beauty and perfection and yet they are meant to be comfortable in their own skin and build their own self-esteem. In a country where nobody goes hungry, commercial life conspires to encourage a diet of sugar, salt and fat. Even when kept safe at home, for fear of risks outside, the drip-feed of entertainment on the screens of their computers and TVs is suffused with commercial, persuasive intent.

Few books about childhood or family, if any, have focused on the slew of time that children now spend as consumers. This world of consumer kids is not just about shopping and advertising, but about playgrounds, streets, bedrooms, the friendships children make and the new technologies they embrace.

Our story

The two of us met through connections that spanned a range of countries. Agnes is an academic, who lectures, researches and consults in marketing, primarily in the UK, France and the Netherlands. Ed is a campaigner, with a track record in marketing for the public good, helping to start initiatives, from the Jubilee 2000 coalition on Third World debt, the Fairtrade Mark and, most recently, the shoppers' rights group Consumer Focus. The woman that brought us together, on the end of an email, is a radical economist from Boston, USA, called Juliet Schor. Nestled high up in the remote mountains of the French-Italian border in 2005, very far from the nearest billboard, Agnes was reading up on pioneering research by Juliet on children's mental health and their consumer involvement. A morning email across to Juliet, asking whether anyone was doing similar research in the UK, got an answer that afternoon – 'you need to work with Ed'. Well, we took her advice and this book is the result.

Three years on, there is now a good deal of research, some of it by us and some by others, which together reveals a fascinating picture of childhood and the way that companies interact with our families without us necessarily realizing it. Perhaps we are so used to it that we can't quite see it or understand it. The creep and reach of marketing into the lives of children is a story that cries out to be told, both because of its rise to economic prominence and, as we shall see, its questionable effects. Chasing profit is what companies do and, in today's consumer world, the children's market is a gold-rush opportunity for those prospecting for profit. Children really are good as gold.

The child catchers

To be sure, there are upsides. Life as a consumer is a story of fun for kids, with all of the pleasures and joys that unfold from their engagement with film, foods, toys, gadgets and games. By and large, children embrace these as opportunities, although, as we shall see, they are not uncritical. However, the downsides, we believe, are no less real and result, as night follows day, from the practices of the companies that we call the child catchers. These are businesses that are making calculated choices to target children at a younger and younger age. They play on their dreams and exploit their vulnerabilities. At the same time, they simultaneously re-sell nostalgic images of youth back to adults in a society that doesn't really want to grow up and can stay young by buying for its children. All of this, of course, has an environmental edge to it, too. In the context of climate change, we are being asked to cut wasteful patterns of consumption at the same time as we are raising a new generation of eager consumer kids.

The inner world of children is shaped by an outside world which promises happiness, freedom and fulfilment. These three wishes come not from a magic lamp but from being a consumer. As adults, we are all complicit in living out this consumer promise and perhaps even believing in it. What we have not confronted is the subject of this book, which is the dramatic step-change in the extent of commercial exposure that children now face. The commercial world that consumer kids inhabit, on phones, TVs or computers, is now far less mediated by adults than ever before. When opportunity becomes overload, this has a psychological effect and the evidence we set out clearly suggests that the more materialistic children become, the less happy they, and their family lives, are likely to be.

Young people have their own words for this. For each chapter, we introduce the theme through what one of the children in our research has to say. And it is down to the children that we talked to that this is not in any way a book of panic. Instead, inspired by them, it is a call for hope and action. Later on, we look at the resilience of children and some of the positive ways in which young people are responding to the consumer world. We talk to some astonishingly successful young entrepreneurs, young mayors and young feminists. We look at how pocket money can provide an effective way for parents to help their kids through the commercial jungle and we explore what schools, and society more widely, can do to give children the chance to be more than consumer kids and to shape the world around them.

We start by taking a look at the latest facts and figures on consumer kids and expose examples of marketing to children, the scale and sophistication of which will shock many parents. We look at the industry behind this – the child catchers – who are the unseen influence on families up and down the country. These are the companies that help to shape the world around children, in turn shaping children's own sense of who they are and what matters to them. We then look at the different scenes in which commercial opportunities and pressures play out for families, from fashion and food through to technology and social networks. Your children, in short, are their market.

Part One: Catching Children

1. Your Children, Their Market

'I just spend money all the time. Nothing I can do . . .'

Shannon, age 11

Let us introduce you to Lorna. She is 8 years old. She lives in Nottingham and, like many children, she enjoys getting letters. Even so, her parents were surprised when the letterbox started filling up with personalized letters from credit companies offering her own credit card. She was, most said, pre-selected. A card was ready at a 'modest introductory rate', although 'modest' still added up to the equivalent of 3 or 4 percentage points APR for each year of her life.

Of course, as you would expect, Lorna's credit history, like most primary school children, was impeccable. She'd missed out on pocket money once for minor in-house anti-social behaviour (involving her younger brother, his toys and subsequent tears) and she still had a Christmas gift voucher from her grandmother to spend, but otherwise she had never yet defaulted on a loan. In ten years' time, as a student, she may be deep in debt, but whatever marketing database of good credit risk she was on had clearly failed to track anyone's date of birth and missed the simple fact that she was still in Year 3 of primary school.

A voracious credit market regularly throws up examples like this. Lorna's parents wrote to complain, and were understandably irritated when yet more personalized offers for loans and credit cards came through for her over the following months. Now they guard the letterbox in the morning, to make sure that they screen what Lorna receives.

Lorna's credit offers are just a few of the 4.6 billion items of marketing material that come through our doors each year.[1] As it happens, in this instance, Lorna's parents had protection in law. There was no way that Lorna could really enter a world of personal debt at primary school, because the credit card is one of the few consumer products that under-18-year-olds can't sign up to. However, a girl of Lorna's age, in a world where 8 years old is now the average age for a first mobile phone, can sign up to an astonishing range of other commercial products and inducements.

As her family sees it, parenting today means being on guard not just against junk mail, but also against junk food, junk drink, junk entertainment and junk culture. Lorna is as bright and chatty as any 8-year-old, but one way or another, her childhood (and the childhood of every one of the UK's 11 million people aged 15 or under – 5.6 million boys and 5.4 million girls) is touched by commercial pressures and opportunities as hungry businesses are finding ways to groom children for profit.

In this first chapter, we will explore the commercial life of children, exposing the scale of contemporary children's marketing and the child catchers behind it, before moving on, in Chapter 2, to look at the sophistication of some of the tactics they deploy. Then we will explore key markets, including fashion, food, technology and social networks, for catching consumer kids.

The consumer lens

If we go shopping with today's children what will we find them buying and spending? Well, there are some things on their shelf that adults would remember from their own days – one in five 10-year-olds, for example, still reads the *Beano*.[2] However, it's the sheer amount that they spend which marks out this generation from the last. Children up to 19 spend a remarkable £12 billion from their own pocket money or part-time jobs.[3] They wear a hefty measure of this as £1.53 billion is exchanged in shopping centres for clothes and shoes. They eat and drink almost £1 billion, gobbling up £860 million in sweets, soft drinks, crisps and snacks. (Healthy food doesn't feature very heavily when they are spending their own money.) The record labels and software houses take nearly another £1 billion with £440 million going on music and £340 million exchanged for computer software. The balance goes mainly on looking and smelling great as children accumulate an ever-growing array of potions and lotions for a better looking body, a prettier face and sleeker, shinier hair.[4]

This £12 billion sounds like a sizeable and attractive

children's market, but it doesn't include the far, far greater sums that parents spend on children for clothes, toys, TVs, phones and holidays. As we will see, £12 billion is only a small part of the astonishing total value of the children's market in the UK.

This is also a global phenomenon. The rise of consumer kids is not unique to the UK, or indeed to UK and the USA. Every European country has a similar story to tell. Even in China, the newest consumers are the 312 million children under the age of 15. Clothes sales for children have doubled in four years and among the favourite brands mentioned by Chinese youth are Nike, Louis Vuitton, Sony and Nokia (as well as Korean movies like *My Sassy Girl* and Korean musicians such as *Rain*). One research firm, Access Asia, reports that:

China's children are bombarded with media messages from all angles, all the time – from billboards, posters, TV at home, TV in taxis, cinemas, magazines, food packaging, lunch boxes, clothing, text messages, websites, store shelves, radios, etc. This new global generation has a world view that their parents' generation never dreamed of, has access to better healthcare, better education, more and better toys and electronic gadgets and not only a wider choice of careers to aspire to, but choice, full stop.[5]

Ben Page from Ipsos MORI is a seasoned trend-spotter. He describes children today as 'massively sophisticated consumers'. They have unlimited access to information.

Even from the age of 12, there is no sense that there are things they are not allowed to know. They inhabit a bigger world, with more cash-intensive hobbies and a social life that involves travel to gigs and festivals rather than popping next door. 'All activities,' he concludes, 'are scrutinised through the consumer lens.'[6]

So a shopping trip with today's child opens up a world of commercial opportunity and engagement. However, a house full of sweets, clothes, music, gadgets and toys is not just difficult to tidy, but may have diminishing returns. Many parents talk of their children becoming bored with what they have. Four out of five children under the age of 12 receive over ten toys a year, although close to two-thirds of those toys are then thrown, unbroken, away.[7] Of course, the reason is that, for children just as for their parents, the consumer promise is that there is always more just around the corner . . .

Every little girl's dream

So what relationship do children have with the things that they own? How do they feel about their possessions? To answer this, let us describe one of our research projects.

It was in a bright, colourful classroom on a sunny day in the southwest of England that a small group of primary-school girls gathered in a circle and opened our eyes to the maelstrom of feelings that children experience in today's commercial world. The research tool was simply a picture of a Barbie doll and the question put to the children was whether Barbie should be counted as a 'cool' or an 'uncool' thing to buy.[8] The children's discussions were passionate and fierce but as we listened that afternoon we found that their contribution went far further than that, as we stumbled into a turbulent inner child's world that was in part a reflection of a ferocious billion-euro rivalry between two toy companies.

Love her or hate her, Barbie is surely the world's most famous toy. Launched in 1959 as a 'teenage fashion model', the doll was created by Ruth Handler and named after her daughter. The inspiration for the doll was Lilli, a sassy cartoon character from a German adult magazine. In Handler's mind, she wanted to create a doll that would 'project every little girl's dream of the future'.[9] Since then, over one billion Barbie dolls have been sold worldwide. The conglomerate behind the dolls, Mattel, claims that three Barbie dolls are sold every second. And, although instantly recognizable, she has also been versatile. Barbie has had close to 100 careers, from president to mermaid.[10]

It is natural for dolls to evoke strong feelings. For many people, our closest toy, doll or teddy bear, stays with us for life, whether in memory, in the attic or passed down to the next generation. Dolls are designed to work as imaginary friends, something on to whom children can project their hopes and fears. However, the reaction of these contemporary girls, and this was subsequently borne out by other children over the course of our research, was not quite what we expected.

Quite simply, far from being loved, Barbie provoked reactions of rejection, hatred and violence. As soon as the image of Barbie appeared, the children expressed their dislike. One girl immediately responded, 'Urgh, no, please turn the page, no, please!', a second joined in, saying 'That is so not cool! Ugggh!' and a third pleaded 'Turn the next page, so not cool at all!' Another simply said 'No!'

But it did not stop there. The girls went on to share, one after another, how they had turned their dislike of the doll into play where they tortured their Barbie. Maiming, decapitation and being put in the microwave were just some of the punishments used. Sold as cute, feminine and beautiful, Barbie was dropped out of windows, burnt, broken and had her hair shaved off. One girl seemed to sum up the situation: 'I still have loads of them so I can torture them.' Her friend agreed, 'Me too, coz they're not particularly cool unless you torture them.'

It wasn't just the girls, boys enjoyed a bit of Barbie torture too. One said, 'The one thing I like about Barbie is that they're quite good at destroying.' Another, in response, explained that 'My sister had one a very, very long time ago and I did like putting soap over them and burning them and breaking them.' While a third said, showing with his hands what he meant, 'You grab their hair and pull their heads off.'

Even though some of the girls actually did play with Barbies, there was an agreed code that it was not cool to admit to enjoying playing with them. Playing with Barbie was presented as a last resort option ('when I don't know what to do') rather than a toy of choice. For most, this was a toy they felt they had outgrown – as though disavowing Barbie was a rite of passage and a rejection of their past.

As one 7-year-old girl said, 'I think I am a bit old for Barbie now. I have got a whole box of them but . . . they're under my bed.' Even so, the violence and hatred was far more than could be explained by a simple repudiation of a previous life stage.

All kinds of woes could perhaps be read into this new phenomenon of young Barbie-barbarians. But, in reality, as we looked deeper, it confirmed this is not some *Lord of the Flies* episode of feral children turning to brutality. It was more subtle, as if the children involved were reacting viscerally against a product that tried to package and sell a very particular fantasy of how they should be. They were, in short, exhibiting their reactions to the world of hard-sell.

In a commercial world where kids are encouraged to grow up fast, Barbie is hated because she is babyish. She is also hated because, although promising to be a playmate or friend, to love and be loved in return, she is a commodity. There is no magic, only betrayal. While Barbie masquerades as a person, she actually exists in multiple selves. The children never talked of one, single, special Barbie. She was always referred to in the plural. Most children not only had more than one Barbie, they had a box of Barbies, and not just a box – a very large box. A box is a place to put things, not a cherished friend. Barbie has become inanimate, an 'it'. She 'should be a human', as one girl put it, but clearly for the children she is not. Losing any individual warmth she might have promised, Barbie symbolizes excess and disposability. When they talked about owning a Barbie, the implication was always one of excess – having too many Barbies.

But having too many Barbies is, of course, just what the marketers at Mattel want.

Bratz battle it out with Barbie

Mattel dismisses the implication that the magic might be wearing off. 'Annual sales of 94 million Barbies are proof that the doll is widely loved by children,' it says.[11] But news of girls torturing their Barbie is doubly sensitive to the company as it faces a ruthless struggle with its competitor, toy company MGA Entertainment. MGA is the inventor of Bratz: older, sexier, sassier, doe-eyed dolls. Bratz had only just hit the shelves when we talked to our 7-year-olds but now they outsell Barbie dolls in the UK by two to one.[12] What we had uncovered was the evidence of collateral from a vicious brawl between rival competitors for children's mindshare. With both companies fighting it out on screen, at shop checkouts and in court, the competition has not gone unnoticed. Investigative journalist Eric Clark found that:

> Barbie's role as a doll representing woman as a sexual object has been supplanted by Bratz. (Interestingly, mothers whose own mothers squirmed at Barbie's impossible shape now see her as the traditional safe doll.) Bratz is the doll of the Britney Spears generation, with her skimpy clothes, thick make-up and crazes for boys and fashion. The spin-offs reinforce it: *The Bratz Superstyling Funktivity Book* for six-year-olds has 'luscious lip tips', 'design your own sexy skirt', and 'tips

on being an irresistible flirt' . . . It is all part of the sexualizing of younger target groups for marketing reasons. Always a selling instrument, sex is now aimed firmly at tweens (so-called because they are classified by marketers as falling 'between' early childhood and teenage years). It is meant to make them feel older, more empowered, more likely to demand successfully what they want.[13]

The success of Bratz marketing is clear across products. It is now one of the top video-games, only just tailing the massively popular *Need for Speed*.[14]

Pester-power

The 'need for speed' captures perfectly the mindset of today's consumer kids. There is no question in our minds that, by and large, children enjoy and embrace consumer life as a thrill and a pleasure. Our research paints a picture of children who see themselves as enthusiastic consumers – a 'shopping generation'.[15] They enjoy buying and, as good consumers, care about getting the right thing. One girl, age 14, describes it like this: 'It reminds me of chocolates. When you've bought something and you feel proud, like it releases a happy hormone.'

Children as young as 8–10 years old are often already keen consumer kids. As one girl, Becky, 10, from Oswestry put it with clear logic, 'the things in the shops need buying!'[16] From Becky's age and above, it is clear too that children are often at the head of the marketing curve. In the field of computer games, some products come directly from the work of young gamers, helping to generate ideas or test pre-release versions. Online, more and more children are generating their own content, including music, film, comment, image and personal biography. As we will see later, in the field of technology they are often innovation leaders. Adults, be warned – it's keep up or keep out. 'If you're not on MySpace, you don't exist,' says one 18-year-old, Skyler.[17]

It is perhaps no surprise to reveal that most children are used to getting their own way. As one 12-year-old boy told us, 'I just kept asking her, and in the end she just gave up and got it.' And perhaps more parents do just give up and get it. In what marketers identify as the 'I'm sorry' syndrome, today's parents pay for treats and gifts as if to compensate for a lack of quality time: I'm sorry I work late; I'm sorry we don't eat together; I'm sorry I'm not home. Any mum or dad who has gone through a separation will recognize the temptation. If sharing custody means less time with your child, you may spend more freely on them or even compete to be more generous.

To be a parent can feel like trying to be a genius at finding new ways of saying 'no'. If you don't get it right, then children have their own ways of changing your mind. They will go the easy way or the hard way. When parents say no most children resort to 'direct action' – including temper tantrums and tears. Around three out of five children say they pester their parents to get what they want and that they get annoyed or slam doors if the answer is no.[18] Pester-power is alive and well. As one girl said, 'I have certain moods when I'm like yeah, let's go shopping. I don't think my mum wants to go with me ever again for putting her in debt'.

Parents are caught up in the commercial net just as much as their children. The trends associated with the anxieties of parenthood are a marketing dream. Worried about gangs? The Essex-based company, Bladerunner, can sell you stab-proof children's T-shirts. Worried about who your child is talking to on their phone? The Teddyfone lets you listen in, in secret, to every call. Fearful of abduction? You could soon get a school uniform with satellite tracking sewn in, from Trutex, the country's favourite. Or, if they are pre-school, you can use a 'toddler tag' from Connect Software, which comes in badges and bracelets. Concerned about internet safety? Why not buy Net Nanny, the screening software? Think your child could be talented? Then sign up to Baby Einstein, their toys could just help make your child smarter.[19] If you prefer creativity to general relativity when your kid grows up, their products also include Baby Mozart, Baby Van Gogh and Baby Beethoven.

The cost of heeding such advice can be high. Vicky Tuck, the principal of Cheltenham Ladies' College, claimed over Christmas 2007 that today's 'helicopter parents' are buzzing protectively around their offspring and 'hindering their child's ability to learn and become self-sufficient because they are constantly hovering overhead, supervising and directing'. The 'least selfish thing' a parent can do for their child, she says, somewhat brazenly, is to send him or her to a boarding school . . . like hers.[20] Cheque books out all around. In fact, all schools are increasingly caught up in commercial marketing, from collecting vouchers for sports equipment and computers through to competing for grants to do up their playgrounds. As the posters go up and teachers press children to take part, it may feel like a wall of marketing to parents. But it all works – families who get involved are found to be 30 per cent more likely to shop with the company concerned.[21]

Adulthood and childhood converge

We can see other ways in which the commercial net is tightening around family relationships. An increasing number of studies show that children have an astonishingly strong influence over parents' decisions in major household purchases such as cars, holidays, leisure and even loans.[22] We talked to one 8-year-old boy who wanted his father to take out a finance deal he had heard about on the radio because he thought his dad deserved to be able to afford a BMW. The old idea, you could say, was one of marketing primarily to parents as a way of selling products for children. That now belongs to a bygone age. Today, marketing to children is the way to sell products for parents. This is particularly true for new technology. Researchers in Austria concluded that in many cases children introduce new products into the family and become role models for their parents to learn from or experts whom parents admire but don't really understand.[23]

Targeting children rather than their parents makes profit-sense on another level. After leaving their teens, adults retain their product preferences from earlier years. It is also true, perhaps most intriguingly, that adults cling to many of the same values as teenagers in an attempt, like Peter Pan, to prolong childhood. It is as if nobody is happy being their age. The companies that track marketing trends talk of 'age compression' and the emergence of 'kidults', where adolescence is stretched at both ends and reaches through to later life. Some believe that by 2012, 30 will be the new 21, the official age when you become an adult, as many will still be living with their parents and will have put off marriage until later. Adults staying younger older, kids getting older younger . . . it is not just that modern society is turning children into adults, but that it is also turning adults into children.[24]

This process can be captured in a single word that makes or breaks companies and their products. It is whether or not they are 'cool'. As a result, many products now sell according to their symbolism rather than their function. The generation of consumers who, in the late 1950s, gave rise to the wonderfully informative magazine, *Which?*, focused on price and value. This was about straightforward consumer choice. Now what is symbolically cool and what is not defines what sells.

£99 billion market

So, if we take into account not just what kids are buying on their own, but what their parents spend on them, what is the size of the children's market? Pulling together these numbers gives a total child-oriented market in the UK of

£99.12 billion[25] and over the last five years it has grown 33 per cent.[26]

Little wonder then that corporations are eager to have a slice of this large and growing pie. As we shall see, the infiltration of commercialism into almost all spheres of children's lives over the past decade is such that there is no easy line to draw between what is commercial or not commercial for children. Children inhabit a seamless, branded world where celebrities, toys, TV shows and electronics are almost indistinguishable.[27] What is designed to persuade and what is designed to entertain is hard to tell apart. Marketing can rarely be isolated from the world they live in, except in its most visible form of adverts on billboards and commercial breaks on TV. Companies that are marketing to children are far more numerous than those we see on TV screens. Hello Kitty is a marketing phenomenon for girls that does not advertise direct, but seems to have licensed every product imaginable – from a lavishly pink Hello Kitty laptop by NEC through to a pink Hello Kitty AK47 assault rifle: a perfect gift for the young lady of the house.[28] Visit the Sanrio Hello Kitty shop in Bluewater Shopping Centre in Kent and you can see the range of products on display . . . along with a sign on the counter that reads 'we are not responsible for your child's purchase'.

Other companies engage children in market research to help in product design. Levi Strauss was first to recruit 'cool' kids to advise them but it's now common practice to attract 'kid engineers'. Brainstorming among young consumers is supposed to have led Heinz to produce its 'E-Z squeeze' bottles.

And as the direct marketing industry can collect marketing data from children without parental consent from as young as 14, promotions encouraging children to text or log on with their details have been hugely successful.

Who is marketing to children? Everyone along the chain in a £99 billion market. It is the stockholders of Mattel Inc., the brand managers for hi-tech gadgets and the buyers of the children's clothing range at major retailers. It is the small agencies selling information about kids to big consumer corporations and it is the giant media conglomerates which profit from the space and time sold to the highest bidder. It is the websites which provide free 24/7 entertainment to kids whilst giving advertisers from around the world unlimited access to the child audience. It is sports stars who cash in on their fame to endorse products. It is the shop-keepers who put junk food at the check-out. As the profit motive seeps into all aspects of our lives, the number and nature of the child catchers continues to grow.

View from the captured child

What is the child's view of marketing? Children mostly enjoy what the consumer world offers them. But they also feel that some things are not right. The young people we spoke to were quick to point out that the good times of consumer life also come with downsides. There appears to be three key groups of problems: feeling under pressure to buy; not having enough money to buy; and being ripped-off and put down.

Pressure to buy

The first challenge is when children feel as if they are under pressure to consume. After all, in a consumer society, what you have can be the key to how you fit in. As one 15-year-old boy put it, 'When all your friends are talking about that stupid game and you haven't got it, it makes you feel left out.' For girls, this is often about clothes – as one 14-year-old said: 'There's so much nice stuff [clothes] around and it's just getting nicer and nicer. It's like, I want that and that and that.'

Girls are also conscious of feeling under pressure to buy products to make them look good. In the words of one of Lily Allen's songs, 'if I buy those jeans, I can look like Kate Moss'.[29] This pressure can play on teenage vulnerabilities in terms of self-esteem and self-image. Jodiel, 15, explained: 'You know, when you are in a dressing room and it looks so pretty on the model and it's like it doesn't look like that on me. That makes me really angry and makes me want to stop it all.' We look at this more closely later on in this book when we examine the new focus of the fashion industry on children.

The pressure to consume can lock children into spending. As Sharon who introduced this chapter told us: 'I don't want to be a shopaholic but I just spend money all the time. Nothing I can do . . .' In some of our focus groups children, particularly girls, touched on this issue of young shopaholics – about spending pocket money as soon as it comes in, borrowing money from friends, buying more than one version of the same thing, and being impulsive but then ending up in guilt and remorse.

Can't buy

The second problem is when children (and their parents) can't afford what they are being encouraged to buy. The children that are most interested in consumer life are, in fact, those from households with the least money. They are more likely to be 'brand aware', to wish their family 'could afford to buy more of what I want' and to be bothered about the make of the family car.

Parents struggle hard to protect their children from shame – and to make sure that their children's lunchboxes are as full of branded items as their classmates. In this way, snacks like crisps or chocolates are not seen as luxuries but as a way for their children to participate in conventional behaviour. This connects with research that suggests that, when they do get it, children in poorer households get *more* pocket money than others – particularly at primary school. It has long been recognized that not wearing the 'correct clothes' can lead children to embarrassment and bullying.[30] In one UK study, children from poorer backgrounds said they would not talk to children who were not wearing the 'right' trainers.[31]

This is poverty twisting the knife. In a consumer society, all the marketing and media that tells others what they can have also tells you what you can't. Inevitably, every new product that promotes inclusion, whether the trainers on your feet or the clothes you wear, can also create exclusion. As Camilla Batmanghelidjh, founder of the charity Kids' Company (which provides emotional and educational support to vulnerable young inner-city people), says: 'The poverty in Britain is worse than in poor countries because it is so isolating. The discrepancy is staring you in the face all the time – on TV, in the shops.' She talks of the children she works with, of the urgency of 'returning their childhood to them'.[32] While many of the worst forms of poverty have been eradicated, these are its new, contemporary variants: the lack of money in lockstep with the lack of dignity. It is not enough to be poor in today's world. You have to feel it at every turn.

Ripped-off and put down
The third challenge is when children actually want to buy things, but are put down or ripped-off in doing so. The children we spoke to feel passionate about being discriminated against. They feel that they are treated as second-class consumers. Sam, 15, said of sales people in shops that 'They don't respect us as much, they don't listen as well.' A girl, two years younger, agreed: 'They take advantage of you. Cos we're younger and they don't think we're going to do anything about it.'

Part of this is wrapped up in perceptions of crime. One girl, only 12 years old, talked of 'the way you dress and that they think you're going to rob something or someone'. Another girl, three years older, said, 'When you go in, you can see them looking at you like hmm, I bet she hasn't got any money to spend in here, she's going to steal something, and everyone looks at you.'

Seven out of ten children say that they have felt ripped-off when they've bought things. They talk of offers and special deals that are 'too good to be true' and are subject to conditions in the small print. Then there's misleading pricing which mean that they end up paying over the odds for mobile phones, CDs, computer games, gifts and magazines.[33] Feeling that someone is out to take advantage of you can translate into taking advantage of others. Touched by the profit motive, we found evidence of kids ripping each other off in the playground, in part because that's what they see the commercial world doing to them.

Many times, too, they feel let down by what they get. Advertising sets up false expectations but experience teaches them that things don't live up to the 'hype'. Hair and beauty products for girls are one example. 'All these shampoos and conditioners don't really do anything,' said one 16-year-old girl. Similarly, boys are cynical about computer games: 'I think wow this looks really good, the graphics are good and then you play and it wasn't like this when I saw it on TV.' Even very young children have grown to expect disappointment, as one 7-year-old boy explained about Action Man: 'I think I was interested in them [Action Men] because when they advertised them they showed them really like, in places that suited them, but when you actually got them, you didn't actually get the setting . . . it was just your bedroom.'

Media bedsits

It is hard for today's child to escape the influence of the child catchers because they have made their way firmly into children's bedrooms. Children in the past may have chilled in their bedroom by leafing through a book, playing fantasy games with toys or just chatting with friends. Today, children's bedrooms have been transformed into hi-tech, intensive media bedsits with more gadgets and goods than would have been shared by a whole family a generation before. They go to their rooms not to switch off but to switch on.

The array of what kids can switch on in their rooms is vast and multiplying. A TV set is almost compulsory. Close to 90 per cent of teens have a personal TV but so do almost 60 per cent of the 5- and 6- year-olds just starting school.[34] This trend is not driven by income: 98 per cent of tweens from deprived families have their own telly, in stark contrast to 48 per cent from affluent areas.[35] The sets are not sitting idly by, either. Unlike the toys which are thrown away, the TV gets good usage. Two-thirds of children aged 5 to 16 watch TV before they go to school in the morning and a similar proportion watch telly in bed before they go to sleep. The poorer the household, the higher are these figures. About sixty per cent of children also watch TV during meals and in bed before going to sleep, instead of curling up with a book.[36]

If telly is a tool for dozing off, the more interactive items of technology are also becoming a more widespread feature in the child's bedroom landscape. More than a third of all children have their own PC or laptop, while two-thirds have their own games console.[37] The number of children who access the internet from their personal space is rising fast with almost a quarter of all UK children able to surf the net away from their parents in the privacy of their room.

The mobile phone, perhaps along with iPod, is the most prized piece of personal kit. Both symbolize freedom, growing up, independence and fun. Almost half of primary-school girls now have their own mobile phone (39 per cent of boys) and this rises to 98 per cent of senior-school girls (90 per cent of boys).[38] The mobile phone connects children to their friends and, if that magic were not enough, it operates as an object of beauty to be admired, compared, rated or rejected in the tough reality-show setting of children's playgrounds and streets. Adults rate mobile phones top for their convenience, but children rate convenience as the least important benefit.[39]

In fact, a visit to the bedroom of a British child of 11, just starting secondary school, might yield a music system, TV, phone, text messaging, mobile phone, computer, instant messaging, voice over internet protocol, email, games console, DVD or VCR, MP3 player . . . In short, this is a remarkable media zone where a quarter of each day, from waking up to going back to sleep, is now spent devoted to machines.[40]

It is salutary to just take a look at the numbers relating to children's screen time. In total, children today spend an average of 5 hours and 18 minutes every single day in front of a screen. That's 2 hours 36 minutes of TV; 1 hour 18 minutes on the internet; and 1 hour 24 minutes on a games console.[41] Total screen time, then, is around 2,000 hours a year. If we consider that children aged 9 to 11 spend 900 hours in class per year[42] and children age 6 to 12 spend an average of 3.5 hours a day with their parents (and presumably less after that age), children's time in front of a screen is more than double their time in class and more than one-and-a-half times what they spend with parents.

The screen can no longer be classed as an electronic babysitter that keeps children occupied. It is a whole, electronic world in which they are immersed and which is underpinned firmly and securely by a profit motive. The conventional paradigm of childhood as a life stage that revolves around family and schools has had to change. It's the commercial world that dominates the time of today's children.

£99 billion is big money, but in calculating even this total, we have not included those purchases that parents tell us they make that are not for children but are influenced by them, from where to go through to what to drive. And when the marketing of youth back to adults as cool is also added on top, it becomes clear that young people, or at least young people as seen through the lens of business, could be described as the dominant force in the economy as a whole. As Jon Savage puts it in his history of teenagers: 'The teenage market has swept everything before it. It is the spearhead of western values throughout the world, for good or ill. It is a huge, huge industry that involves everybody.'[43]

The children's market is unlikely to slow down as spending power increases and childhood and adulthood continue to converge. For children, the way in which they experience and respond to all of this is in itself shaped by the commercial media culture which they have experienced all their lives and which encourages them to be, and to enjoy being, consumers.[44] The situation is exciting but it's getting out of control. It would be easy to characterize a child's relationship with the commercial world along the love-hate lines we saw in our look at Barbie. The truth is more challenging – that marketing today is neither love nor hate for children, but the very air that they breathe.

How this came to be and how children are caught up in this seamless world of commercial persuasion is the subject of the next chapter, where we look at the profitable techniques and tactics that are at the forefront of marketing to children. Let's move from the child's bedroom to the executive board-room.

2. Blitz Marketing

'Because companies are very rich, they can do what they want.'

Tyrone, age 10

It's a war. At least that's how some marketers see it. Trade journals and marketing conferences pound out the same terminology time and again: battle, target, weapon, hit, win, power. The required reading for many an MBA is Machiavelli's *The Prince*[1] and the 6th-century Chinese military treatise by Sun Tzu, *The Art of War*.[2] Today's commercial strategy is rather like military strategy. It's all about meticulous campaign planning; scrupulous psychological analysis of 'enemy' thinking; strategic placement of undercover agents; and penetrating hostile lines. In this chapter we look at how some companies catch children, watching and stalking them until commercial messages become embedded in every aspect of their lives and friendships.

Surveillance techniques

'There is £5 billion out there, burning a hole in UK teenagers' pockets' cries the publicity leaflet for a youth marketing conference sponsored by *Marketing* magazine. 'But they don't part with it easily,' continues the blurb. 'Media sophisticates from an early age, today's teens distrust hype wherever they see it, from product advertising to political campaigns. So how do you get your brand message heard?' The market research firm BMRB runs a database (Youth TGI) which can help you 'understand how pester-power can work for your brand'. Their database 'helps users to target parental expenditure by focusing on the key markets where kids pester the most'.[3] This is a revealing offer given the marketing industry guidelines of the Broadcast Advertising Clearance Centre, which say explicitly that 'advertisements must not encourage children to pester'.[4] BMRB says that the database provides 'extensive insights into the media consumption habits' of children of different ages, all so that markets can 'pick the most efficient media vehicles to hit your target'. Indeed, the logo for the Youth TGI database is a lopsided archery target, with an arrow in the bull's eye, which is presumably meant to indicate the children that companies are aiming at.

Marketing conferences from Centaur offer an alternative act of aggression to 'hitting', promising instead the chance to 'stamp your mark on tomorrow's generation'.[5] Other battle tactic promises include 'learn how to tap into the consumer psyche with creative campaigns'. One of the most popular recommendations within the industry is to get the kids to do the work for you. According to Dr Scott Gallagher, Director of Online Partnership Marketing at BSkyB, '76 per cent of consumers don't believe the information in your advertisements but 68 per cent of consumers do trust the advice of their peers.'[6] Now with unprecedented access to the places where children talk to their friends, such as the social-networking sites and virtual worlds we will look at shortly, getting kids to market to each other is becoming child's play. It's called 'brand advocacy' in the trade and, as 'user generated content' (i.e. people writing their own blogs, creating their own home pages, posting their own music, and divulging the most intimate details of their private lives . . .) continues to grow, the potential for getting kids to spread the word about products is huge.

'Tweens' are a key focus in the commercial literature, but when companies use words like 'targeting tweens', it is easy to lose yourself in the jargon, forgetting that this is simply an Orwellian cover for saying what they mean, which is 'targeting primary school children'. Another marketing conference, this time sponsored by Revolution, explores the role of 'customer advocates' and 'the impact that user-generated content can have on your brand'. It asks potential delegates: 'Are your advocates your secret weapons in the battle to secure positive brand buzz?'[7] What are 'customer advocates'? They are friends. We just wonder how children would feel if they thought their best friend was being lined up as a 'weapon' and aimed right at them.

Stalking

Be under no illusions, someone is stalking your child.
Sounds like paranoia? Well, not according to Seana Mulcahy,
an industry insider and author of an interesting little piece
entitled, 'Most Consumers are Clueless' in a MediaPost
column called Online Spin.[8] 'What most consumers aren't
used to is how they're tracked by us and the company we
keep,' she says, '. . . there are many Netizens [sic] that aren't
too savvy online'. She's writing about the 'Do Not Track List'.
This is an idea being mooted by consumer advocates which
would allow us to opt out of targeted online advertising in
just the same way as signing up to the 'Mail Preference
Service' or the 'Telephone Preference Service' stops us from
getting piles of irritating junk mail and those annoying
phone calls selling windows which always come just as
you're sitting down to dinner. But, as Ms Mulcahy points
out, the problem is that most people don't know they're
being tracked and targeted in the first place. Terms such as
'junk mail', 'cold calls', even 'spam' have entered into everyday use. But what about 'behavioural targeting'? How many
of us know about that? And how many of us like the idea
of our children's behaviour being monitored by predatory
advertisers?

One piece of research we conducted revealed that about
85 per cent of children's favourite websites collect some sort
of personal information[9] – email address mainly but we
found sites collecting the user's name, address, postcode,
city, country, date of birth, gender and age. Most of this
information is 'compulsory', in other words the child can't

use everything being offered on the site without divulging these personal details. Fifteen per cent of sites demand information to participate at all. Another 35 per cent offer ringtones, wallpaper, newsletters, screensavers or 'the chance to tell your friends' in exchange for the information. Except exchange isn't really the right word. Exchange implies some sort of fair deal where both parties know what's being given, what's being received and why. The transaction involved in a child exchanging personal details for 'free stuff' is much less transparent than it might seem at first. Let's take an example.

Laura, aged 9, signs up to a toy website so that she can make a Christmas list to send to all her friends and relatives. Already, she's made public the sorts of toys she likes. This information, along with her personal information, will be stored in a database. The host site now knows just what toys to advertise to Laura and they may well also be able to send adverts to Laura's mum and dad, aunt and uncle, and granny and grandpa if she's given their details too. This data might then be 'fused' with information gathered from tracking software ('cookies') which are placed on Laura's computer both by the host site and companies advertising on the site. Privacy regulations are very quiet about cookies even though these pieces of code monitor where Laura goes on the internet, what sort of links she clicks on and how long she spends in different web areas. This 'spyware' can also scan the text of her conversations with friends and try to understand what other sorts of things she might be persuaded to buy. After signing up to the Christmas list, Laura will find herself increasingly tempted to buy stuff she sees during her 1.9

hours a day on the computer because someone now knows she likes soft toys in pink; someone now knows she talks endlessly to her friend Carla about her pet rabbit; someone now knows she has a new Nokia mobile phone; someone now knows she always clicks on the big flashing adverts; someone now knows she can easily be lured away from the site she's on with a more exciting offer; and someone now knows she's a 9-year-old girl who lives in Luton. Someone now knows rather a lot about Laura and knows the right buttons to press in her mind.

Legally, Laura has probably agreed to 'someone' knowing all this by ticking a tiny box at the end of a very long, boring privacy statement which she hasn't read and wouldn't understand even if she did. Laura may also have agreed (without knowing it) that she is over 13. But ethically, has Laura really agreed to accept adverts targeted specifically at her? We don't think so. In fact most kids don't want any adverts at all interfering with their fun. As one boy said to us, 'Every 15 minutes on telly, three minutes of advertising are on. Why do you need it on the computer as well as the TV?'[10]

The truth is that Laura and her parents have no idea that because she was tempted with the idea of making a Christmas list she is now being 'behaviourally tracked' or, in other parlance, stalked. She didn't agree to this. She couldn't. At 9 she doesn't have a sophisticated understanding of the business models driving the internet. And as Seana Mulcahy concludes in her article about her own peers in the behavioural tracking industry, 'My guess is that most of these publishers and tools providers tend to be less than transparent, with a what-they-don't-know-won't-hurt-them mentality.' Our guess is she's right. Our other guess is that in the excitement she describes about 'what behavioural tracking can deliver to the bottom line', few in the industry have even begun to think about the implications for children.

Privacy invasion

Our research shows that children and parents don't think about the commercial implications of giving out information online: they are much too preoccupied with stranger-danger.[11] And, indeed, on the surface stranger-danger is much more alarming, while commercial intrusion appears to be pretty well regulated. A glance at websites used by children shows that most sport a privacy policy and many take particular care with children.[12] Miniclip, for example, won't ask children under 13 'to disclose any more personal information than is necessary for them to participate in a particular activity'.[13] However, scratch the surface and we see that many of these policies are not worth the cyber-paper they are written on. One in four of the third-party advertisers on these sites do not have a privacy policy at all and those that do offer little protection to children, so the minute kids click on an enticing advert (which they may or may not realize is an advert) anything they divulge is up for grabs. Take an Orange advert on the Miniclip homepage. Children are invited to send their first name and surname, a contact number and an email address in return for a free sim card. There is a privacy policy on this advert but there is nothing specifically to protect children and, it seems, not a lot to protect the privacy of adults either. According to the terms, simply by using the service an individual has agreed to their information being used for marketing and profiling purchase preferences. The privacy policy also notes that 'by using our services you consent to our transferring your information to countries which do not provide the same level of data protection as the UK if necessary for providing you services you require'. It goes on to reassure customers that, 'Unfortunately the transmission of data via the internet is not completely secure. Although we will do our best to protect your personal data we cannot guarantee the security of your data transmitted to our site, and transmission is at your own risk.'[14]

Miniclip, of course, takes no responsibility for Orange. The advertiser is Miniclip's REAL customer, the one who generates the revenue. The Miniclip site is only able to operate at a profit because it sells space to companies who want a slice of the juicy kids' marketing pie.

You would be excused for not having read disclaimers on a host-site privacy policy. In fact, we came across only a very tiny number of parents who had ever read anything on a privacy policy. They're designed not to be read: often featuring tiny writing and arcane English and they are so, so long. However, if you do read them, you may discover that you agree to any legal issues with the website being settled under Californian law, which is the case with BEBO, the most popular teenage social-networking site.

One of the big problems in this area is that privacy laws are not unified internationally and there is currently a hotchpotch of self-regulation and national and international legislation. The implementation of the Children's Online Privacy Protection Act in the USA is an example. It stresses the role of the parent and states that information from under 13-year-olds should not be collected without specific parental permission. However, on every single one of the sites we investigated it was easy for a child to disclose personal information with no verifiable parental consent at all. In fact, 70 per cent of the sites made absolutely no attempt to encourage parents to be involved.[15]

The sites Piczo, Cheatplanet and Popcap absolve themselves of the need to involve parents by stating on the data collection page that the site is only intended for those over 13 (Piczo and Cheatplanet) or 18 (Popcap). As these sites are among the most visited sites by children under 13 according to our survey, such a warning clearly has little effect. Sites which are really only for children, like Disney, Cartoon Network and Barbie, do one of two things: either they ask for the parents' email address so that permission can be sought (Disney, Habbo Hotel and MyScene), or they simply ask kids to tick a box to say they have asked their parents (e.g. Cartoon Network UK). There's a problem with both of these approaches. A kid is desperate to get on this fun site. Will they really go downstairs, interrupt their mum and ask their permission? Or will they just tick the box and get on with the game? We'd say 99 per cent of kids will go for option 2. What about giving mum or dad's email address? Well, if the child actually does this it does activate a rapid message sent to the supplied email address offering the recipient a chance to cancel registration. (On some sites the child can't register until parental approval is secured, but on others the registration and site activities go ahead until a parent puts a stop to it.) Of course, the system administrator has no idea whether that email address really belongs to the child's parent. It's really completely useless. It's not only useless, it also contravenes another piece of regulation, namely Section 19.33 of the Code of the Direct Marketing Association which states clearly that parents' personal information must not be collected from children! The codes are not really thought through and we might be excused for thinking that simply putting the onus for protecting kids on the shoulders of parents is just a convenient cop-out.

Privacy from our parents

Another reason that using parental consent as a protection for children's personal information is unlikely to be effective is that kids really don't want their parents hanging around their private online lives. After all, our parents wouldn't have checked out behind the bicycle sheds. Indeed, researchers Sonia Livingstone and Monica Bober argue that children see parental involvement in their internet activities as a much greater threat to their privacy than giving out information.[16] In their survey, 69 per cent of 9 to 17-year-old daily and weekly users of the internet said that they minded their parents monitoring their internet use; 63 per cent of 12 to 19-year-old home internet users had taken some action to hide their online activities from their parents and 40 per cent had used the internet to play games by changing their identity. Getting them to ask their parents really isn't the answer to these privacy issues. Companies themselves need to take more responsibility.

Conscription

Companies are not just stalking kids online; they are also recruiting them to fight in the battle for brand domination and market share. Close on half a million young people in the UK alone have been enlisted by big youth brands, and that's the figure from just one recruitment agency.[17] Kids are regularly signed up through the internet to be 'insiders', 'informers' and 'lifestyle representatives' for big corporations. In order to find out first-hand how this works, we decided that one of us (Agnes) should go under cover:

> So now I'm Angie Harrison, age 10. But because, like any normal 10-year-old, I usually lie to get on the good sites my cyber age is 14. OK? So I go to the www.dubit. com website where I'm offered the chance to hang out with other teens by creating my own avatar and chilling in the chat room. Sounds good. I sign up. Then I get this welcome email:
>
>> Don't forget you can create your own mini home-page, upload your pics, and get exploring the island and its buzzing community! Remember – the more you can tell other people about yourself, the more likely you are to meet some interesting people! We'd like to give you the opportunity to turn your opinions

into cash, too – through joining our Informer team. Loads of companies like MTV, Sky TV and the Government want to know your points of view, and they're prepared to pay you for it – so click here to find out more. It's all part of the Dubit way of getting young people heard, so don't be left out of the debate!

I like the idea of this 'cash for questions' so I sign up to be an 'informer'. I give my email address and a password, my first and last names, my gender and my age (14). I hit a snag here as they want me to give my parents' full names, address, phone number and email in order to ask for their permission because I'm under 16. I do all that, but I also want to get on with earning some money so I create a new Googlemail account and sign up again as a 16-year-old. I get to the next stage where they want my full address, phone number and then a host of information about my hobbies and inter-ests. I give them the lot and then get told that I have to wait to see if I am accepted as an informer. By now I really want to belong to this club because it seems pretty exclusive and rather hard to get into: major incen-tives for a precocious 10-year-old. The next day I get the email. I'm in. I've been approved by the panel.

The next Friday I get my first survey. I have to fill in my gender, age and postcode. However, I'm then told I can't take part because the quota for my age, gender or postcode has been filled. Next week I check out my emails on the Wednesday (to make sure I don't miss out again) and find another survey. I rush to the page to find that the survey is now closed. The same thing happened the next week. I'm feeling rather despondent now. So much for getting my voice heard.

Three weeks later I (the real Agnes) get a call to let me know that my errant daughter Angie has signed up with Dubit. (Her sign up as a 14-year-old has registered on the system.) Did I know? I said I did but didn't know much about it. I was told that she had signed up to take part in surveys about things like sports and health. I asked if all the clients were charities or government organizations. I was told yes, more or less, as Dubit does lots of government things and also stuff for companies like Wrigley. I was a little confused by the link between national policy and chewing gum but the Dubit representative explained they do surveys of people from age 7 to 25 and that the kids get between 50p and £2. When they get to £25 they get a cheque. I asked if the whole point of the survey was to get information from kids and she said that the Informer programme was about just that. I asked where Angie would have heard about Dubit. Most likely recommended by a friend, came the reply. Would Angie have received anything before I gave my permission? No. The representative double-checked that I was happy and I said I was.

The next week, as Angie, I went back on Googlemail and found another three surveys which I wasn't allowed to take part in. Then I did a recruitment questionnaire

for Barnardo's which asked about whether I had a police
record or regularly attended a Youth Offenders' Centre.
I decided to give up . . .

Dubit has tens of thousands of informers aged from 10 to
24. Every weekend Dubit runs a survey for its clients (Coke,
Nike and some public service organizations as well) and,
indeed, the kids who fill it in are offered money. However,
the drawback of not being able to claim any money until
you have amassed £25 is that some kids have to complete
50 surveys before they see a penny. And for some surveys
kids get absolutely nothing: just entry into a prize draw.
What's more, because not every survey will be relevant to
you, it may be a long, long time before you see any reward.
Given Angie's luck, it may be a very long time before she
even gets to fill a survey in, let alone be paid. However, the
kids in there know it's an elite world and that because Dubit
'only allow certain people' to be informers, then the chances
of winning are greater. It's worth hanging on in there: not
for the money, but because it's exclusive.

From Barbie Girl to Barbie Secret Agent

If being an 'informer' is cool, being an 'insider' must be
the ultimate. According to Dubit's sales pitch to clients they
'recruit and manage inspiring young people to act as brand
ambassadors or lifestyle representatives for companies and
causes across the UK'.[18] By using these kids, they go on, 'we
have been successful in creating believable campaigns that
really do have measurable effects on the bottom line'.

One of Dubit's clients is Barbie. The new Barbie Girls website offers chat, fun and girly things, but it is also a merchandising bonanza. Girls need to have bought a Barbie MP3 player to fully access the activities on the site. At the time of writing, this retails at £49.99: not within the pocket-money budget of most 7-year-olds. And, of course, it doesn't stop at the player itself, because this MP3 player has its own docking station and its own 'wicked mini magnetic accessories'. The mission for the agents, should they choose to accept it, is clear: take the MP3 player everywhere they go and sell, sell, sell to all friends and contacts. Dubit's insiders are 'screened to ensure a fit with campaign' and so the agents they are signing up for this assignment are '50 special girls aged 7–11'. As we set out in the introductory story about Sarah, these little primary-school children will be armed with their very own, brand new MP3 player and will be tasked with taking it everywhere they go: to school, to Brownies, to dancing, to swimming and to friends' houses.

But just showing it off is not enough: they also have to produce photographic evidence of their selling techniques. Then they have to create their own fan website where they promote Barbie Girls to as many people as possible. They also have to get their friends to sign up to www.barbiegirls.com and they have to go on all their favourite sites, promoting the Barbie site and the products with relentless energy. And, most exciting of all, they get to have a party where they invite all their friends round and show them what cool stuff they have. What do they get in return? Well, free stuff, of course, a paid-for party and, most important of all, the promise of being the coolest girl on the block. But there is more. For the girls who 'evidence their promotions really well' there is a bonus incentive: a massive star prize from Barbie. So, in a nutshell, Mattel has 7-year-old girls working for them on commission by exploiting their friendships. Perhaps using this is their revenge, given our findings, related earlier, about Barbie-torture.[19] Meanwhile, Dubit continues to offer kids the opportunity to 'promote brands on the street for free stuff, prizes and cash'.[20]

Inappropriate tie-ins

Whilst Mattel may be guilty of promoting its products in the wrong way, more and more advertisers are promoting the wrong product to young people. Summer 2007 saw the *Transformers* movie take £28 million in three days in the UK and $70 million in its opening weekend in the USA. The film had a level of violence which gave it a rating of 12A, i.e. children under 12 must be accompanied by an adult. However, *Transformers* was promoted to children as young as 3 years old through a tie-in with Burger King. The tie-in was designed to make those interested in the film buy the burgers and those interested in the burgers see the film. But 3-year-olds can't see the film without negotiating with their parents, nor can 4, 5, 6, 7, 8, 9, 10 or 11-year-olds. The way this sort of tie-in works (apart from selling more burgers and more film tickets) is to dangle the carrot of the unobtainable in front of kids in order to make it even more attractive. A big part of childhood is about doing stuff you're not supposed to be doing. The number of 10 and 11-year-olds around the country vying with each other to see who would pass for a 12-year-old and get into *Transformers* was doubtless significant and was equally doubtless a planned part of the marketing campaign. Juliet Schor has suggested that when ratings were upped in the USA more young kids went to the cinema because this attraction of the forbidden proved a huge marketing pull. Be that as it may, it's clear that TV and cinema tie-ins are powerful around the world. According to a Young Media survey in Australia, nearly 90 per cent of pre-schoolers have asked their parents to buy food with a favourite character on the packaging.[21] We are pleased to report, though, that Burger King can take credit for what it has done since the *Transformers* campaign. Twelve months after Ed went public with a critique of their tactics around *Transformers*, the company has responded by moving to end the practice of running marketing promotions and tie-ins targeted at younger children.[22]

Just plain inappropriate

Whilst many children may be happy to find their way into films that are rated as over their age, they might find some of the website marketing we found completely inappropriate. Our survey of kids' favourite websites, which we will describe in more detail later, threw up a sobering number of unmarked links to gambling, dating and cosmetic-surgery companies. On Mousebreaker, while we were writing this, we counted eight gambling ads on the home page alone. In fact, apart from the chance to win some Led Zeppelin tickets, all that was being advertised was '£5 free', 'Win up to

$6,000', 'Win cash prizes', 'Extra Bonuses' and a picture of a James Bond look-a-like offering the chance to 'Be a Real Gangster'. None of them were labelled as adverts but were actually entitled 'Hot Links'. So Agnes decided to go under-cover again and assume the persona of Angie Harrison, the precocious 10-year-old who is struggling to have her voice as an informer heard on Dubit:

> I like the look of this '£50 extra' and click on the button to proceed. I end up at the Party Poker site where I'm confronted by a mean-looking King of Spades and a huge red and yellow flashing button telling me to Download Now! In very small writing on the left there is an 18+ certificate and a link to responsible gaming. (Isn't it interesting that these sites talk about 'gaming' rather than 'gambling'?) Angie, frankly, has no interest in reading this and goes straight to the download. I give my name, email, gender and verify that I am over 18. The software is downloaded immediately and in minutes Angie, aged 10, is 'part of the world's largest poker room where 80,000 people play every day'. Sounds like fun. As I click on the screen to start playing I'm told several times that playing for real money is much more exciting:

>> Start playing for real money today! We hope you've already enjoyed our great play money games, but we've got much more to offer, including great prize

pools and jackpots, exciting promotions, and lots of exclusive bonuses. To take advantage of these great features all you need to do is log in and make a deposit to start playing for real money. You can even use your real money account across all our games. Join the action. Make your first deposit today![23]

I go to a registration form where I enter my name, address and phone number. Then I get asked for my passport number and decide to back off. I also uninstall the programme so my mum and dad can't find it. A pop-up immediately tells me that Party Poker are really sorry that I have wiped them off my computer but they tell me that I can play using my browser and hit my screen with another enormous flashing box urging me to PLAY NOW! I'm fed up with this hard-sell so I try to close the window. With no warning, what looks like a Microsoft message box pops up and asks me if I'd like to win $150. I just can't get it to go away . . . Incidentally, later that evening Agnes got her first ever junk text message with a dubious looking offer. So, from going on a games site Angie Harrison, age 10, has now become part of a targeted gambling network.

When I finally do get rid of the box, I have a go on the cool gangster thing instead. As soon as I click on the James Bond guy, a dinner-suited baddie thrusts a gun straight in my face and tells me:

Demand begets supply, begets money, power and greed . . . Chaos prevails in the underworld as small timers fight for control of gambling, prostitution, booze and dope . . . An undisputed kingpin must emerge to fill the power vacuum, regulate the rackets and reign as the Mastermind . . . GangsterMind is a FREE, browser-based game where you are a ruthless Gangster thirsting for money and power. At the helm of an organized crime gang, you will . . . instil fear in the hearts of your enemies to protect your assets and expand your territory. This action-packed game is full of excitement, loads of fun and it's FREE! Sign up today and join now to become the Mastermind![24]

As Angie, I'm actually rather sickened by this. I like having fun and being a bit naughty but this is scary. And, in fact, the commercial operations of the site, GangsterMind, are rather scary too. There are absolutely no contact details if you did have any complaints you would like to vent and there is nothing marked 'privacy policy'. A 'User Agreement' has to be signed, but this is much more about the intellectual property rights of GangsterMind rather than protecting individuals who have stumbled on to the site. I did find a paragraph on information disclosure as I scrolled down the tiny writing in a tiny user-unfriendly box: '12. Information Disclosure: We cannot ensure that your private communications and other personally identifiable information will not be disclosed to third parties.' Great!

We also found other sites, such as Ebaumsworld (www.ebaumsworld.com) which is in the top 25 sites for under-14s, that carry content inappropriate for children. This used semi-naked women in suggestive poses to advertise 'intimate dating' and 'hot girls'. When we went back a year later, in the course of writing this book, to have a look to see if anything had changed, the answer was 'sadly not'. On the second page we encountered we were offered the following links: 'Wanna see pics of girls who live by you?', 'How to attract women', 'Hot amateur girls!' and 'No girlfriend?? You've got to read this!!' Just like Mousebreaker, none of these links are marked as advertising and (unlike Party Poker) none of these links have any warnings of unsuitability for under-18s. The 'Hot amateur girls!' link, which promises to let you 'rate these hot teens', takes us to Sugar Loot (www.sugarloot.com). This site is obviously aimed at teenagers and its purpose is clearly to sell but we found some devices designed to make the site 'sticky' i.e. to make you stay there long enough to make a purchase. As soon as we registered, we were encouraged to join the 'contests'. These range from 'prettiest eyes', 'hottest guy' and 'best couple' to 'tell us your gossip contest'. We click on the gossip one and this is what we get:

WE'RE LOOKING FOR SOME JUICY GOSSIP! Tell us yours. It's easy to enter, here's how it works: Record a video of you telling us something crazy, weird, wild or funny about you that we would never have guessed. It could be the fact you still sleep with your stuffed animal giraffe, or that you crush on your friend's boyfriend, or you like to eat peanut butter and pickle sandwiches, or you once sent a sappy love letter to a really lame celebrity. Anything that Gossip Girl herself would looove to find out. (p.s. No acting necessary on this one – your personality is what we're looking for!) Upload your video performance. Get everyone you know to vote for you.

Rob Parsons, founder of the charity Care for the Family tells a sad tale in his book *Teenagers – What Every Parent Has to Know* about the effects of 'contest' sites like this. Chloe was at a party and before long she noticed everyone was shrieking around the computer: 'Minging!', 'Lush!', 'Fit!' The other kids were loading up their pictures and rating all the other contestants in the competition, 'How sexy am I?' When Chloe got home that night she sought out a picture she thought made her look OK and dashed to put it on the site along with her friends. As the scores came in, her friends got an average of 7.6 but Chloe got a rating of 2. Over the next few months she became withdrawn and a bit listless. She lost interest in her activities and her school life started to suffer. Her grades fell and she started hanging out with a set of girls who were constantly getting into trouble. These 'hot' contests play on the raw insecurities of teenagers. And to what end? To sell records, make-up, skateboards and teen pulp fiction. Once you find yourself caught up in Sugar Loot you find yourself bombarded with glitzy teen stuff to buy because, of course, the ultimate aim of setting up websites focused on teenagers is to separate them from the £5 billion that 'is burning a hole' in their pockets.

360-degree marketing

Really successful marketing is present offline as well as online. Some campaigns are designed to follow children wherever they go: these are called IMC (Integrated Marketing Communications) in the marketing text books or 360-degree marketing in the more trendy industry e-newsletters. A great example of this is the relaunch of Bazooka Joe, a comic-strip character created 50 years ago, who comes with his own bubble gum. His hallmarks are a baseball cap and an eyepatch. We remember him from our youth when the sweet shops on the way home from school had two trays: a penny tray and a halfpenny tray from which you could choose from exquisite items like Fruit Salad, Black Jacks, Space Ships, Penny Dainties, Bubblys and . . . Bazooka Joe. If you chose Bazooka Joe you got a small slab of pink bubble gum wrapped in wax paper imprinted with a cartoon story featuring the hero's exploits. You chewed the gum, blew bubbles which splattered on your face, picked the bits off, left the gum stuck on the underside of the kitchen table and that was it until next pocket money day. But when Bazooka Joe is relaunched it won't just be a matter of supplying village sweet shops and the bubble-gum experience will extend far beyond messy mealtime habits.

Topps, the confectionery company which was founded in 1938 and owns the Bazooka Joe brand, has just been bought by a consortium led by Joe Eisner, the former CEO of Disney. He paid $385 million. Here's what he has in mind for the humble gum. 'There's no reason why there can't be Topps movies, Topps Internet, Topps television, Topps mini-series and Topps publications,' he says. This is no standard marketing manager talking about increasing sales of his product lines. It's about a total wrap-around marketing bonanza. And Eisner has all the right credentials to make this happen. At another point in his career he was CEO of Paramount Pictures where he oversaw *Raiders of the Lost Ark*. He's also been involved in sports and says somewhat curiously about his new brand: 'It's all about sports and sports stories.' Presumably, he wants the brand to touch every aspect of a kid's life including every one of their leisure activities, so there really is no escape.

What's particularly interesting about Eisner's proposed wrap-around communications approach is the way he plans to exploit childhood memories or nostalgia. He notes that the heroes (with the exception of Harry Potter) in the recent big kids' movies were created in comic books about 50 years ago (e.g. Spider-Man, Superman and X-Men). This is important to him because he's 'hoping that Bazooka Joe has that same little piece of your brain, or somebody's brain'. He's certainly got a little piece of ours and just reading about the launch transported us back to our youth before you could say tuppence ha'penny. This nostalgia marketing is incredibly powerful because it relies on unconsciously formed emotional connections which we'll look at in detail in Chapter 7 where we'll see just how strong they can be. After all, Marcel Proust conjures up a magnificent 3,200 pages of fiction from a sudden flashback to a childhood sensation of eating little sponge cakes dipped in herbal tea.

Some American business school academics have drawn on the work of psychoanalysts to provide a recent bank of theory and evidence to demonstrate the power of childhood memories on brand preference.[25] They urge marketing managers to make more use of this technique in their branding activities. However, a number of marketers appear to be one step ahead. Gillette shaving products (owned by mass global marketing giant Procter & Gamble), Sure deodorants (owned by P & G's arch rivals Unilever) and Shell, the international oil company, have begun to create good feelings about their brands in the very young so that, presumably, they'll have acquired the right brand habits by the time they grow up. All of these companies have recently placed 'advergames' on www.miniclip.com. Gillette was the first to buy this sort of publicity with its 2005 jet-ski challenge which featured M3Power razors and attracted 80 million game plays in its first few months on the site, making it the most successful advergame ever. According to Miniclip's own publicity for advertisers, site users are predominantly in the age category 10–24, meaning that about half of the audience has no use for the product at all . . . yet. When these kids come to choose their first personal hygiene and shaving brands you can bet they're now more likely to reach for Sure and Gillette and when they start driving they'll head for the Shell service station. Far beyond just tapping into nostalgia, this sort of product placement is manufacturing the nostalgia of tomorrow by catching our children young.

The activities of child catchers are no accident or spillover from an adult world. Marketing to children is conducted like a battle plan, designed to hit every part of a child's life. In the chapters that follow, we will trace the story of how, armed with such battle plans, child catchers touch children in four key settings: food, fashion, technology and the world of friendships and online networking. But first, it is worth saying something about responsibility – or the lack of it.

We have found that intimate and sophisticated marketing is lined up against children, with their own friends used as weapons. Internet advertisers hold huge amounts of kids' data and their privacy is poorly protected. Advertising online is currently not well regulated and, because legislation is patchy and advertising is borderless, a lot of internet advertising seen by children is completely inappropriate. Too many advertisers, when challenged on this, trot out a standard line that we have heard time and again: children today are savvy and, anyway, parents – and not business – are responsible for how children grow up. But the fact that parents accept that they take responsibility for children surely doesn't absolve others who have a degree of influence from doing the same: a responsibility shared does not mean a responsibility halved. Responsibility and influence have to operate hand in hand. Ironically, if you read the industry press, you find that many companies are in fact rather keen to accept responsibility, because they want to show off the influence they have. They want to prove that what they do works. Euromonitor, for example, has surveyed the lifestyles of 8 to 12-year-olds across the world, concluding that 'they are starting to develop their sense of identity and are anxious to have products that will cultivate a sophisticated self-image'. And why is this? Well, in part, this is 'due to marketing initiatives that force children to grow up quickly, since marketers have discovered that treating tweens like teenagers is a lucrative business'.[26] Welcome to the war on children.

3. Fashion Child

'There's lots of beautiful women on TV saying how beautiful they are.'   Sophie, age 15

Fashion is getting younger. There is no better place to see this than in Italy, at the world's leading children's fashion show. The market for baby and children's fashion has taken off fast in countries such as the UK, Italy, the USA and Netherlands and at the show you can see leading designers like Louis Vuitton, Dior and Gucci cashing in.[1] Luxury labels like Chloé, Milan-based Missoni and Alberta Ferretti all launched new kids' labels in 2008 and, for marketers, excitement rises to fever pitch.

Up and down the aisles, there are displays from over 400 brands. As you walk through, over your head on enormous banners hangs the word 'bimbo' for all to see. Of course, being in Italy, the word means baby or child but, for English speakers, it raises the question of whether you are looking at clothes for outgoing, 8-year-old party-goers or a recipe for the creation of young bimbos.[2]

After one children's fashion show, the German newspaper *Der Spiegel* identified a fashion industry edging further and further down the age range and dubbed what was on offer as 'crawling down the catwalk'. In this chapter, we examine how baby accessories have become status symbols, how pre-teens are turned into sex objects and how a lucrative fashion industry affects children's self-image and their relationship with their peers. It is good to enjoy clothes, whether as a child or parent, and it is natural to choose clothes that reflect who you are or would like to be, but when what you wear or how you think of yourself is promoted as competitive or exclusive, then it is likely that some kids are being set up to fail.

Designers are increasingly targeting products that intro-duce children to their brands at a very early age. Axel Dammler, of market research company Iconkids & Youth, explains why: 'Children of the age of three don't understand the concept of luxury,' he argues, but of course parents do. 'In our society, the gap between rich and poor is getting wider, and so is the need for people to differentiate them-selves and their children from everyone else. Even if all that means is buying the right polo shirt.' The same point is made by the psychologist Hans-Georg Häusel: 'A well-dressed child is a reflection of one's own lifestyle,' Häusel says. 'People want to set themselves apart from others. Even monkeys pass on their status to their offspring. It's deeply ingrained in our biology.'[3]

So there you have it. With all the determinism of nature, fashion for children (or children as a fashion accessory) is being touted as the culmination of millions of years of evolution. Even so, although we share many things with monkeys, children's perfume probably marks us out as different. Can you bring to mind the smell of a baby? Whether cuddling, feeding or changing them, it's a smell most parents will never forget. The company Burberry, on the other hand, believes that babies should smell like the 'enticing sparkle of citrus fruit, the freshness of wild mint and the insolence of rhubarb jelly'.[4] So it offers Baby Touch perfume, combining these scents, which sells for £30 for a 100ml spray. And in case baby rubs off the scent with its stretching and its sleeping, Baby Touch comes not just in a perfume spray, but also as an all-over baby wash, eau de toilette, baby balm and massage oil.

Big name brands like Givenchy, Bulgari and Guerlain dominate the market for children's fragrance. Jean-Paul Guerlain was among the first into the children's perfume market with the launch in 1994 of his citrus and mint blend, Petit Guerlain. In 2006, Guerlain responded to a barrage of competitors with the release of the even more diminutive Baby Guerlain. Parents can buy it in a tactfully blue or pink bottle, inscribed with the child's name.[5] As Guerlain puts it, the aim is to 'initiate little ones into the art of perfume'. Barbie, with her love of fashion, has obviously read the same marketing script, as her perfume for young girls is designed by Mattel 'to help girls discover their sense of smell'.[6]

Barbie also teamed up with Bonne Bell to offer cosmetics for children, with a new range lined up in 2008 aimed at girls between ages 6 and 9. The partnership brought, in the language of corporate marketing speak, a 'unique beauty experience' for girls. A trial run in 2007 with the company Estée Lauder, including items like Rocking Chick Lipstick, was among the most successful new launches of the year.[7] Two-thirds of children age 11 to 14 now use perfume or after-shave.[8] Bonne Bell already markets to even younger girls with cosmetic confectionaries like LipSmackers.

The simple truth, however, is that babies' cheeks don't need perfume and children's skin doesn't need make-up. The promotion of children's cosmetics is about a sales opportunity, pure and simple: along with the smell comes the sell. For scent makers, it's about starting young in terms of brand loyalty and attachment. The bigger question is whether marketing make-up to young girls encourages them to feel uncomfortable in their own skin and whether selling images of perfection on screen, on page and on billboards reinforces the message that they fall short.

Hot tweenagers

For girls, fashion products are all about attitude – being cute and sexy. 'I'm cool, I'm hot, I'm everything you're not', 'I'm cute, I'm neat, I'm your biggest ever treat', 'Too many boys, too little time', 'Sex Kitten' and 'Flirt!' are all slogans from toys and T-shirts for girls as young as 6 years old. Of course, companies will say that this is not about sex, but about being sexy – a shift from noun to adjective that is an act of grammatical and moral cowardice.

The most prominent and best-selling range of stationery for children in WH Smith, for example, features the Playboy

Bunny. The range is promoted extensively in the UK. *Mizz* magazine, which is aimed at age 10 to 14, has promoted Playboy stationery on its cover and as a free giveaway inside. 'Playboy is probably one of the most popular ranges we've ever sold,' says head of media relations for WH Smith, Louise Evans. When some teenage pupils from Coloma Convent in Croydon, southwest London, asked passers-by in the town centre to sign a petition calling for the items to be banned,[9] WH Smith's response was, 'it outsells all the other big brands in stationery, like Withit [a range of cute cartoon animals], by a staggering amount. That should give you an idea of how popular the brand is. We offer customers choice. We're not here to act as a moral censor.'[10]

The metallic pink gel pencils and heart-covered pencil case have no bare flesh on them beyond rabbit fur but, as Eleanor Kirwan, a teacher at Coloma Convent comments, children are:

> aware of what the Playboy icon is . . . the bunny symbol represents pornographic images. The girls are able to acknowledge that symbols have a deeper significance than that which is on the surface. For stockists and manufacturers to deny this is shockingly disingenuous. I do not vilify the pupils who own Playboy stationery. My criticism is directed at those who buy the Playboy licence and target children. Companies must take social responsibility into account as well. Our argument is that they are simply prioritising financial gain over the moral offensiveness of using children to sell sex.

When she reported this, Rachel Bell, a journalist at the *Guardian* newspaper, also tested out the Playboy stationery with girls that were using it. 'I like the brand because it's posh,' explained 14-year-old Tatiana. 'It makes you feel like you're worth something.' When Bell asked her if she knew what the bunny logo meant, she giggled and said, 'It's porn innit?'

WH Smith's official position does not accord with the views of these teen customers: 'We believe it is a fashion range.'[11] In a way, the company is not wrong. The range does have elements of the fashion formula. The power of children's products like the Playboy stationery is multiplied when they become something that you can take to school and that others collect. It helps to transform your products into 'must-have' items that you look good with, and lame without. This fashion cycle was a recurrent theme in our discussions with primary-school children. Playboy bunnies can be found in primary-school pencil cases pretty much anywhere except for Coloma Convent, but fashion and fads can get an added cachet if the school bans the items. They become even cooler to collect. But cool can come at the price of convenience. As one boy put it, 'First there were Pokémon cards and they got banned, then Yugioh cards and they got banned, then I spend £20 on boneheads and Aaaagghhh . . . THEY got banned.'

Luxury babies

Fashion reaches down much further than to primary schools. Evolution may not have advanced to the stage where fashion shapes the grave, but it does now define many a cradle. How your baby gets around is a perfect example of a product that has moved from function to fashion. You can still find cheap buggies at Mothercare or have them passed down in the family, but the status-conscious no longer have to put up with this. After successful debuts at the trade shows, John Lewis stocks the Starck Maclaren buggy in lemon and charcoal for £200. The shop advises mums and dads that designer Philippe Starck has developed this sleek buggy 'in honour of the hopes, visions and dreams that babies will grow up to have'.[12] But for those parents that really want their children to travel in 'comfort and style', top of the range is a Maclaren leather-clad version for £850. It comes with a handy pocket on the hood for your iPod, in case you tire of the sound of the little dears.

Maclaren, though, is not at the head of the innovation curve. The Bugaboo range, including the Cameleon, the Gecko and the Bee, was among the first to offer a wide choice of colours. The Cameleon comes in once-washed deep, dark-blue denim for £650 and, after it featured in the TV series *Sex and the City*, the company brought out a special limited-edition pushchair for £1,100 – if you can get one, of course.

When baby tires of life on the road, a beautiful Calla designer highchair will do nicely. Baby can also frolic in Gucci Baby outfits or the booties and tiny fur slippers made by Baby Dior. Or, why not try black patent-leather ankle boots by Petite Maloles? With top quality leather and a lining in 100 per cent goat's skin, they are a perfect gift for a newborn. Tiffany offers a sterling silver rattle, while Hermès can furnish the proverbial silver spoon (£265 with silver baby fork) and marries childhood and couture in its own exclusively priced version of a rocking horse. At three months, they'll be in a brown woollen all-in-one designed by John Galliano for Dior, retailing at £98. After a year, girls could enjoy a wool dress for £88 designed by Ralph Lauren and Missoni tights or pre-faded jeans. Marie-Chantal sells cashmere baby jumpers and diamond children's necklaces for £600. Marie-Chantal, a real-life princess, is married to Pavlos, the Greek crown prince in exile, and has, as you might expect for someone with 216 pairs of shoes, a reputation as a style icon.

Despite the fact the birth rates are in decline across the West, or perhaps, paradoxically, because of it, the luxury baby business is already worth £10 billion worldwide and is set to double in value over the next five years.[13] In a survey for 'BBC Money Programme', two-thirds of mums said that they spend more money on children's clothes than on their own.[14] At the most exclusive upmarket nursery schools, the drop-off and pick-up of children have become fashion parades in their own right. As one mum commented, 'I live in London's Notting Hill where a lot of these sunglass-wearing, 4X4-driving yummy mummies run a fashion parade at the prep school gates every morning. Given the level of competition in every bone in these women's (bony) bodies, I'm not surprised they're acting it out through their poor kids.' As for herself, she says, 'I'm proud to watch my 2-year-old muddy his Start-Rite shoes and Gap combat pants.'[15]

The birth of children's fashion

There is no doubt that children lap up fashion. As one commentator wrote in the *New York Times*, children between 8 and 12 'are discerning consumers. They think a lot about what they are going to wear, whether their outfit matches their peach-sparkle nail polish, how clothes sit with a teal-colored cellphone ("Can you believe Mom didn't know what color teal is?"), what kind of sushi they are going to eat, and what to read after books like "30 Guys in 30 Days".'[16] This sounds like a New York thing, or perhaps the writer had been reading too many PR reports over his sushi and self-help books, but perhaps he's not far off. We asked one of our tween daughters whether he'd got it right. He needed to get out and talk to children, she said, because nobody but nobody did all of those things . . . although, when she thought about it, they might do some. He's right, the daughter went on, that it matters what you wear. 'Every child,' she added, 'knows that.'[17]

Every generation has its own sense of what to wear, from today's trends of 'busting low' with beltless trousers and visible underwear to the flared jeans of your authors' youth. Enduring classics, like jeans and T-shirts, spring up from time to time as do brands that yo-yo constantly in and out of fashion, like Converse shoes. So, where did it all start? Where does children's fashion come from? According to Sarah Smith and Louise Heard, children's fashion was born in London in the 1960s. 'As the first "teenagers" moved into parenthood in the 1960s,' they explain, '"Swinging London" led the world in all things fashionable, and young designers fresh from art school didn't want parenthood to preclude them from expressing their individuality. And so they created miniature stylish versions of their own clothes for their offspring.'[18]

Designed for the shop Biba in London's Kensington Church Street and for her son Witold, born in 1967, Barbara Hulanicki's clothes, together with others such as Kids in Gear and Clothkits, proved a big hit with young parents. Biba advertised its wares with the children's story 'Once upon a time, Sam and Alice went to Biba to buy some new clothes. On the second floor, they found lots of special houses. Everyone was dressing up and – like magic – looking much happier.'

Hulanicki explained that her son 'was the first Biba baby. He was my inspiration for creating childrenswear . . . I thought he would look adorable in a polo neck or romper suit and I hated the blues and pinks available elsewhere. I wanted him to fit in with the 60's lifestyle. No Biba baby would be seen dead in those colours.' The styles took off – black, in short, was the new blue and pink for kids. The clothes were designed for children of all ages, from nappies in fuchsia, black and purple for toddlers through to a teenage collection called 'Lolita'. Parents loved them, but did the children? Hulanicki recalls the time with a laugh when Witold was interviewed for TV on the King's Road about his fabulous maxi coat, the first designed for children. 'Really feels difficult to play in,' he answered.[19]

Children's fashion is enjoying a heady renaissance, fuelled by parental spending. You can find tiny versions of Rolling

Stones T-shirts and mini Converse shoes. You can find traditional chic at the French label Bonpoint or the shops and
catalogues of Rachel Riley. The parenting magazine *Junior*
tracks all this. On its fashion pages, it demonstrates how to
dress a toddler in cardigan and top, grey trousers and brown
shoes for £496.[20]

Such a set of clothes will not last long, as toddlers grow
so fast but, of course, parents and relatives enjoy spending
money on their children. So, if you have the money, good
luck to you. And there is something subtly different in
buying fashion for children today compared to the 1960s.
Now, fashion is part of the pecking order for all. 'I've been
buying childrenswear for a long time,' says Lynne Crooke,
buyer for Selfridges. 'In the past two years there has been
a definite move towards parents wanting to show off their
affluence through what their children wear.'[21] As Alex
Theophamous, founder and director of AlexandAlexa.com,
an online children's fashion store, puts it, 'buying these
collections will help you to extend the fantasy through your
children'.[22] So, we are back to monkeys again.

For children, clothes can show who they are and how
they fit with peers and friends. Perhaps as a result, pester-
power for clothes is high. Around two-thirds of children
from the age of 7 pester their parents for the right pair of
trainers.[23] Fashion is seen as a short cut to self expression
and a way of experimenting with identity. Parents can be
persuaded to hire organizers for children's beauty and
fashion parties for 4-year-olds and up, allowing them to walk
the (living room) catwalk at a birthday photo-shoot.[24]

In the same way, some of the favourite internet games for younger girls revolve around dressing and choosing accessories for an online doll (avatar) and seeing the changes come alive, and boys can choose different fantasy or celebrity characters to role play in a video-game. Even here, brands rule. Online sites like Stardoll and Cartoon Doll Emporium, for example, report that children are 'practically begging' for name-branded clothing for their virtual dolls.[25] Branded clothes are imbued in our culture. In the summer of 2007, as one urban myth runs, a teenage driver, up for a count of dangerous driving, was asked by the youth court judge what gear he was in when the crash happened. 'Gucci sweats and Reeboks,' he replied.

We buy it so our kids aren't pushed out

So, children enjoy clothes and they enjoy being able to choose. Ashia, a 12-year-old Muslim girl, speaks about her clothes as if they are part of her: 'Yeah, I'm a proper jacket person,' she comments, 'I like shoes but I'm not a very shoey person.'[26] An enthusiasm for the right clothes shows up across children's ages, but reaches a peak, in terms of popular labels, in the 13 to 15 age range.[27] From 16, children become more settled in their choice, picking from different ranges and styles as they wish. Sixteen-year-old Laura, for example, comments that 'I don't even like shopping at H&M because everybody at school wears those clothes. You can tell immediately how much they spent there.'[28]

The connection between how you look and who you are inside is explained by Robert, age 7, who sees himself as a 'skater boy' in the clothes he wears. In fact, when he is actually going skateboarding, he will wear any old clothes. Most of his sports clothes are worn for everyday use rather than in real activity. Sports clothes conjure up associations of masculinity, athleticism, strength and power. It is the image, not the practicality, he buys into. 'If you were like going out with your mates you'd probably wear your cool stuff because you don't want your mates to say they're rubbish,' he explains. The same obviously holds true for his dad, as Robert goes on to explain that, 'because now I've got into skater things he's sort of getting spikey hair and he's got sort of these skater trousers.' As his parents, Tony and Mary, see it, this is all a very profitable way for marketers to tap into their desire to do the best for their children – including trying to buy the one thing they can't provide – popularity with peers. Tony told researchers, 'The thing is that us gullible parents keep buying the stuff and as long as we keep buying they'll market it,' and Mary chipped in, 'We buy it so our kids aren't pushed out.' Her husband agrees, 'Exactly, they know that and that's why they market it in that way.'[29]

Fashion bullies

If clothes are sold as making you feel not just good, but better than others, this could explain why fashion bullies in and around school appear to be on the rise. This is not new, of course.[30] The children's book *The Hundred Dresses* by Eleanor Estes dates back to the second world war and tells the story of Wanda, a Polish girl. She finds herself teased and friendless at school, made fun of for wearing the same shabby blue dress each day. In response to the bullies, Wanda sits down to draw 100 dresses that she claims to own.

Escaping the pressure of 100 dresses is one reason why school uniforms tend to be popular, at least with parents. In Germany recently, there has been a mass parents' campaign to make uniforms obligatory across schools. As one schoolgirl, Jennifer Jansen, puts it, 'if a skirt is too short, they call you 'slut' at school', she says. Showing part of your belly is okay, she believes, but a skirt should not rise above mid-thigh if you want to avoid opprobrium. Without a school uniform, the line between what is in fashion and being a 'slut' is a thin one.[31] In the UK, four out of five state schools have school uniforms, although for primary schools, it's fewer. Wales stands out as the big exception, with 36 per cent of its schools having no rules on uniform.[32] Even with a uniform, though, competition thrives – 100 dresses become 100 accessories, whether mobile phones, backpacks or shoes. What you wear and how you compare is now a major source of pressure for children. Tweens across the UK believe that the third most stressful part of being a child today (after tests and school) is having the right clothes or the newest gear.[33] Across the Atlantic, the film *Mean Girls*, starring Lindsay Lohan, tells the brutal story of fashion cliques in high school. The increase in pressure is borne out by research too. Dorothy Espelage, Professor of Educational Psychology at the University of Illinois, has studied teenage behaviour for 14 years and says she has recently seen a clear increase in 'bullying related to clothes'.[34]

The perfect me . . . and consequences

In a world in which the lottery of who is beautiful and who is not counts in myriad ways, being attractive translates into power for boys and girls. The more attractive you are, the more others tend to like you. The happier most adolescents are with their bodies, the more they like themselves.[35] As a result, anything that tips the lottery in your favour, in terms of how others see you or how you see yourself, must be a good sell. A decade ago, only around a quarter of girls under 14 said that it was important to be attractive to the opposite sex. Today, it is half. With boys, there is a similar rise.[36]

Of course, it is more profitable for the beauty industry if beauty is something perfect that you continue to strive for rather than something you can actually achieve. 'People want to see the girl next door,' Louis B Mayer was said to have suggested to Joan Crawford, who put him right, replying 'Louis, if they want to see the girl next door, tell them to go next door!' The beauty you see in marketing and advertising is never about the girl next door. It's unobtainable because of the host of tricks that the beauty industry deploys in the images it creates. As a video produced for Dove, the brand that has made a name for itself with its campaign for 'real beauty', explains: 'You have probably heard the expression, the camera never lies. Well, we have got news for you. It is all a lie.'[37] The Dove campaign was started by Silvia Lagnado, now Group Vice-President at the London-based company Unilever, after, reportedly, she showed a home video to her board which featured some of their own daughters talking about how they were made to feel about themselves by the beauty industry. Dove has now produced a series of short online films, easy to download, which all build on the concept of self-esteem.[38] However, before Unilever scoops credit all round we should point out that whilst the Dove brand may be about selling a more attainable image of beauty to young girls, another Unilever brand, Lynx, ends up as selling the image of girls as sex objects to young boys.[39]

The search for the perfect me is increasingly leading young people to take up tanning beds, body building or body slimming. Once the preserve of Olympic cheats and body-builders, anabolic steroids are taking off fast among the young. The charity Drug-Scope estimates that steroids are now the third most commonly used drugs by teenage boys, after cannabis and amphetamines. Nurse Deborah Jones, who works at a harm-reduction centre in the Wirral, explains that steroids are much easier to obtain now, either online or through the local gym. 'Parents will pay for gym subscriptions because they don't want them on the streets,' she says. 'They see it as the healthier option, but it can expose them to the steroid culture.' From teenage years, young boys strive for the perfect body. 'It's all about being big, muscular, toned, and they can gain that much quicker using steroids than they ever can working out,' she says. 'It does take over.' The dream is to have the rippling six-pack with the golden body. Many end up, though, with the significantly increased risk of health problems such as liver damage, high cholesterol and stroke. Worse, rather than offering an escape from teenage angst, boys using steroids may also tip themselves into teenage hell, suffering from added acne, extreme mood swings, depression, bigger male breasts and a lack of sex drive. Nurse Jones compares young men that use steroids to girls who suffer from anorexia in that, regardless of their true size, they still see themselves as 'tiny, scrawny, weedy'.[40]

Plastic surgery is also on the rise among young girls. One in ten girls has argued with their parents about wanting cosmetic surgery.[41] Some think 'I hate my body', while others simply seek to improve it, but plastic surgery for young people can be the biggest financial decision that they have ever taken and there are significant health risks.

One might imagine that the search for the perfect me has been a constant throughout history, even if there are new ways to act on it today. However, in a revealing study of the diaries of adolescent girls in the USA over the past 100 years, Joan Jacobs Brumberg has argued the opposite. She found that, whereas girls of earlier eras focused on 'good works' as the key to getting on, today the focus is far more on 'good looks' and improving physical appearance. Teenage girls today are focused on their bodies and it is this subject, more than any other, which dominates their emotional landscape.[42] In the UK, Rebecca Coleman of Lancaster University has explored the inner world of early teenage girls and found that how you look is central to your sense of who you are.[43] In an international study by Dove, the UK emerges as the country, more than anywhere else, including the USA, where girls find it hard to feel beautiful when surrounded by the images of perfection and beauty pedalled by the marketing industry.[44]

A key insight of marketing is to play to our vulnerabilities and then sell it back to us. Images of beauty and perfection are splashed over every corner of commercial spaces because someone wants to make money by tapping into that anxiety and concern. It seems harmless and, on an advert by advert basis, it may well be, but our research suggests that the sheer accumulation of imagery is creating discomfort and harm among children. It can be no more than a nuisance: as one 14-year-old girl told us, 'It's quite irritating when they're advertising lip gloss or something, and they've always got perfect hair and their skin's so smooth. It's just like what are you advertising.' But, in an example of how advertising can give you the blues, another girl, age 15, described to us how she was left feeling: 'Also, you know when you have those feelings, you're having an off-day, but everything seems to point at the thing that you're annoyed at, it's like everything. That's irritating, but that's just a coincidence. When there's lots of beautiful women on TV saying how beautiful they are, and you've got loads of people around. But I suppose that's just when you're having an off-day.'[45]

Lost innocence

For girls, the focus on body image and beauty as the key to improvement and success, is something that the commercial world exacerbates rather than challenges. It can be hard as a parent to take on the world, with its wrap-around imagery of beauty, perfection and predatory sex. In recent years, parental protests have forced a range of retailers to withdraw push-up bras, saucy knickers and black lace lingerie for girls as young as 9 years old.[46] One chain has promoted a pole-dancing kit in its toys and games selection.[47] The kit invites you to 'unleash the sex kitten inside . . . simply extend the Peekaboo pole inside the tube, slip on the sexy tunes and away you go! Soon you'll be flaunting it to the world and earning a fortune in Peekaboo Dance Dollars'. The £39.95 kit comprises a chrome pole extendible to 8ft 6ins, a 'sexy dance garter' and a DVD demonstrating suggestive dance moves.

If your daughter's doll, whether Barbie, Bratz or Hannah Montana, wears black miniskirts, feather boas and thigh-high boots, then it will not surprise you that primary schools such as the Hamp Community Primary School in Bridgwater have got into deep water over whether girls can come to school in a G-string.[47] Head teacher Mrs Roxburgh banned girls from wearing thongs, saying that girls could face possible embarrassment while changing for PE or playing out in the playground, falling over, or doing handstands. Some of the girls' parents were outraged that their daughters' underwear had been brought into question. One mother of an 11-year-old girl complained that 'They're fed up being treated like children. It's unbelievable.'[48] Perhaps this is what we have lost sight of, that children are children.

Outside of the reach of the head teacher, advertising goes out of its way to compound the focus on portraying women as objects not just of beauty but of sexual desire. Women are twice as likely to be shown with their clothes off as men in television commercials, according to American research, while an analysis of magazine adverts published over the last 20 years has shown a dramatic increase in the sexual imagery. Today, one in two women (49 per cent) is shown partly dressed or undressed in adverts, up from one in four 20 years ago (28 per cent).[49]

You might hope that when it comes to marketing to young people, there is a more responsible attitude to the use of sexual imagery. The truth, at least for older teenagers, is the opposite. It is worse. The models in their adverts, compared to those aimed at older adults, are far more likely to be dressed provocatively and twice as likely to be doing something sexual.[50]

In the film industry, 17-year-old star Emma Watson, who plays Hermione in the Harry Potter movies, has been electronically enhanced on posters to make her look curvier. Indeed, the film industry makes the last male preserves of merchant banks, political parties and golf clubs seem like equal opportunities paradise. In the top-selling films for general release, there are three times the number of boys and men as girls and women. The most common role for female characters is that of a secretary or other clerical staff (although singers and princesses also make a regular appearance). Researchers have concluded that women are three times more likely to run a business or have a professional job in real-life than as they are portrayed in films. There has been little change and little improvement over the last 15 years.[51]

The same bias emerges in modern music and music videos and confirms how often the role of females centres on sexual imagery. In music popular with teenagers, around one in seven songs, and much higher among rap and R&B artists, contain sexually degrading lyrics.[52] In music, teen singers of the same age have marked their shift to a more edgy, adult stage by coming out as sexual icons, as the ill-fated Britney Spears did at the 2001 MTV Awards, displaying her 'mature' image in a nude body-stocking.

The marketing of Disney's film, *Pocahontas*, is an example of how sex and race can be packaged and sold in an unquestioning way. Ziauddin Sardar analyses the marketing of the film in a forensic essay, 'Walt Disney and the Double Victimisation of Pocahontas'.[33] In Disney's sanitized screen epic, he argues, what had been a war of colonial settlement and expansion became, in modern family entertainment, a paean to cultural diversity. Two people of different races fall in love, with Pocahontas first to find the love-light burning in her eyes. This, for Sardar, is like Anne Frank falling in love with a German officer. It is a contemporary version of the conquerors' myth of available, willing women, wanting more than their own world can offer. Pocahontas is given a cartoon makeover, and probably cartoon plastic surgery, in becoming the most sexually endowed of all the female forms that appear. As Mel Gibson exclaimed in the accompanying television documentary, 'I mean, Pocahontas is a babe, isn't she? You've got to say it.'[54] In reality, the true Pocahontas was probably 11 or 12 years old in 1608, when the story takes place.[55]

Too much too young

Now, fast forward 400 years. Do you remember Chloe? We told the story earlier of how, when she was a young teenager, she and her friends discovered the 'how sexy am I?' online quiz. When her average score came in as 2, she seemed to lose all interest in her hobbies and sports. The author, Rob Parsons, says that 'teenagers like Chloe need to know that however they look, whatever they wear, and whatever happens, they are loved. Letting your teenagers know that you love them unconditionally is crucial if they are to discover a sense of purpose and value in the world.'[56] But her story is not unusual. The campaign group Women in Journalism has helped to shine a light on a series of teen and tween magazines and websites, including *Sugar* magazine, that have run modelling competitions for girls as young as 13, asking them 'want fame, freebies and fit lads?' *Mizz* magazine website put up galleries of 'lush lads', some shirtless with the tagline 'rate our hotties', and *Bliss* magazine asked readers (girls aged 14 to 17) to rate different parts of their bodies (boobs, bums, tummies, thighs . . .). Teen magazines always walk a fine line between reflecting the world they find in their readership and responding to the concerns of the outside world, and on some issues, like sexual health, they have played a trusted and invaluable role for children. However, remember that the ages given are the official ages for marketing purposes. The true age of children readers is always younger. As Peter Hutton and Annabelle Phillips of MORI explain, 'As a rule of thumb, always assume when marketing to young people that the magazines and media always attract an audience two or three years younger than you expect.'[57]

As sex is widely represented in the media, advertising and marketing, children learn that this is something that fascinates and delights adults. But the images to which adults are used affect children in quite a different way. When they are young, the bombardment of sexual imagery that they don't understand can be off-putting and scary. The connection between sexy and the act of sex may not be made. It is simply all part of an overall encouragement to have skinny bodies and buy the things that make you more beautiful, pretty and, above all, grown up.

At a teenage stage, the prevalence of sexual imagery is likely to encourage early sexual behaviour. The United Nations children's programme, UNICEF, in its 2007 survey found that the UK was the worst country for children to grow up in.[58] There were many factors that contributed to this result, but how children in the UK relate to their peers was one. In other wealthy countries, UNICEF reported, between 15 per cent and 28 per cent of young people have sex by the age of 15. For the UK, the figure is 40 per cent. Yet at the same time, only 43 per cent of teenagers see their peers as 'kind and helpful', which, as Judith Woods writes in the *Daily Telegraph*, 'adds a terrible poignancy to the figures, suggesting as it does a culture of underage sex taking place in an emotional vacuum'.[59] Libby Brooks, in her book *Story of Childhood: Growing up in Modern Britain*, comments that 'Today's young women are reputedly the most sexually confident, most sexually active generation ever, yet a third say that they have been coerced into sex and many more express regret at starting their sexual lives so early.'[60]

However, it is not only precocious sexual behaviour and what children learn about sex and sexuality as they grow that is the worry, but how it affects their idea of what it means to be a girl or boy. The feminine ideal emerges as a more passive one. Girls are encouraged to take a romantic vision of the future, whereas for boys, according to Brooks, 'sex is characterised as an act on its own and one that underpins their masculinity'.[61]

What happens to children whose value comes primarily from their sexual appeal or behaviour is described in an exhaustive report from the American Psychological Association on the sexualization of girls. The results include emotional distress, anxiety, low self-esteem, eating disorders and depression. It affects their schoolwork, with girls dropping out on subjects like higher-level maths. Some girls appear more resilient, including girls from black and minority ethnic communities that reject the images of white beauty that surround them. Boys end up with an idea of girls as sexual objects, which is a belief that can jeopardize their ability later in life to form and maintain intimate relationships. And on top of their psychological scars, girls can lose out in terms of their own sexual self-image and therefore, ironically, have less of a chance to have a healthy and happy sex life in future.[62]

We turn next to another human instinct, food, but it may help first to summarize and draw conclusions from what we have learned here about the fashion industry and its lucrative foray into the life of the young. Children tend to enjoy the world of looking good. However, as with many of the examples in this book, what we find is not simply that there are upsides and downsides to children's consumer life, but that – and this is really striking – there is such little effort to distinguish between the two and, therefore, so little effort to promote one and limit the other. We found a sense that, for all the fun of clothes, there may also be a significant cost if the market creates a culture of competition among the young. A culture of comparison can turn sour if children learn what society seems to validate as beauty and what children internalize for their own self-image is whether they have sex appeal. On this, the research is clear. It is not prudish. It is fact. The sexualization of our children where children of a younger and younger age are exposed to more and more provocative imagery – too much, too young – exacts a heavy price, now, soon and later.

4. Food Child

'Am I twice as healthy today, because I have had two diet Cokes?'

Jed, age 7

We all enjoy a winner. Competitions and lotteries have an uplifting effect on us. We're surrounded by reality TV contests, football leagues, cricket matches, board games and pub quiz nights. But now, brace yourself for the Product of the Year contest, where hundreds of the edible goods that jostle on the shelves of your local shop fight it out to take the mantle of the UK's favourite new thing to eat.

Invited to judge, we walked through the portals of the Institute of Directors in London's Pall Mall, our expectations high. Spread out on tables and in fridges all the way along the central room of the building were entries from every major food company. The UK's food and drink industry is big business. It is the largest manufacturing sector in the country, with a turnover of £66 billion. It employs 500,000 people and buys two out of every three potatoes, lettuces, tomatoes, hops, pigs and sheep leaving our farms (the other little pig goes to market overseas). However, to be honest, the competing offerings from the UK's best food innovators and marketers were . . . a complete and utter let-down.

Every company seemed simply to mimic existing products or aped competitors' offerings, with zero change in substance and tiny adaptations in presentation. Each product was heralded by a breathless folder announcing promotional hype prepared by the PR team or agency: the beer with not too little and not too much alcohol; the crisps still packed full of fat but fried in obscure oils that are 'lower in poly-unsaturates'. You say it once and it sounds good but repeat it and, like all PR puff, it dissolves away to nothing really new, nothing you really need and in all probability nothing you would really enjoy. There on the table, for example, was the 'brand new' chocolate offering, except it was the same size, same format and probably same ingredients as the others. The only new thing about it was its name, Heaven (a result of extensive market research). This is to compete, no doubt, with the successful Divine Fairtrade chocolate that has plumped up the children of ethical consumers for ten years. Divine won 'Millennium Product of the Year' in 1999 though, with chocolate farmers from the Kuapa Kokoo cooperative sitting on the company board, at least it was a genuine innovation. Product of the Year was not a true competition but a banal example of herd mentality announcing that great marketing is somehow all about sticking to the script.

One of the shared directions for the herd was its focus on children. This focus was not on new products either, but on repackaging and reformulating a classic success in marketing to children – junk food. The difference was the glossy new veneer of 'better health': Smarties with the artificial colours taken out; gummy chews in which sugar and artificial ingredients fuse with 25 per cent fruit juice for a natural feel; everywhere you look, saturated fat, but lower than before . . . 'junk lite' that the marketers called the trend for 'permissible treats'. Retailers 'will not want to miss the opportunities for profit from sugar consumers'. Sugar consumers! There you go, children in a marketing nutshell. So how did junk food becoming reinvented as health food? Keep hold of this question as you read because, to trace the full story, it is worth stepping back a few years.

The 1950s' child is bonny and bright

Compared to any previous generation, we live in a new world in terms of our diet. Foods that used to be considered treats have become an everyday option. Industry and technology have combined to cut food prices, just as we have more money in our pocket. Food comes to us from astonishingly complex networks of distribution. We have choice over what we eat and where we eat it. However, evolution has bequeathed us a physiology with a preference for variety and taste and a weakness for sugars and fats. The result is a phenomenon known as the 'nutrition transition'. This describes the see-saw shift over time from a significant section of the population getting less than enough food and nutrients to a point at which they get too much. Remarkably, this is happening simultaneously in many poorer countries, where you can see children that are malnourished and obese in the very same village and even in the very same family. According to the World Health Organization, the largest chronic health problem worldwide is not HIV/Aids but obesity. More people are overweight (1 billion) than starving (800 million). In Egypt, 25 per cent of children are obese, while in Zambia and Morocco, 15–20 per cent of 4-year-olds are obese.[1]

The nutrition transition has taken place over generations in the UK. The grandparents of some of today's children would have been teenagers in the 1950s. The 1950s, more than any other decade, are thought of as 'the good old days' – a time to which people hark back with nostalgia. And, perhaps surprisingly, that is exactly what one study did find, when comparing children's diets in the 1950s to today. The study found that diets in that 'age of austerity' were close to today's healthy eating guidelines.[2] The researchers suggested that the increase in soft drinks and snacks was the major factor in the deterioration of children's diets. Children also exercised more then, but even if children today were as active as their 1950s' forebears, they would still be losing out in comparison in terms of their intake of several key nutrients, such as fibre, calcium, vitamins and iron.

One of the children that benefited from a 1950s' diet is the tall, avuncular figure of Sir Don Curry KB, CBE, FRAgS. Don Curry is the UK's favourite farmer – at least that is our view, though it is possible that we may now never again be asked to judge a competition such as the Product of the

Year. Growing up in the countryside, he remains true to it, farming 250 acres in Northumberland with arable and lowland grass.

Don was catapulted into the position of advising the nation on how to chart a way forward after the disaster of the foot-and-mouth outbreaks in the early years of the new century. Drawing on the input of farmers, campaigners such as Deirdre Hutton (now Chair of the Food Standards Agency), environmentalists and industry leaders such as Iain Ferguson (now Chief Executive of Tate & Lyle), Don Curry tore up all the received wisdom of farming policy before him. Reporting to Government in January 2002, he said that the future of farming in England lay in business models that encouraged farmers to be stewards of land and nature and to improve the health of people.

The real innovation of his widely welcomed report 'Farming and Food, a sustainable future' was that it provided the first national strategy anywhere in the world to make a link between agricultural policy and health and nutrition. When Ed met Don for the first time, Don asked him to help make the link he had established on paper happen on the ground. He said the problem is that the connection between the families that eat food and the people that grow it has been broken. Our changing tastes and the complexity of where food comes from has helped to make this happen. We used to be self-sufficient in beef. Now we eat prime, import steak and export the low-value parts. In poultry we export the legs and extremities of chickens and import the breasts. If farming is to survive in Britain, we need to reconnect the next generation, those who are children today, with quality food and its origins in nature.

And how should we do this? We need, Sir Don says, a response to the issues of diet and nutrition as consistent and coherent as the decades-long road-safety strategy. This is a good analogy. Back when Sir Don was young and walking to school, the number of children killed on the road was climbing fast as more cars came on to the road. It seemed, to some, inevitable – just as the rise of overeating may do today. Cars were becoming cheaper and more available and people wanted them. But when parents started to campaign for more road safety, the country rallied to launch an urgent, sustained and consistent programme of action: a government-led initiative, combined with industry action and individual education and support. The School Crossing Patrol Act of 1953 gave lollipop patrols the power to help children cross the road safely. It gave us the bushy-tailed road safety character Tufty the squirrel and the 'Lookout club'. Many other initiatives built on this, including driving tests, the green cross code, speed restrictions, drink-driving campaigns and zebra and pelican crossings. There were 797 child fatalities on the roads in England in 1953. Today, despite many more cars on the road, the figure is 169.[3] In short, nothing in society is inevitable. Fundamental change, from companies to families to children, is possible if you organize to make it happen.

The 21st-century child comes in all shapes and sizes

Is young obesity really such a problem that we now need fundamental change? Many cultures celebrate an overweight kid. What to one person is a child piling on the pounds is, to another, a healthy kid ready to grow. The scientists have their definitions of what counts as overweight or obese, but their definitions are nonetheless lines in the sand. Scientists' opinions do not necessarily tally with how the parents see their child. Parents, as we shall see below, are notoriously poor at judging whether their children are overweight. In part, this is because media coverage – with examples such as a 14-stone 9-year-old – encourages a sense that obesity is an extreme condition, associated with neglect and abuse. Any parent would want to distance themselves from that. What is beyond doubt is that the accepted measurements of obesity used today tell us how things are changing among children and give us a risk profile for those that fall the wrong side of the line.

Obesity, or being overweight, is not in itself a disease, but what it does without parallel is to increase the risk of picking up a remarkably wide range of diseases, not only chronic ones that stay with you through your life, but also more immediate problems. Obesity causes high blood pressure, increased cholesterol and even clogged arteries among children. If children are obese, they are more likely to face distress, discomfort and psychological problems. If they eat the wrong foods, without key vitamins, minerals and essential fatty acids, children end up less able to concentrate, less likely to learn and will do worse academically. If you are obese at the age of 2, you are nine times more likely than your friends to end up obese when you are adult. It used to be that children lost their puppy fat as they grew older, but these days, we are told, have now gone. Type 2 diabetes was once known as 'late onset' diabetes because you had to be over 40 to get it. Now, it is increasingly found in adolescents and this is put down to the rise in obesity. When writing this book, we talked to the Chief Executive of a big Birmingham hospital about type 2 diabetes. Was he still finding a considerable increase in type 2 diabetes in 12-year-olds? His response was to say forget 12-year-olds, as we are now seeing type 2 diabetes in 5-year-olds.

Let's go over the facts briefly. Obesity in children under 11 has risen by over 40 per cent in ten years and the UK now has the highest rate in Europe. Overall, up to one-third of children are now overweight or obese.[4] If current trends continue, half of children will be obese or overweight by 2020[5] and, by 2050, Britain will be a mainly obese country.[6] Obesity is not the only dietary concern relating to young people, of course. The eating disorder anorexia is on the rise and there is too much salt in young diets. Four-year-old children, for example, have double the amount of salt in their food that health professionals recommend.[7] As with obesity, both of these dietary problems can be amplified by commercial trends, from skinny celebrities and 'size zero' models through to the sales success of snacks. Now, 92 per cent of children consume more saturated fat than is recommended while 86 per cent consume too much sugar and 96 per cent do not get enough fruit and vegetables. If the

Product of the Year was measured by what is eaten, do you think you could guess the top six foods that children in the UK eat more of than anything else? We'll give the results below.

How do you like your food? Yellow or green?

Manchester is a beautiful city shot through with invisible lines that divide better-off neighbourhoods from rougher parts of town. The lines are the *de facto* boundaries across which money and power do not cross. On the wrong side of the line, the washing hangs out of windows and balconies, rubbish collects in the street and the chintzy uptown food shops give way to all-purpose corner stores. Obesity is something that affects rich and poor alike, but a diet rich in fresh fruit, vegetables and oily fish, for example, is harder to find in poorer areas.[8] What emerges from research on 'health inequalities' is how much it matters for your health which side of the line you grow up on. As a result of these and other health inequalities, boys in the centre of Manchester can expect to live almost eight years fewer, and girls almost seven years fewer, than their contemporaries in more affluent London neighbourhoods like Kensington, Chelsea and Westminster. Food and drink is 28 per cent of the household budget for those on a low income and families in poorer neighbourhoods have, in general, diets low in fresh fruit and high in fat.

It all comes down to a battle between 'greens' and 'yellows'. Maisie, the 23-year-old daughter of an ex-miner, gave up vegetables when she was 14 years old. She's a mother herself now and when you ask her about healthy eating, she knows what constitutes a balanced diet and knows what to feed her daughter, but she also confesses that she would have made her parents' life hell if they had tried to force her to eat her greens. She is not alone. Just 27 per cent of children in the UK eat fruit every day, compared to 42 per cent in Germany, 38 per cent in Italy and 34 per cent in France.[9] You might find tomato on her pizza, but Maisie is from the generation of children that have fallen in love with 'yellow' food – waffles, chicken nuggets, cereals, chips and crisps. Yellows 1, Greens 0.

In a world where both parents now work outside of the home in two-thirds of households compared to under half in the 1980s, children increasingly control their own eating patterns. People are working longer hours and journey times to work have also increased. The time spent preparing meals has dropped from 2 hours in 1980 to 20 minutes in 2000 – although, refreshingly, it has apparently climbed back one more minute over the last year. Family members may eat at different times, making convenience food easier. Breakfast and packed lunches for school are prepared in the morning rush, when mothers are particularly busy. Lack of time is the single most important reason for buying convenience foods.[10] With convenience foods, not everyone has to eat the same thing or at the same time. Instead of just setting down a meal in front of children, as previous generations may have done, you can offer them choices. Four out of ten children regularly choose their evening meal.[11] And so, the food industry has developed more and more products – many of which are high in fat, sugar and salt – that target this new way of eating and markets them heavily both to parents and children. Parents in the UK now tear the wrapper off six times the number of ready meals consumed by families in a country like Spain. Yellows 2, Greens 0.

All parents have to evolve sophisticated tactics when feeding their children because food time can be a battle. Mothers still bear the burden of food shopping and preparation and face the risk of buying nutritious foods that their children will not eat. The main concern is to make sure that they do eat enough, and have the fuel to grow and be active. So, boys eat nearly four times as many biscuits as green vegetables (by weight) and girls eat over four times as many sweets and chocolates (again by weight).[12] Consider the state of the school lunchbox. Parents struggle hard to ensure that their children do not go without – and make sure that their children's lunchbox is no less full than those of their class-mates. In a perverse way, having less healthy food is about status and not losing face, because having crisps or chocolate biscuits is a way for your children not to stand out in their class. You certainly don't want other people to think that you are letting your children go hungry – to see you, in effect, as a bad parent. Again, the food industry has products for all of this, competing for space in the lunchbox, knowing that it is easier to put snacks in, even if they are less healthy, because you can be pretty sure that your child will eat it when you are not there. Yellow 3, Greens 0.

Of course, yellows may be the team with the money and the wealthy backers to exploit the success, but the underdog greens are set to make something of a comeback. The 2006 *School Dinners* TV series by Jamie Oliver and his 'Feed me better' campaign has kick-started a widespread renewal of interest in school food, with local authorities and the organic food sector among the pioneers. By September 2009, every primary and secondary state school will be working to better food quality standards. Although new healthy menus and showing the red card to chips and the infamous turkey twizzlers have not taken off in every school, with meal take-up dropping in some cases, those schools that have involved children in planning the switch to healthy menus have proved the most successful.[13] The number of children that are becoming vegetarians, a clear green option even if you do have to work a little harder to get a balanced intake of nutrients, has risen to 6 per cent of toddlers and 10 per cent of teenage girls.[14] Yellows 3, Greens 1, and everything to play for.

So, what are the top six foods eaten by children? Stand up the much-loved potato as the one vegetable that makes it – and, in fact, the potato makes it into three of the top six slots. The top six are, in order: white bread; crisps and savoury snacks; chips; biscuits; boiled, mashed or jacket potatoes; and chocolates. Before the British Potato Council issues a release celebrating this book as a triumph for potato power, we are obliged to point out that the latest guidance from the Food Standards Agency pulls the rug from under their celebrations, pointing out that 'Did you know that we should be eating at least five portions of fruit and veg every day? You can choose from fresh, frozen, tinned, dried or juiced. But remember that potatoes don't count because they're a starchy food.'[15]

Parents fighting back – the campaign on junk food

The success of children's junk food in commercial terms is awesome. Of these, the most profitable 'big six' are sweets and chocolates; soft drinks; crisps and savoury snacks; fast food: convenience foods; and pre-sugared breakfast cereals. In each and every case, British children are among the top consumers internationally. Remember what we said in earlier chapters about how kids spend their pocket money? Well, overall, the confectionery category, for all the family, is now worth an estimated £6 billion per year. The top sweet for children aged 8 is Maltesers, but by the time they are 10, Maltesers have slipped to number three, behind Cadbury's Dairy Milk and Galaxy.[16] British children spend far more on sweets and fizzy drinks than their European counterparts: in fact children aged 5 to 9 spend more than £100 a year on sweets and a similar amount on fizzy drinks – that's over twice as much as France and the highest spend of any country in Europe.[17] They are also far more likely to snack 'on the go', spending £433 million on their way to and from school.[18] Every second Scottish girl or boy aged 13 eats sweets every day.[19] Around half of children aged 8 to 15 eat from a fast-food outlet at least once a week.[20]

Soft drinks now come in all forms – with tonics, shooters, zips, shots, crushes, fizzes and spikes. We led the way, for better or worse, when in 1770 English scientist Joseph Priestley was the first person to put fizz into a drink – in this case putting carbon dioxide into distilled water. If he had also invented a time machine, he might be flattered or, as a father of four, horrified to find that in the 21st century, teenage girls in the UK drink two-thirds more fizzy drinks than milk.[21] Drinking your calories fills you up less than milk though, and significantly less than food, so you need more. Not surprisingly, children who drink soft drinks are more likely to gain weight.[22] The marketing for soft drinks is perhaps more assertive than any other part of the commercial assault on children. Soft drinks are poured into children with multi-million pound aspirational marketing campaigns, using athletes, celebrities and the packaging of an 'active lifestyle'.

There are problems, too, with the young and the marketing of alcoholic drinks. In the UK, 27 per cent of 15-year-olds get drunk regularly compared to 3 per cent in France and 5 per cent in Italy.[23] In total, over 800,000 children below the age of 15 are regular drinkers in the UK, according to Frank Sodeen from the charity Alcohol Concern. A record number of children – around 7,000 – are in treatment for alcohol abuse and the number of children admitted to hospital because of drink has risen by a third over the last decade. [24] The *Food Magazine* found that the most popular teenage soap on TV, *Hollyoaks*, was awash with drink, featuring alcohol in a remarkable 40 per cent of scenes, either in a prominent way (18 per cent) or in the background (22 per cent). The magazine also compared the £800 million a year that the drinks industry spends promoting its products with the government budget of not quite £4 million for safe-drinking campaigns.[25]

The issue of what is spent on advertising and marketing junk food has become hotly debated over recent years. For every £1 spent on advertising fruit and vegetables, the food of which we are supposed to eat at least five portions a day, £70 is spent advertising chocolates and snacks.[26] Over the last few years, over 300 consumer and health organizations have combined to challenge the advertising industry over rules for the promotion of junk food and the result, in the teeth of virulent industry opposition, shows signs of progress.

There must be downsides to being a marketer. If everyone knows that you sell only what you are paid to sell, surely people are less likely to believe what you say. Perhaps it then becomes easier to take positions that overstate and exaggerate to win the point. So, when health professionals and academic researchers started to make the link between the marketing of food and our worsening diet, the most natural thing for the marketing industry to do was to run a campaign to deny it. The result was the Food Advertising Unit, which started its work 'with an involvement in the public policy process – in particular, talking to those in Government, Parliament and Whitehall, and seeking to de-couple the debate about food advertising from the debate about children's health. There are many that believe these are linked, but try as we might, we can find no evidence to support that view.'[27]

Over the following years, the evidence piled up, culminating in a magisterial review in 2003, commissioned by the Food Standards Agency. The undeniable conclusion was that the promotion of less healthy food is something that contributes to children eating less healthy food. It seems obvious – after all, if it didn't have that effect, why would food manufacturers spend so much money on marketing in the first place? Since then, the evidence has firmed up even further. A study by psychologists at the University of Liverpool in 2007 showed that children aged 5 to 7 ate 14–17 per cent more calories after seeing ten adverts for food during a cartoon show than children seeing ten adverts for toys. Those aged 9 to 11 who watched the food adverts then ate 84–134 per cent more calories than the group that viewed toy ads.[28] Who would not agree with the 14 to 15-year-old boy who told *Which?* that 'you only have to see the Pringles ad and you want one'.[29]

And they had the backing of parents. As one woman, Pam from Teignbridge in Devon, told *Which?*, 'I am a parent and a community dietician and am exhausted in trying to combat the advertising messages that undermine my parental role and my work.' Another, Emma from Chingford, commented that 'I get extremely annoyed with the yoghurt and cereals that are endorsed with cartoon characters. My three-year-old is becoming increasingly aware of these products and is starting to make a fuss when I choose the healthier (and probably cheaper) alternatives that of course don't have such appealing packaging.' Research by the regulator, Ofcom, revealed that foods high in fat, sugar and salt account for 80–90 per cent of all TV food advertising spend,[30] while a survey for *Which?* showed that four out of five parents think that TV ads for unhealthy foods shouldn't be allowed when children are most likely to watch.[31]

The response by the Food Advertising Unit was to hire other academics to try to discredit the findings, something that failed to convince the authorities at the Food Standards Agency. Something had changed. Before this, companies didn't necessarily have to believe their food products were wholesome and healthy. They simply had to hire someone to suggest that they were. Their bluff had now been called, as this was no longer a debate about whether to take action on food promotions to children, but what should constitute that action. Meanwhile, a wider alliance of people, including one of your authors (Ed) working at the National Consumer Council, was now pressing the regulators to introduce rules to get a better balance of food promotions to children and limit junk food ads, starting with TV. The Children's Food Campaign was born and, as it gathered support in 2003, the Food Advertising Unit responded and their chief, Jeremy Preston, suggested a head-to-head debate with Ed in front of an industry audience at their annual conference.

Into the lion's den

Jeremy is a career children's marketer, having run a breakfast cereals business for 13 years before joining the Food Advertising Unit. When he and Ed faced each other on the platform Jeremy introduced himself, as so many from the industry find comfort in doing, as the parent of two sons. The core of his argument was that, fair enough, companies sell what children want to eat. 'My previous company,' he explained, 'launched a child's breakfast product with minimal sugar, no salt and no fat, advertised by Michael Owen. It failed to meet any of its objectives because kids didn't like the bland taste.' So don't make it bland, Jeremy, was the murmur across the audience, but he went on to argue that this simply couldn't be done. 'I have also sat in tens of focus groups watching children trying to eat bland cereals. In the vast majority of cases, the only way they find them palatable is to sweeten them.' This was the choice of the nation – sweet, sugared cereals, flavoursome food and happy kids or bland food, down-in-the-dumps toddlers and a smile only on health tsars in government. It is 'a known fact' he went on 'that overweight parents tend to have overweight children – sometimes it is genetic, but parents with unhealthy diets and lifestyles often consciously or unconsciously wish these upon their children.'[32]

Other marketers there on the day took aim at the idea of restricting adverts for junk food. 'If I genuinely thought that an ad ban would solve the problem of child obesity I, as a parent and citizen, would sign up right now,' said David Kershaw, Partner at M&C Saatchi, but as Ed quickly produced the Children's Food Campaign petition for him to sign, he added that it would not work and, worse, would be a smoke-screen for 'the real causes'. He was right, of course, that restricting adverts doesn't solve the whole challenge of child-hood obesity, so you need to do more. Even so, as Ed pointed out, those who argue that we can't do everything shouldn't get in the way of those who want to do something. Later, as the campaign heated up, this point hit home. A feast of food companies came in to lobby the Secretary of State for Health, one after the other, invariably starting by saying that, sadly, they bore only a small share of responsibility for child-hood obesity, perhaps a few per cent at most. 'A few per cent?' was the cheery reply from the key health adviser, Professor Paul Corrigan. 'That is wonderful. That will make a real difference, alongside everyone else.'

Ed's contribution on the day was to warn companies not to believe everything that they read from industry lobbyists. With the public mood becoming rapidly more concerned with food and obesity, their competitors could well be ahead of them, and if they were credulous enough to swallow what the Food Advertising Unit had said, they probably already were. In particular, he tried to bust what he described as the five myths that were regularly trotted out when industry commentators defended the marketing of junk food to children: 1. there's no such thing as good or bad food; 2. marketing doesn't target children; 3. advertising doesn't change minds; 4. advertising grows market share not markets; 5. it is parents that are at fault.

Traffic lights

The first of these myths was key, as you can only find ways to promote a better balance between good and bad food if you can distinguish between the two. At the time, in 2003, Ed said:

> Food lobbyists say that there is no such thing as a good food or a bad food, only good diets and bad diets. This is pure sophistry. It is like saying that there are no good apples or bad apples, only good or bad barrels.

Of course, we can make these distinctions at different levels, depending on what we know of the likely balance of people's diets. The proof is that food labelling claims and logos send a different message to consumers – 'lowers cholesterol', 'maintains heart health', and so on and so on. You can't promote food as good and pretend there's no food that's bad.

In truth, most nutritionists would find it easy to say which are junk foods, that you should eat in moderation, and which are more healthy foods of which, in general, you should eat plenty. But can you design a set of scientific rules that bears out those judgements? This is when Mike Rayner steps into our story – or rather back in, because he was one of the co-authors of the original Food Standards Agency review. Mike is an academic with a heart – a pun he has got used to, having set up and directed the Health Promotion Research Group at the British Heart Foundation. He is short with a thick, black beard and eager eyes, looking more like someone you would find glued to a computer game than the gastronome he is. His brain works at double speed.

Sitting down to a coffee one afternoon some time after the Food Advertising Unit event, Mike showed us the bones of a model he had developed for scoring products by the quality of the nutrients that they contained for standard sizes. This was designed to draw a line between healthier foods for children, which would be good to advertise, and less healthy foods, where cutting back on advertising could help. Shortly afterwards, the 'traffic lights system' was born, which points to the fat, saturated fat, sugar and salt content of foods as you buy them. Having ironed out a few anomalies, such as mackerel, which is high in fat, and dried fruit, which is high in non-milk extrinsic sugar, that were 'red-lighted' despite their nutritional value, this system is what you can now find on the front of packs on the shelves of Sainsbury's, Asda, Co-op, Boots and Marks and Spencer. The colour coding of traffic-light red, amber and green for nutrients like fat, salt and sugar makes it easier to see the quality of the food that you buy for yourself and your children. Tesco, the biggest retailer, made a big play of carrying out trials of the traffic-lights system, but refused to come on board with its competitors when push came to shove, opting for an alternative system – meaning that parents have had to get to grips with competing ways of putting nutritional information over.

Buy junk, get more free

The supermarkets tended to keep their heads down as the Children's Food Campaign developed or, alternatively, presented themselves as working for children's health. Yet, if there has been one single big boost in the marketing of junk food in the last 20 years, it is what supermarkets have done in terms of in-store promotion. In fact, you could argue that this has done far more to promote junk food for families and children than any on-screen advertising. These promotions began in earnest in the early 1990s at around the same time as obesity began to increase. Prior to 1992, the only form of in-store promotion that could be run in a supermarket was single-pack price reductions, like '50p off' and 'half-price'. After this, developments in electronic point-of-sale scanning technology allowed different individual items to be linked in a shopping basket and the multi-buy promotion was born, typified by what marketers call BOGOF and the world knows as 'Buy One, Get One Free'.

For most grocery categories, this is fine. If you get a pack of toilet rolls for free it has no impact on how fast you use toilet paper. However, family food categories such as snacks, crisps, biscuits, chocolate, cakes and soft drinks fall into a group that is termed 'elastic consumption'.[33] In short, this means that the more you put in the kitchen cupboard, the more gets eaten. As a rule of thumb, if you put 100 per cent more snacks in the kitchen cupboard, they disappear in only 10 per cent more time.[34] Anyone with children can confirm this. All this has combined with a change in the balance of power between manufacturers and retailers. Supermarkets now drive the promotional activity and food manufacturers (of branded or unbranded goods) pay for it. What is particularly prized are the 'gondola ends' (the end of aisles) as 100 per cent of shoppers pass these, whereas only a proportion pass down any individual aisle (only 20 per cent, for example, typically go down the chocolate aisle). These gondola-end locations are in very short supply and retailers want to maximize their return from this space. They therefore get reserved by those who can pay the fixed costs (about £100,000 for a single week in a leading chain) and those with the biggest brands, as these sell best.[35] The other preference is for promotions from the categories with 'elastic consumption', because it is in the interests of supermarkets for us, the shopper, to return to our normal purchasing habits as quickly as possible after the promotion ends. If we still have a cupboard full of toilet rolls, we don't buy more. It's hardly surprising that supermarkets far prefer promoting junk foods to more healthy foods.[36]

The truth is that advertising is only one of the more visible components of overall marketing. More balance in the way food is advertised to children has to help, but to address the broader issues by focusing on advertising alone is like trying to catch a bus by jumping on its trail of exhaust. There will be enough loopholes to keep marketing teams busy for years. Rupert Howell puts this well. Based at ITV, he is past president of both the Institute of Practitioners in Advertising and the European Association of Communications Agencies and known for his advertising success with the Tango soft-drink brand. Howell remarked at another Food Advertising Unit event, 'I think banning advertising is like putting a picket fence around a flock of birds and expecting them to stay there. I mean, it might look pretty, but is a total waste of time. Because of merchandising, point-of-sale, catalogues, programming, movies, all this stuff, there's just no point doing it.'[37] He is not far off the truth, in our view. The moral is that if you want to encourage responsible advertising to children, then you have to take an approach that addresses the full mix of marketing and not just part of it.[38]

The reinvention of junk food

Companies that have found ways to make truly healthy food sell are still rare. For most (as we witnessed at the Product of the Year show) the approach has been to sell pretty much what you already have but this time under a new mantle of health. After all, health sells but who is to say what is healthy?

A cinema advertisement for Kellogg's Frosties, for example, showed children playing football with Tony the Tiger. A voiceover stated 'Train hard, eat right and earn your stripes'. The commercial finished with a scene showing a bowl of cereal and a packet of Frosties on a table. The Advertising Standards Authority, on receipt of a complaint, noted that a 30-gram portion of Frosties with 125ml of milk contains more sugar than a jam doughnut, a custard tart or a flapjack, and so concluded that that implication of healthiness was misleading. But there is always a way around the rules. After the débâcle over Frosties, Kellogg's used cartoon characters to package another high-sugar cereal, Coco Pops Coco Rocks, as part of an 'active lifestyle'. One advert, on children's TV, ran with a caption 'run around, have fun and eat a balanced diet'. On this occasion, when the complaint came, the Advertising Standards Authority concluded that the advert was just offering good advice about diet and exercise.[39] With this leeway, Kellogg's has since run adverts claiming that Coco Pops are a source of calcium, vitamins and iron, neglecting to mention that one-third of them is sugar.[40] To their credit, the company has now closed the Coco Pops and Frosties advergames and websites, but there is still a contradiction between Kellogg's putting 'healthy lifestyle' information on the outside of 250 million packs of cereals such as Coco Pops and Frosties and the less than healthy lifestyle associated with what is inside.[41]

Sweet and crisp companies are taking the same tack. Starbursts, for example, are advertised as 'bursting with real fruit juice' when in reality they're 61 per cent sugar. Walkers are the UK children's crisp of choice, featuring advertising with Gary Lineker, who has done more than any other celebrity to boost crisp sales and therefore salt in children's diet. Walkers advertise their crisps as carrying as little salt as a slice of bread. Well, yes, but as investigative journalist Felicity Lawrence has shown in her book *Behind the Label*, there is a serious problem with the amount of salt in everyday bread too. Besides, detecting salt is not easy. Parents are told that they have to lower their children's salt intake, but on labels, the salt is described as sodium. You then have to translate that into salt and then compare it to the recommended daily amount. As with the 70 or so different types of food-assurance labels to be found on British supermarket shelves, it is all a bit of a maze. Parents and children alike can be baffled and bamboozled by claims and counter-claims as to whether a product helps or hinders finding a balance in your diet.

When there is complex health information on products such as Guideline Daily Amounts, few parents or children take the trouble to stop and try to work out what it means. That is not how we shop. Typically, we make rapid decisions based on short-cuts, habits and forces of desire that are deep in our subconscious. So, here is how it really works. While conscious awareness about health concerns is on the rise and makes parents think twice before buying that chocolate cereal as a treat for the kids, the mere presence of health labelling and advice on a pack gives a split-second, emotional reassurance that it is all okay. Perhaps as a result, one in two children aged 2 to 4 have pre-sugared cereals for breakfast (and only 1 in 25 have any kind of fruit) and these are cereals that come with health advice – eat a balanced diet, take some exercise – prominently displayed.[42] In the seconds it takes to make food choice, the halo of health in the form of nutritional labelling is now helping to sell the same junk foods that accelerated the health crisis of children's diets in the first place.[43]

It is not, we should add, all bad news. One of the most hopeful approaches is one that has been pioneered in the UK by Gerard Hastings, a partner with Mike Rayner in the Food Standards Agency review. It is called social marketing and its motto is 'if marketing got us into this mess, maybe it can also get us out . . .' Social marketing is a fusion of the techniques of marketing research and design with the values and ethos of public benefit. The core idea is that health organizations can promote better public health by marketing it with care in the same way that companies market their products. One family that has benefited is Coral, who works in a local health-food shop, and her daughter Olivia. Coral knew that she needed some help with Olivia, who was 9 years old, but had to wear age 14 to 16 clothes. So she was delighted when a promotion was run for a food and exercise programme at her local leisure centre in Catford,

South London. Olivia became a passionate member. After nine months, she reported that 'I wear 10–11 clothes and I love them.' 'I enjoy the sessions,' she added. 'I feel much fitter now and I've just got a lot more confident about everything really. I know all about foods and which ones are good for me.'[44]

However, the balance of evidence is that the way food is promoted still contributes to children eating much less healthily than they should or than they did in the past. We have an obesity crisis on our hands. Food marketing has seen off public concern and, remarkably, junk food has been reinvented as a healthy option. So why do we put up with it? Some research completed for the emerging social marketing programme at the National Health Service in 2007 suggests the answer.

Fooling me, fooling you

The research shows that the decisions we make on how to feed ourselves and our children are emotionally and psychologically complex. Surprisingly, we may be more likely to tolerate poor food and drink for children. Researchers have found three processes at work here.[45] First of all, we fool ourselves. As noted above, many parents discount the weight of their own children, sometimes despite having been advised by doctors that they are obese or overweight. To most parents, their kids look normal or they look underweight. Why is this? Subconsciously, no parent wants their child labelled 'fat' or 'obese'. Parents fear that such labels will put children at risk of other problems, like bullying or eating disorders. As one mother put it, 'I think it's totally wrong to make children aware of their weight – my daughter is bigger than some of the other girls in her class and I'd worry that she'll stop eating and become anorexic because she would think she is fat and the others would call her names. She is already asking me if her bum looks too big.'

Second, happiness trumps health. It is common for people to believe that their children are healthy so long as they are happy. Because their emotional and psychological well-being comes top, parents put this first, even where this runs contrary to their long-term health. It is easier to feed children yellow foods like potato waffles, chicken nuggets and chips if you know they'll wolf them up. Watching children clear their plates gives any parent an emotional buzz. Which is why, with a little marketing, feel-good products for children sell well. Walkers calls its crisps 'little slices of happiness' while Cadbury's promotes Snaps with the strapline 'your happiness loves Cadbury's'. As one mother puts it, 'To me, healthy is about them being happy, like smiling, sleeping well and not worrying about things. I don't really think about whether they are physically healthy because I can see that they are. If they were ill, I would know.'

Third, couch potatodom can be made to feel like it is an active choice. Health can feel like a drag and takes away the little things that make life worthwhile such as a night in front of the TV or your favourite biscuit. Health, for many, is something only other people can afford or it's the privilege of stay-at-home mums who have the time to cook. Parents believe that their children are already doing enough sport in school time and they don't want their children to roam around outside. It is not just stranger-danger, but traffic and other, older children that they worry about. As a result, we are far more receptive to commercial brands that link sedentary living with associations of pleasure, fun and rewarding family experiences. They suggest we have made a choice, that the opportunity to do nothing is a symbol of success, a privilege earned and a reward for all our hard work. No wonder we attach a high status to entertainment products like high-definition TVs and games consoles. As another mother put it, 'We both work very hard all week to provide a nice home for our family. When it comes to the weekend, we want to sit down and enjoy what we have at home . . . We all watch TV together and it is nice we can enjoy what we pay for.'

Pester-power

These three factors – self-deception, a focus on happiness and the triumph of the couch – unpick the bindings of parental responsibility. One more syndrome helps to make it an explosive mix – the rise and rise of pester-power. Food eases the dynamics of family life. Snacks can be used as a parental tactic to reward good behaviour, to appease children, to break up the day or to help get things done, from homework to tidying rooms. Meal times can be fraught, whatever the age of the children. Again, treats like ice cream or pudding can help encourage eating vegetables – so-called 'food trading'.

The idea that everyone has a right to choose what they

want when they want it means that telling children what to do can have negative connotations for parents. Many want to offer their children the choice that they never had in their own childhood. But what children want is wide open to commercial suggestion, starting with the way that food is branded and packaged. When asked by the National Children's Bureau what they liked about how food looks, children talked about brightly coloured packaging; the use of characters and celebrities; jokes and humour; fun factors, such as yoghurts in squeezy tubes; specially shaped packages; free gifts and collectable items like wristbands, tickers, trump cards and toys; and limited editions. 'Healthy food is not packaged attractively – it doesn't draw you to it,' commented one girl, aged 13. Meanwhile, the rebranding of junk food as healthy food helps to disrupt the messages that children receive about healthy eating. 'It's confusing because different people are saying different things,' explained one girl, aged 14. 'When you see a celebrity promoting something, you think, well they eat that and look great, so I can too,' said another girl, one year older.[46]

So, how do children persuade their parents? 'I go on my knees and beg,' says one 8-year-old boy, and a girl of the same age agrees: 'I do try and persuade her in a sweet voice.'[47] When out buying, though, there is rarely a need for children to be on their knees, even if the words shopping centre and tantrum go together like horse and carriage. Supermarkets won't tell you this, but research shows that shopping is an unpleasant task for many parents if they are on a tight budget and have children in tow. They will race through as fast as they can, taking no risks, generally sticking to the safety of convenience foods that kids pester for. Promotions are predominantly for less healthy food, at least with the exception of Marks & Spencer. As one mother put it, 'Last week they have three packs for the price of two on chicken nuggets so we bought them. It was good for us because we spent less and the kids got nuggets every night till they were all gone.' If children are suggestible to the packaging and marketing that companies use to grab their attention, parents are certainly suggestible to what their children ask for. Over three-quarters of parents will typically comply when children ask for cereals (77 per cent) and around two-thirds when they ask for crisps (68 per cent) and biscuits (63 per cent).[48]

The official advice from the food marketers on pester-power is that we have a crisis of parenting, not a crisis of marketing. Parents should simply do more to take responsibility. Bob Eagle of the Food Advertising Unit, which we met earlier, argues that 'There has been a lot of debate in the media recently about pester-power. But surely the point is that we have to learn to understand "no" – which part of the word "no" does one *not* understand?' Most people would agree with the sentiment and some parents probably do need better parenting skills or support to set those boundaries. One mother in the National Children's Bureau research talked about her difficulty with this: 'She has got really naughty recently and I don't know what to do about it. She won't sit at mealtimes, she won't eat her dinner, she demands iced lollies for breakfast and she won't listen to me or her dad . . . so we just give in.'

However, to accept, as almost everyone does, that parents have first responsibility is not the same as saying anything goes. Parents should not have to swim against a tide of marketing. After all, to ask parents to say 'no' is deeply disingenuous, as the child catchers know more than anyone how to fire up children to get round their parents and how to make parents feel good by saying yes. As a result, children are learning to 'over-indulge' as a way of life. If food is a battle, then it is one in which the odds are stacked against parents that want to do the right thing – not because they want to be bad parents, but because of the opposite. They want to see their children happy and they feel good when they are. It is a powerful combination.

5. Techno Child

'I have seen a lot of things I don't really want to see.'

Jordan, age 8

Kyle is 11. Every morning he sits at the kitchen table and slurps his cereal, eyes fixed on kids' TV. When he gets back after school he slings down his bag, leaps on the sofa and hits the remote: bit of MTV, *The Simpsons*, *Hollyoaks* . . . By 5.30 p.m. he's a bit bored so he grabs a bag of crisps and heads for his bedroom where he logs on to the internet, catches up with a couple of mates on Bebo and spends the next hour trying to get his character to the next level on Runescape. Whilst on Runescape he takes the odd call from his mobile phone and downloads a few snippets from YouTube. James from next door comes round and they slog it out in a boxing match on the new Wii until his mum chucks James out and calls Kyle down for tea which they eat in front of *The Bill*. He gets nagged into doing his homework after this, but he does it as fast as he can so he can wrestle with *Grand Theft Auto* on the new PS3 for an hour before bed. Snuggled down under his Man Utd duvet he's got his iPod playing Arctic Monkeys and *Big Brother Live* on his telly to get him to sleep.

Technology is no longer part of children's lives – it is part of them. In this chapter we look at how the breathtaking pace of technological change has revolutionized children's daily lives forever and how commercial forces harness the power of the technologies which permeate our children's lives. We look at TV, computers, video-games, mobile phones and the stars of the screen.

Gary Rudman has been doing qualitative market research among teens and young adults since 1991. He suggests that 'technology is everything. Other products – jeans, skate-boards, skis – are all interesting, but they don't dazzle and truly excite. Because technology is the focal point of teen existence today – technology is what generates heat. With technology embedded, ordinary items can be magically transformed from also-rans to must-haves.'[1] But it is not just technology's contribution to cool that's exciting children. The new functions, new gadgets and new ways of doing what young people have always wanted to do, including creating their own stuff, chatting to friends, quizzes, sharing photos and learning to flirt, are creating a new interactive and digital world out there.

Sherry Turkle noticed the beginnings of this in her remarkable book *The Second Self – Computers and the human spirit*, published in 1984, where she made the following observation: '[The] question is not what will the computer be like in the future, but instead, what will we be like? What kind of people are we becoming?'[2] She was prescient in many ways. Asking what the computer – or any other piece of technology – will become is to indulge in fruitless speculation. She could never have dreamt that 25 years after the publication of her book, kids like Kyle would possess the power of the computer on a tiny mobile-phone handset which would be attached to them like an extra limb. She couldn't have guessed that beneath his duvet he could plug himself into an information superhighway offering him unfettered 24/7 access to a sparkling universe of fun and games or a menacing underworld of violence and depravity. Even the most brilliant scientists have been prone to make the most extraordinary understatements when attempting to shine their crystal ball on the wake of their innovations. Our personal favourite is Alexander Graham Bell's announcement in the 1870s about the first telephone: 'I do not think I am exaggerating the possibilities of this invention when I tell you that it is my firm belief that, one day, there will be a telephone in every major town in America.'

We can't predict technology, and no doubt the role that machines will play in the lives of our children in another 25 years would shock everyone today. However, we do know quite a lot about human nature and, given that turning the clock back is neither possible nor desirable, we can try to adapt to what's happening to our kids in their technological lives and try to concentrate on the undoubted positive impacts. Monitoring the effects of technology on our daily habits and values is an activity which will have to become part of our routine.[3] For the moment, let's have a look at what Sherry Turkle found in one of the first studies of kids and technology.

Techno child 1984 was a young mind fascinated by the challenge of understanding and engaging with rudimentary computers and primitive programmes. Techno child might be in nursery school working out how to progress on the Speak and Spell console. Techno child might be a junior-school student writing a series of commands to make an on-screen space ship take flight. Techno child might be a young adolescent allowed into the video arcade for the first time, desperately trying to beat the system on Space Invaders. And techno child might be a 15-year-old girl discovering how the skills developed in mastering and controlling a computer can help forge her own identity and self-image as someone in control of her own life. Techno child operated in a kind of 'man versus the machine' way: the two were still quite separate entities.

Through long hours spent with children in all sorts of locations and settings, Turkle made the discovery that children's engagement with the computer changes quite radically as they hit different phases of growing up. Part of it is just to do with the way children's thinking skills and social skills develop in biological terms. Later on, we will look at how children's minds and how their brains work and develop over time and how this affects the way in which children process marketing information. For now, we can note that the idea of children developing in stages – most famously articulated by Jean Piaget in his three key stages of child cognitive and social development which are reflected in most school systems round the world – chimes with how Turkle concluded that children relate to computers. Those at nursery or infant school (age 3 to 7) approached these new pieces of technology in their lives in a very metaphysical way. Young children had a burning curiosity to know if the machines could think or feel and – a major preoccupation – if they were alive. When the game wasn't going their way lots of little kids would accuse the computer of cheating which led some to believe this meant the computer was alive because, as one little boy claimed, 'if you cheat you're alive'. Others believed that even if computers were not alive they certainly could think. One child playing Merlin (an interactive computer toy on which you can play games such as noughts and crosses) observed that 'Merlin saw my move, but he didn't light up a square for me. He doesn't let me light up.' He saw human motivations in the computer. For some these motivations were also imbued with feelings, emotions and 'human' characteristics rather than pure logic: 'Oh yes, this is not a regular toy. It is very mean.' The under-8s debated where computers came from; if they had a mother; whether having batteries made them more or less alive and which of these questions would help define the difference between a computer and a human.

Rules and secrets

By the end of junior school the 1984 child-machine relationship had moved away from metaphysical considerations to concentration on gaining domination over the machine. For children in the next stage of development the appeal was the rule-based nature of computer games. Kids shifted from getting narky with a 'naughty' Speak and Spell game to engaging, in highly competitive fashion, with the simulated, bounded realities offered by video-games. For a number of 7+ young people these universes opened up the opportunity to be in control: a possibility which might not have been available in their real lives: 'You walk out of the arcade and it's a different world. Nothing that you can control.' Perhaps, ironically, control is granted by the rules. If you know what the rules are you can work out how to get better and better because there is a clear benchmark: beat your previous score or, in today's video-games, get on to a new level. It is a certain and reassuring (if sometimes frustrating) space to inhabit. It is also intriguing because there are secrets involved. The 'webmaster' in charge (a term that resonates with this culture of domination and deference) knows how to get to the next level, but you don't: it's a secret. Discovering the webmaster's secrets holds an excitement of its own and entire websites are now devoted to uncovering them. Today, metaphysical mystery has given way to a more cynical view of mastery. The honest endeavour of working out the secrets or cracking the codes has mutated into cheating – with entire sites devoted to how to circumvent the rules on the most popular games.[4]

The allure of video-games is strong but, in 1984, Sherry Turkle concluded that a heavy involvement with the virtual world affected the way that children related to the real one. She compared how children play video-games with how they interact during face-to-face role-play games. In the latter there was 'empathy, understanding, recognition, negotiation and confrontation with others' – in virtual games there were simply rules and a system. Recent research in the UK, however, is far more hopeful. Free time soaked up in on-screen play, indoors and alone, may be the end of play as we knew it, but it is not the end of play. In particular, more sophisticated games and the arrival of massive multiplayer games have heralded a new phase: not 'man against the machine' but 'man versus man on the machine'. Researchers from Brunel University, Nic Crowe and Simon Bradford, have spent three years studying teenage gamers who spend hours on web-based games. They conclude that multiplayer online games give children a freedom to explore but without their parents worrying about where they are in an age when, in real life, they are not allowed out by themselves because of safety fears. Far from becoming pale prisoners of their own bedrooms, regular play was good rather than bad for their imagination.[5]

In Sherry Turkle's research the third stage of relationships with computers involved their role in facilitating children's experimentations with identity. Some older teens enjoyed the freedom of computer programmes to create something 'unique' – reflecting that heartfelt desire of the teen to be different. As one girl said, 'Nobody could have done that exact same thing.' For others, working with a computer made them think not only about programming a machine but how they themselves have been programmed throughout their childhood. Some young people heading towards the responsibilities of adulthood saw how their upbringing and education by parents, school, the church or the government was all a form of programming. This posed fundamental questions about the freedom to create an identity. Other youngsters began to use computer analogies to appreciate how they might be able to programme their own lives. For one girl who had inhabited a world of drugs, drink and sex, engagement with the machine brought with it the realization that she really could take control of her life just as she had taken control of the software and hardware sitting on her desk.

Techno child today

These stages of child-machine engagement still apply today. Children still take refuge in the certainty offered by rule-based games and tears of frustration are still shed when machines don't play fair. The role of computers in forging teen identity has burgeoned at a phenomenal rate as social networking and blogging have become essential elements in adolescents' very presence on the planet; as Skyler told us in an earlier chapter, 'if you're not on MySpace, you don't exist.' But there are two big differences between techno child of 1984 and techno child today.

The first is that technology is portable, ubiquitous, trans-ferable and ever-ready in a way never dreamt of a few decades ago. Today's techno child is 'always on'. Technology is not only a part of children – it is a part that is soldered on and painful to remove. Try taking a teenager's mobile phone away for a day and watch the writhing and raging of cold turkey. A recent study found that the majority of 16 to 24-year-olds would rather give up alcohol, chocolate, sex, tea or coffee than live without their mobile phone for a month.[6] And technology doesn't just affect waking hours. The Sleep Council complains that children who fall asleep while watching TV, listening to music or using other electronic gadgets are more tired in the day as a result.[7]

The second big difference between then and now is the wholesale infiltration of every technology platform by powerful commercial forces. These include the companies that have helped to spread the technology and, perhaps legitimately, want to get their money back. But, one way or another, precious little of the technology used by children to play, communicate, learn and progress is now free of some corporation using it for profit.

We are going to explore this phenomenon through the different screens that children today use to interact with technology. Remember our finding that children spend twice the amount of time in front of a screen as in class? Well, here we unpack this to see how a ubiquitous commercial culture operates through some of the many screens kids stare into on a daily basis: the computer screen, the video-game screen, the tiny mobile-phone screen and the giant silver screen. First, let's look at a factor that has been feeding into this change: the amount of time children don't spend outside, any longer.

Nature deficit disorder

It seems to be a characteristic of modern life that children are increasingly cut off from nature. Paid-for entertainment, perhaps, or urban life has displaced the free-range roaming of children around the world. This condition has a name. It is 'nature-deficit disorder'. When you first read about it, it comes across as a Cassandra-like prediction of doom for a generation that is, inevitably, far more urban and, perhaps less inevitably, lives more of its days indoors. However, the more we have looked at the evidence, the more it does seem that growing up less connected to the natural world suffocates some part of young people's well-being and development.

Psychologist Aric Sigman estimated recently that there are 1.1 million 'concrete children' aged 8 to 12 who have never visited the UK countryside. 'Twenty-first century youngsters,' Dr Sigman warns, 'are more likely to have holidayed abroad than to have explored England's fields and farms.'[8] In truth, the worry that children are losing contact with nature around them is not new, even if trends of urban living have accelerated. Sixty years ago, in a world of war and industrial waste, JRR Tolkien wrote *The Lord of the Rings* to try (among other aims) to awaken children's imagination and to re-enchant the land and nature around them.

The point is that if fewer children have direct experience of nature, they care less about the natural world. As Robert Pyle wrote some years ago, 'What is the extinction of the condor to a child who has never seen a wren?'[9] Perhaps this was the kind of concern that prompted a team at the

Department of Zoology, University of Cambridge, to look into how much primary-school children know about nature. They compared what children knew about species in nature and the characters and species in the world of Pokémon, invented by Satoshi Tajiri and inspired by his own child-hood memories of collecting creatures in the wild. They found that 8-year-olds could identify 25 per cent more Pokémon characters than wildlife species. The research conclusion, delivered with the dry wit of a team of trained zoologists, was that 'conservationists are doing less well than the creators of Pokémon at inspiring interest in their subjects.'[10]

Trees

There is a wealth of evidence that the natural environment plays an important role in helping children to develop. Take trees. There are researchers who have dedicated their time to the interaction between nature, trees and health. If trees could give Nobel Prizes – and they might choose not to, given that Alfred Nobel started his career as an armaments manufacturer by blowing up trees along the Neva river outside St Petersburg – then Frances Kuo would be first on the list. She founded the Human-Environment Research Laboratory at the University of Illinois, USA, in 1993, combining psychology with environmental design. Kuo and her colleagues have proved that people need trees. They need to see leaves from their windows. They need to sit and play in green spaces, with trees around. Trees draw people out from behind walls of brick and glass and, in doing so, help to nurture children and build a sense of community. More specifically, Kuo's research suggests that access to green spaces for play, and even a view of green settings, enhances peace, self-control and self-discipline in children living in inner-city areas – particularly, she found, in girls. Access to nature can even help reduce the symptoms of attention deficit disorder.[11]

The benefits do not stop with trees. It is not hard to work out that children are happier and healthier when they have opportunities for free and unstructured play anywhere outdoors but, of course, just as the woods were a source of folklore and fear centuries ago, so traffic, strangers and crime mean people don't venture far today. We know this affects parents but the extent to which children also play in fear of the outside world has recently been uncovered by Green Alliance and Demos, with help from the work of Ken Worpole. (Worpole, by the way, is the persistent researcher and campaigner that any self-respecting public park in the UK would nominate to run against Professor Kuo for Nature's Nobel.) Worpole has found that children would certainly like to spend more time out of the house but are often frightened to do so. As one girl, from Wick, said, 'I feel most comfortable in the garden. Because I know that there's no strangers there, and no one can get me or anything.' Another child, a boy on the streets of Huddersfield, said, 'If you kick into the road, it's really dangerous to get the ball back.'[12] It is not necessarily as if he could have kicked it on the grass either. The ubiquitous signs saying 'no ball games' are the visible evidence of a culture that can't help telling children what they can't do instead of what they can. When asked about their local parks and playgrounds, the majority of a sample of 500 children described them as 'boring': 45 per cent said that they were not allowed to play with water, 36 per cent that they were not allowed to climb trees, 27 per cent were warned not to play on climbing equipment and 23 per cent were disallowed from riding bikes or playing on skateboards.[13] No, no, no, no, no.

Incarcerated children

Traffic is another factor that keeps children indoors. Where traffic speeds in town come down to 20 miles-per-hour, children's casualties are cut by 70 per cent. In Home Zones, areas designed to cut car use, children are 30 per cent more likely to play in the street and to know their neighbours better.[14] In the rest of the country, the statistics show that 90 per cent of children own a bike, but only 2 per cent cycle to school.[15]

Crime also plays a part. Every year, one in three children age 10 to 15 is the victim of a theft or assault – most often in the street or in public places.[16] This means that young teenagers are perhaps the most vulnerable group in the UK. Even the most informed parents might be shocked to learn that the odds against any child reaching the age of 16 without at some point being the victim of crime are now 20–1 against. We know this from the systematic tracking of the Howard League for Penal Reform, which has researched the experience of more than 3,000 primary- and secondary-school children over a period of seven years. The majority of children have been assaulted, or had property stolen or damaged. Most are committed in and around schools and playgrounds or on the journey home from school. When you add this all together, a remarkable 95 per cent of children have been a victim of crime on at least one occasion.

It is possible that crime is at a peak in children's early years in secondary school, when they are prey to older children. What would it say about our society today if 13 is in fact the age at which you were most likely to be a victim of crime? If it were older, say 32 or 45 or 53, there would be such outrage that any government in power would be thrown out if it did not turn things around. However, as Frances Crook, Director of the Howard League says, children are rarely consulted about crime and the impact of crime on their lives:

If they were, adults would discover that children are frequently the victims of crime perpetrated by other young people. Two thirds of children do not report crimes against them to parents, teachers or the police, as they think adults will not listen to them or the crime will be viewed as too small to bother with. To children, however, in a child-sized world, playground theft is serious enough and does matter. It is ironic that the very institutions where children should feel safest – their school environments set up and patrolled by adults – are where children are most commonly victimised.[17]

This is, in part, a spillover from consumer culture. Street-wise kids replace the distinctive white iPod headphones with cheaper versions and different coloured leads, because they know that, even in a hoodie, white leads say 'I've got what you really want.' Indeed, the most common reason given by young people who commit crimes, apart from boredom and wanting money, is so that they too can fit in with others.[18] Similarly, some young people boast to their friends of having taken 'designer drugs', whether they have or not, but again with the aim of looking cool and fitting in.[19]

Of course, it is also true that for many or most of these incidents, young people are perpetrators and not just victims of crime. The Home Office, for example, conducted a 24-hour snapshot of the UK and counted over 66,000 recorded reports of anti-social behaviour. This was a Wednesday, mind, not a Saturday. Around 60 per cent of these were reported to be down to young people. Perhaps as a result of anti-social behaviour orders, the number of young people in custody has doubled over the past decade.[20] According to the United Nations, the UK 'locks up more children than most other industrialised countries'.[21] If you add together the costs of crime and the costs of courts, custody and care, then the full costs of youth crime add up to £13 billion per year, a figure that dwarfs the £1.6 billion spent by the government on positive prevention and youth programmes.[22] Even so, the adult population prefers to see the balance swinging towards getting tough rather than giving love. When asked as local residents (rather than as parents), the great British public would rather keep teenagers indoors and off the streets. One MORI survey found that a remarkable 75 per cent of the adult population said they supported a legally enforceable evening curfew on teenagers.[23]

It is all about risk: risk of traffic and abduction, risk of drugs, street crime and gang culture. These are all risks which touch young people. As a result, one way or another, children end up indoors far more than would have been the case for any previous generation. Children can be world citizens on the internet but are often afraid to go outside their own front doors. This has a real cost. The planner Kevin Lynch argues in his classic worldwide survey, *Growing up in Cities*, that urban children are now kept safe at the price of being starved of experience.

There are brave moves afoot to encourage parents to forget about stranger-danger, set aside worries of a risky world and set their children free. One of the most persuasive campaigners is Tim Gill, former Director of the Children's Play Council and author of a forensic book, *No Fear: Growing up in a risk-averse society*. He practises what he preaches. When out in the park one day, his 9-year-old daughter, Rosa, complained to him that some boys were 'bullying' her and her friend. He suggested she try to sort it out herself, which she did and the situation evaporated:

One day a week now, Rosa comes home from school by herself, with an older child who lives up the road. And she was really keen to do it. In fact, at the beginning of term it was the biggest thing that was going

to happen to her that term. Now, it's, 'Oh yeah, whatever? So I walk home from school.' But of course, the
first day it happened, we were sitting here waiting for
her, looking at the clock. So yes, it is scary. But we are
very clear that it is good parenting to do that.[24]

The computer screen

Returning indoors then to today's techno child and looking
at our first screen, here are the headline statistics on children
and computers. By the age of 6, one in four children now
has their own personal computer. By the age of 16, you are
in a minority if you don't have one of your own and, on
average, you'll be spending over three hours on it, online,
every day. Communication is the big attraction, with almost
half of all children using the computer to talk to their friends
on instant messaging or social networks. Otherwise, it is
for playing games, having fun and for school work, too.[25]
87 per cent of children can access the internet from their
own house and a sizeable minority do so from their own
bedroom.

Our own research has shown that most parents believe
that computers in general and the internet in particular are
a power for good and that if their children are not 'connected'
they must be losing out, particularly in terms of educational
advantage.[26] Children simply won't 'get on' without a broadband view of the world. This now strongly entrenched
attitude is surely a tremendous boon for the manufacturers
of software and hardware and the myriad organizations
who use the internet to sustain up-close-and-personal

advertising campaigns of the sort not possible on TV. The internet-enabled computer has become not a desire or a want, but a need as basic as food and shelter. While kids do use the internet for studies, the latest figures show that they are really much more interested in using it to hang out and have fun. There's no great surprise there really. It's like the telly-addict father justifying getting Sky for all those wonderful documentaries and educational programmes which, of course, no one ever watches: they are too busy watching reruns of the soaps and obscure sporting fixtures.

The idea that accessing the world wide web provides a quasi-mystical passport to better grades and a better future is being fuelled by a whole range of different advocates, even including reputable organizations such as the Ofcom Consumer Panel, who recently produced a report which flagged up a social need to 'change the attitudes'[27] of parents from lower socio-economic groups who have no desire to have the internet in their homes. It seems that they have won their battle already as, according to research just out, only 3 per cent of all children never access the internet. But why should families feel pressurized by Ofcom or anyone else to have the internet in their homes? We are not aware of any evidence proving that children with internet access develop greater intellectual capacity or life skills than those without. All we really know is that computers save kids the journey to the library, help children present their work more neatly and allow them to download more pictures to illustrate projects. We've talked to parents who feel that even schools pressurize them into having a computer for their children at home. However, not all are convinced. One parent in the study notes: 'If my kids need access to the internet, I just send them round to their uncle's. They don't seem to go that often, so I presume that they don't really need it.' What kids really 'need' it for is to do what they used to do in the park: playing and chatting.

Where does this pressure to connect come from? Well, it is certainly the case that advertising and selling via the internet creates vast wealth for the corporations who understand how to manipulate it. Although the roots of the world wide web are planted firmly in the laudable cause of the transfer of knowledge around the world, the internet today is undoubtedly a commercially driven machine. Two of the most popular children's websites[28] are YouTube and its parent site Google, a firm with a market capitalization of $146 billion,[29] derived almost wholly from advertising revenue. This advertising-driven business model is a ubiquitous and intrinsic component of cyberspace, but we discovered that no research had actually monitored commercial activity on children's websites – so we decided to do just that.

Here, again, we are going to take you on one of our research projects. We started by joining forces with the internet safety charity Childnet International and the National Consumer Council and began with a 'mystery shopping' exercise where we logged on to kids' sites and made systematic notes about the commercial activity we found there. We knew which sites were the most popular from a survey we had run with children looking at media use and happiness – something that we will explore later.[30] We looked at the top 40 kids' sites. Only one had no commercial activity on it (the BBC). The remaining 39 sites were funded by two sorts of commercial activity: selling goods and services (both virtual and real); and hosting third-party advertising. Then we went to talk to children and their parents. We talked to pairs of friends in their own homes and larger groups in schools. We convened discussion groups with mums and dads. We crossed the length and breadth of the country and included families from all sorts of social backgrounds.[31] This is what we found.

E-shopping

Almost half of sites used by children offer e-commerce opportunities. Many of those targeted at the very young are owned by toys and games brands and are little more than entertaining shop-fronts. On the highly popular www.barbie.com you can find hundreds of Barbie dolls, accessories, cosmetics, clothes, DVDs and other merchandise which can be purchased then and there from online retailers or purchased later from the many outlets advertised. Another site like this is www.diddl.com, devoted to the proliferation of cutesy mice. Both these sites offer kids the chance to create a 'wish list' (of their own products, of course) which they can mail to friends and family. The subject line of the email comes ready written to make it easy for the tots, so don't be surprised if you suddenly get one of these popping into your inbox around birthdays or other gift-giving occasions: 'Great birthday ideas from Barbie', 'These things from Barbie make me smile'. This is pester-power at its worst. One of the problems with these nag-and-pester-lists is that they aren't covered by Advertising Standards because they are not strictly advertising: i.e. Barbie and Diddl have not paid to advertise on someone else's space, they're just doing it in their own back yard. If branded sites were covered by regulation, things would be a bit clearer. Advertisers are specifically advised against suggesting to children that they should ask their parents to buy stuff for them. What's more, the promoting of email spam falls foul of the Advertising Standards Authority codes and it is against the Direct Marketing Association guidelines to give out other people's emails over the internet. Parents have mixed feelings. Glenda, who's the mother of senior-school children, told us, 'My daughter's done the Bratz one. It's cute and all that . . . But it's really cynical as well. I think it's really clever. It takes all the surprise out of gifts.'

Other sites try to get children to make direct impulse purchases – such as cute soft toys and other character-related paraphernalia from www.neopets.com or ringtones which can be downloaded on to a mobile from www.streaming-clips.com. Wallpaper, music, screensavers, skins, furniture for your Club Penguin igloo and cool new outfits for your avatar can all be bought online. Parents have to be quite tough, like 9-year-old Sam's mum: 'My daughter does look on e-Bay because she's really into *High School Musical* at the moment. Bought the T-shirts and all the gumf that goes with it. She'll call me to look and I'll say, "Add the postage and packaging on it and no you're not having it." They think you're a money tree.'

Until recently, children's direct internet shopping was severely curtailed not just by watchful parents but also by the fact that transactions had usually to be completed by credit cards – which are only available to adults. However, with the introduction of the IDT Prime Payment Mastercard, this has changed. This is a prepaid 'credit card' which can be bought at the local corner shop with no ID and can be used to buy up to £100 of goods at a time on the internet or over the phone. Although the card can only be purchased by someone over 18, a 14-year-old boy in Kent managed to buy a set of graphic porn films called *10xxx* from Amazon for just £6.97; three lethal knives from Tesco (which he signed for himself when they were delivered to his house); and a bottle of Kulov vodka from Oddbins for £8.99. He also set up a William Hill betting account where he gambled £10 on an England v Germany friendly football match. Other underage kids in Glasgow set up a bingo account and started gambling; bought a boxed set of 18-rated horror films linked with sick murders; and ordered in some wine.[32]

Even children without a Prime card can buy things on the net if they really want to. Lots of kids know their parents' credit card numbers and use them to make impulse purchases of anything from iTunes to hard drives. One mum told us the sorry tale of her 14-year-old who ordered a new motherboard for the family computer from the USA, not realizing that the bill would include a rather hefty tax and shipping charge. Parents should be careful about sharing numbers with their children – not because they shouldn't trust them, but because commercial temptation on the internet is strong. Everywhere kids turn they are urged to 'buy now!'

Another way of paying is by mobile phone. All that's needed here is a phone number and children can not only download ringtones and other mobile services but can pay for other goods such as virtual furniture items for Habbo Hotel rooms (www.habbo.co.uk) via their phone bill. We are told that Habbo Hotel currently has no less than 39 different payment methods: that's 39 ways to part kids from their cash. We came across a host of kids who'd been stung by Jamster. They thought they were downloading one new ringtone only to discover that they had signed up to a subscription service which mysteriously wiped out their credit every time they topped up. And it seems that soon our mobiles will be linked to credit cards. A 'pay-by-mobile' system already operates in Japan, where it is nicknamed 'o-saifu keitai' (mobile wallet), and trials are under way in the USA, France and Sweden.[33] Kids are very wary of rip-offs but are also aware of their own vulnerabilities. Rick, aged 14, told us about a site store he'd come across which was selling games: 'The title is misleading because it says Free Games.' He thought that with a title like that and the possibility of paying by your phone, 'You might be less likely to look for the amount of money, the price – you might just text your number.'

Internet advertising

Whilst direct selling on the internet is a big concern, especially with laxer payment methods, a more insidious and certainly less regulated type of commercialism comes in the form of the glittering array of colourful and noisy adverts which dance and sing around the pages of the websites our children enjoy, and, of course, the other forms of advertising which lurk quietly within the content. Hosting paid-for adverts is a massively lucrative activity for sites due to the sheer volume of traffic. The most popular children's games site, www.mini clip.com, currently has 34 million unique users. Around three-quarters of top kids' websites sell advertising space to third parties. As we will see in Chapter 7, 'Who's Messing with My Mind?', the techniques used in these adverts can be sneaky and potentially dishonest. What's more you can't get away from them. While just looking at the home page and one other page on our top 40 sites we added up an astounding 211 adverts selling, cajoling, persuading, tempting and spreading brand buzz. One page sported an amazing 17 adverts.

Kids find this commercial barrage, above all, annoying. 'If they're going to have adverts, they shouldn't be as big and should be at the side, and not make your computer freeze. Just ads for things that help you – bullying, ChildLine,' said one 11-year-old girl.

Children across the age spectrum recognize many, but certainly not all, forms of internet advertising. It's not surprising that they often can't tell what's content and what's a sales proposition as the internet advert really does come in all shapes and sizes. The fast-evolving formats include banners, buttons, interstitials, pop-ups, pop-unders, rectangles, animation GIFs, sponsored links, sponsorships, advergames, demonstrative integrations and homepage take-overs. All of which sounds like a cross between an episode of *Doctor Who*, a woman's magazine feature and a maths lesson. And, of course, each time consumers learn to recognize one format, the industry creates another just to make sure we are paying attention to them – or, conversely, so that they can slip unnoticed but effectively into our minds. We are all now apparently suffering from 'banner blindness' which means we pay no attention at all to the rectangular sash at the very top of our screen – no matter what it is flashing at us.[34] This is seen as something of a crisis in digital-advertising circles.

We asked 7-year-old Sophie where she could see adverts on her screen. 'The top and both sides,' she told us. How could she tell they were adverts? 'They look like it.' And her friend Gemma chipped in, 'It says "ad". Yeah, it tells you what it is. Sometimes the ads move.' Most of the children we talked to told us that they usually identify an advert from its position, its tendency to move, if it has absolutely nothing to do with the content on the rest of the page and, of course, if it happens to be one of the few adverts which is labelled. It's worth noting however that fewer than 4 in 10 of the adverts we covered in the research actually were labelled.

We discovered that, despite what they claim, in reality kids often can't distinguish what's what because the rules of the game change so often. 'I don't think they should write "advert" there because it says play,' says one 10-year-old boy about an advergame. We ask him if it really is advertising. 'Yeah, to play,' he insists. His mate suspects that it is more than about getting children to play the game itself. He's got some idea that the advert isn't completely related to the host site. 'I don't think it is, because it's their own site and it should be their own thing.' Even the tech-savvy 15-year-olds had a bit of an issue recognizing commercial intent.

As we have noted, company websites designed for children are not covered by marketing regulations because advertising is currently defined as when you pay for media through which to promote your products. However, online, that is nonsense. The sites that we have touched on in this book, like www.barbie.com, are 100 per cent adverts. For consumer kids as much as consumer adults, it is worth fighting for a basic right that all advertising should be labelled as advertising and subject to appropriate regulatory standards of truth and honesty.[35] As one girl put it in the course of the research, it is simple: 'don't lie'.

Kids in an adult e-world

Children are not just being encouraged or enabled to purchase children's items. As our 'Fashion Child' chapter has shown, kids are being nurtured by hungry marketers into developing adult tastes at a younger and younger age. We found that this is true for their choice of electronic games as much as it is for their selection of underwear. Our survey showed that the vast majority of the sites popular with children are intended for a wider audience, often students.[36]

Only 31 per cent of the sites most visited by kids aged 9 to 13 are dedicated to children, such as www.beanotown.com or www.cartoonnetwork.com; 29 per cent are general entertainment sites such as www.funkyjunk.com or www. ebaumsworld.com; 21 per cent are interactive gaming sites like www.miniclip.com or www.mousebreaker.com; 16 per cent are social-networking sites like www.bebo.com or www.myspace.com; while the list also includes eBay, the dedicated purchasing site. As we saw earlier, kids use the internet to have fun and hang out with friends – activities which probably haven't changed over the decades – but the difference is that almost 70 per cent of the cyber-locations they frequent are primarily intended for adults. You could argue that this is hardly the fault of companies running those sites. They are aiming to reach adults and surely can't be held responsible if they are extensively used by children and they can't even prevent it.

In reality, though, companies do not seem to own up to what is going on and many may in fact be trading on it. Companies that run major sites are completely aware of the extent to which they reach children yet persist in profiting from adverts for products aimed at adults and in producing adult content. For example, the entertainment site www.stupidvideos.com tells potential advertisers that its audience consists of '40 per cent teens aged 14–18; 25 per cent of young adults ages 19–34; 35 per cent adults, parents, even grandparents ages 35+'.[37] (Interestingly there's no mention of the under 14s, yet our survey showed that this was in the top 50 sites of 9–13 year olds). Aware that the biggest user group is still at school and presumably also aware that younger children are likely to use the site too, this site offers a whole section on 'girls' including videos of 'grind girls' and another section entitled 'sex videos'. It also takes advertising for misleading adverts claiming the site's visitor has won a free laptop and for holidays, green cards and other items aimed at an older audience.

Kids' TV tastes are equally adult: *The Simpsons*, *Coronation Street* and *Friends* are all favourites. So children are exposed to a plethora of enticements to buy cars, computers, financial services, double-glazing and washing-powder in whatever entertainment medium they use. Whilst this publicity is not going to translate into sales to kids today, it is certainly helping to build brand awareness for the future. Most of this happens at a subconscious level, something we return to when we look at how marketing works in relation to children's minds. Yet there are also greater worries for the here and now as advertising for gambling, dating, cosmetic surgery and loans are on the increase.

Here are a few examples we found on popular kids' sites. 'Flirtomatic' is an over-18s mobile flirting service encouraging sexy text messaging. Kids are encouraged to 'chat live', 'check out the most snogged flirters' and 'add loads of photos and videos to enrich your flirt profile'. This appeared alongside a quiz to assess how dissatisfied you are with your body, with an option to sign up for cosmetic surgery to make it all better. Like the letter offering credit to Lorna at the start of this book, we found a host of offers to children on the internet to obtain 'free' credit. Nearly a quarter of the sites visited regularly by children are gaming sites which are highly attractive advertising spaces for gambling services, such as Party Poker which our friend Angie Harrison got caught up in. Kids are lured by offers of 'free' money to gamble with, so we can see that the kids' screen time is being used by corporations to urge them to buy now, pay later, to get stuff for free and to be loyal to the firm for life.

The dominance of commercial and adult-oriented internet sites, together with the relative decline in children's TV programming is leading quite naturally to a new interest in public-service broadcasting for children, or at least its equivalent online. There is a long and proud heritage of public-service broadcasting, including but not limited to the BBC, but the media world online for children is clearly characterized by almost blanket commercial marketing. One way to balance this, therefore, would be to create a new Fund for Public Service Online, a model for which is proposed by the organization Save Kids' TV. As they describe this, it would support new investment in online content and destinations for 6 to 15-year-olds.[38]

Parents' views

Children now know more about computing than their parents and, with an increasing number of even the very young accessing the internet in their bedrooms, it can be hard for parents to know how to cope. So we decided to ask parents what they did to monitor, understand or regulate their children's internet activities. In conjunction with the charity Care for the Family, we asked parents from around the country to share their tips with us and each other.[39] We asked parents for their tips on fashion, sex, pocket money, mobile phones and the internet. The internet was the one that seemed to cause the most concern. As one mother who had been asked to give her tips pleaded, 'I would be grateful to get some tips – I find this difficult as my son spends every minute he has on it.' Although parents may feel they are acting alone with no rule book to follow, up and down the country mums, dads, carers and grandparents seem to have discovered a core of similar tactics. The overwhelming advice revolved around keeping a beady eye on what kids are doing and, above all, keeping the lines of communication open.

Most parents recommended keeping the computer in a family area so that they could walk by from time to time without appearing intrusive. Many used parental-control software but there were mixed views on its effectiveness. Setting time limits for internet access was another popular method of curbing the effects. A number of mums and dads also celebrated the fact that the kids could teach them something for a change and we learned about one 10-year-old who sorted out her mum's PowerPoint presentation for work. Dads working in IT proved an interesting set of people. They really liked the idea of remote control: watching what kids were doing from afar. They might use tools such as SpyAgent, by SpyTech. It's a 'spy software' or a so-called 'password stealer' plus it has other tools that are used together to present a clear picture of what's happening on a given computer.[40]

Mums preferred to talk face-to-face with their sons and daughters. Negotiations and discoveries over computers in family life were used by many adults to find what Gwen, the mother of a 5 and 7-year-old, called 'teachable moments' – daily opportunities to help kids negotiate their brave new world.

The video-game screen

Video-games have been around a bit longer than their internet equivalents and *Grand Theft Auto* is one of the games people love to hate, with its invitation to gratuitous killing, violence and sex with prostitutes. One veteran games reviewer, Frank 'Candarelli' Multari, concluded that:

> The violence in this game is unlimited, I've wasted (the GTA way to say killed) roughly two thousand pedestrians in this game and I am only 20 per cent completed. You can shoot down aircraft, senselessly beat down old grannies to death with a club for no reason at all, shoot random people, steal cars as you run over the person you hijacked, so on and so forth . . . You also frequently spot prostitutes on the street and you can actually pick them up in your vehicle, screw them, and gain life points.

He says it is, in short, a 'crime simulator'.[41] The inventors of such games appear to revel in what they are creating. Mat Sullivan, development manager for Stainless Software, said of *Carmageddon 2*, 'All the people will be part of the physical environment, which will enable us to create spectacular crashes, and remove arms, legs, heads, etc. in a shower of blood.'

Whether media violence causes real violence among young people, or at least desensitizes them to it, is a perennial question of research. Surely adults or children can be exposed to a violent or action film without having a desire to be violent, but does it defuse violent tendencies or incite and encourage them? For some, the jury is still out. For others, the conclusion is that it clearly does connect to violence off-screen.[42] This is a field of many studies and many conclusions. Fiction and games are a way of explaining the world – but where does fiction begin and end? Academic David Buckingham reminds us that whereas researchers might class cartoons as violent, children do not.[43] However, the United States Surgeon General's report 'Youth Violence', from 2001, offers a persuasive synthesis, suggesting that the balance of research weighs towards the idea that violence in the media spills over, at least in some way. 'In sum,' the Surgeon General states, 'a diverse body of research provides strong evidence that exposure to violence in the media can increase children's aggressive behaviour in the short term.' This conclusion was endorsed in April 2007 by the Federal Communications Commission in its 'Report on Violent Television Programming and Its Impact on Children'. If you prefer a better known source, then we might note that Arnold Schwarzenegger has signed legislation in California that prohibits the sale of ultra violent video-games to children.

The way that products are rated is something that the child psychologist and presenter Tanya Byron reported on in a review for government in 2008. Compared to other European countries, the UK has a reasonable framework for rating, but there are inconsistencies. Ratings for computer and video-games come under two separate systems: the voluntary European PEGI system (nicknamed Piggy) and the mandatory British Board of Film Classification (BBFC) system. PEGI offers age descriptors such as 3, 7, 12 and 16, while the BBFC adds separately the descriptors of 15 and 18. There are also icons that you can find on the back of the box to give an indication of the game content, such as drugs, bad language, sex, violence, discrimination or fear. However, as Tanya Byron pointed out, the meanings of the icons were mistaken by many, so that what people thought was a 'multi-player game' was actually a warning of content that included 'discrimination'. What they thought was a sign that a video-game was suitable for a boy or a girl was in fact the warning for 'sexual content'. She recommended a cleaned-up, single system of classification for video-games.[44]

Of course, to some degree, as we saw earlier, ratings can be counter-productive and become an attraction for a younger audience. As one young person put it, 'its bcuz they have lines like "for adults only" or if ur over 18 then click this and such phrases make children want to see'.[45] And if companies push the boat out, they may often get coverage and sales from the moral panic that ensues. An example is the mobile phone game, the *Coolest Girl in School*, which proclaims:

Lie, bitch, flirt your way to the top of the high school ladder. Become the Coolest Girl in School. Coolest Girl in School is Grand Theft Auto for girls. What does every girl across the globe have in common? At some point, every girl wishes she could be the Coolest Girl in School. Coolest Girl in School lets players live out their high school fantasies. Experiment with fashion! Experiment with drugs! Experiment with your sexuality! Cut class! Spread rumors! But try to avoid dying of embarrassment – literally! In Coolest Girl in School fashion and communication reign supreme. Working out what the hell to wear and answering hilarious quizzes makes or breaks you. Students are labelled according to the sub-culture they subscribe to, teachers exist to be manipulated and parents ensure the constant threat of social death. Nobody said being the Coolest Girl in School would be easy.[46]

The focus of debate on labels, however, has tended to be on how to capture and classify what is bad rather than how to promote what is good. In the USA, the movement that, four decades ago, created the long-running kids' programme *Sesame Street* is now arguing for the development of educational standards for different ages and contents. There are no requirements for online commercial content to have any educational value, nor is there any framework for vetting children's websites – or indeed the growing number of electronic toys that claim to be educational. It is an ambitious project, but developing research-based, universal standards for what constitutes educational content would mean that efforts can be channelled into promoting the good stuff online, rather than just decrying the bad.[47]

We need to know the good and the bad, because children and their families (and policy-makers, if need be) want to be able to distinguish between the good apples and the rotten pears in terms of what is offered to kids. In previous years, it used to be easier for parents to gauge what would be okay for children to watch. There was the watershed of 9 p.m., announcements before programmes began and a consistent schedule with text in the listings. Now, on-demand viewing, multiple channels and user-generated content make this far harder. But remember the story of Mike Rayner and the nutrient-profiling system he developed to be able to score food products and distinguish healthy eats from junk food? Well, there are similar efforts underway across a range of other products, notably the field of video and film, sometimes termed as 'digital labelling', as well as the online communities for parental advice that offer their own ratings on toys, games and films.

If the online future is, as technologists claim, the promise of a 'semantic web', then a consideration of what things mean for children must be an essential part of this. The good news about this work is that it starts to turn the debate on the needs of children and families from one of resistance and precaution in relation to the commercial world and, in particular, the online world, to one that seeks to harness the power of the new digital media for positive ends. Without research-based, rigorous systems for assessment, the only possible way to respond is either to let everything go, in terms of marketing, or to try to ban it all – a debate we return to below.

The tiny mobile screen

This brings us to the icon of the last ten years, across the world: the mobile phone. Practically every secondary-school girl (age 11 to 16) has a mobile (98 per cent). Nine in ten secondary school boys do, too. In primary school the figures are catching up, with ownership having increased dramatically over the past two years. There are now 350,000 5 to 7-year-old children that own a mobile phone.[48] While texting and calling remain pretty much universal, new activities are spreading fast as phone technology becomes ever more sophisticated and children constantly upgrade. Using the phone as a camera is becoming almost as standard as using it to talk and text, with three-quarters of all kids taking pictures and nearly 90 per cent of teenage girls capturing mobile images of themselves and their friends. Pictures and videos are swapped free of charge using Bluetooth by 60 per cent of all children (and three-quarters of teens) and about half listen to music on their phone, too. Only a fifth actually access the internet on their phones, mainly because it costs too much, but this may change soon as service providers offer new 'unlimited access' packages to encourage 'WAP' mobile phone internet use. Watching TV programmes on the phone is also taking off – something likely to increase with the proliferation of the Apple iPhone with fabulous picture quality.[49] All this adds up to the tiny, always-on, always-with-me mobile screen becoming a bigger and bigger part of how technology is digging deeper and deeper beneath the skin of children's identity and self-image.

Parents and the phone

The phone provides plenty of those 'teachable moments' mentioned above because most children make a point of doing deals with their parents over who pays. Our own children have approached us with the winning line, 'Well, half of our calls are to you to let you know we're safe – so maybe you'd like to share the costs,' which is a reasonable point. There are strong incentives to drive a hard bargain: with the phone more important even than chocolate, having enough credit is obviously a serious issue. Two-thirds of young mobile users say that their parents (like us) pay for at least some of the cost. The parents in our Care for the Family survey nearly all warned against having an open contract for kids with plenty of horror stories about bills of hundreds of pounds being clocked up by loquacious offspring. Some were really tough: 'Once you have paid out for the first phone the child should be totally responsible for the cost of running it from pocket money or earnings. Even if they mess up one month, do not bail them out. Yes, it will be inconvenient . . . but it probably won't happen again! This is the best introduction to budgeting a child can have.' 31 per cent of children pay for all mobile costs, exactly half are paid entirely by generous parents and 14 per cent of families have a joint arrangement. Over half of families use phone cards, 16 per cent prepaid arrangements, 7 per cent a credit card and just 5 per cent now get a phone bill.[50]

Free mobile calls with a catch

One company is offering to save parents and children all the hassle and all the cost.[51] Blyk is offering children their phone bills for free. Too good to be true? Well, it's not unlimited. Children get precisely 217 free text messages and 43 free minutes every month, but even so, it still sounds pretty good. The question they pose on their site is probably the one you are asking yourself now: 'How come Blyk can give you all this stuff for free?'[52] Simple – children who subscribe agree to receive adverts on their phone. Or as Blyk put it, 'Blyk goes out and finds brands that want to talk to people like you. Blyk charges them for sending you messages, and gives you money back in the form of free texts and minutes.' Blyk is a start-up company, but one with pedigree. It's run by the former president of the Finnish mobile giant Nokia and he has managed to sign up major brands like Coca-Cola, L'Oréal and Buena Vista, part of the Disney media empire. Giving companies more opportunities to bombard people with ads and special offers may sound an unattractive proposition to anyone over the age of 30 but Blyk is likely to be popular with a younger audience. They appear much more willing to accept the trade-off between putting up with marketing and getting something for nothing. They are also, as we have seen, addicted to their mobiles. Peju, 14, from Stratford, East London, said she would definitely be interested in the service because it was free and if the adverts were well-targeted they could even be useful. However, she warned that big brands using the service would have to make sure their adverts did not become too intrusive. 'If there is too much advertising it may get boring,' she said. 'The advantage is that you get to find out about new things and the disadvantage is that it could eventually get annoying.' She also thought her parents would support the idea. 'My parents would be relieved that they don't have to give me money for credit,' she said. She expected many in her peer group to be interested in the service for the same reason.[53]

Not all kids felt the same, though. Amina, 15, from Leyton, East London, said she would steer well clear 'because I don't trust them', betraying cynicism about big business. But she did think it would be popular among her school friends because it was free.

Naturally, phones featured heavily in our parents' tips survey. Finding the best way to pay for phones dominated the advice on offer. However, it wasn't the only important thing. Adults also wanted to share ideas on stopping phones taking over and disrupting family time. Many banned phones at mealtimes and confiscated them at bedtime to stop furtive under the covers texting. One mum wanted the same rules applied to parents: 'I hate seeing parents chatting away on their mobile phone while they are walking along the street with their children, as if the children are too unimportant to talk to.' Theft and mugging were also concerns, as was 'brand-bullying'. Most parents were pretty pragmatic about wanting to sharpen children's cynicism about the marketing machine whilst being acutely aware of the often ruthless law of the playground: 'Buy a middle of the range phone with "some" extra features. Less to go wrong, less attractive to thieves BUT not a bog standard phone that would be an embarrassment.'

Phone porn

Maybe there are other, greater issues parents should be tuning in to. Finance and branding may prove to be the least of their concerns as the phone becomes a whole lot more than a way of telling mum that the bus home is a bit late. According to Rachel Bell of the *Guardian*, with sex education failing to teach young people about relationships, pornography is filling the gap.[54] And what's the most discreet way to access porn if you're a child? Not WH Smith where the magazines are still more or less on the top shelf. Not on the internet at home because parents have either got software or remote spy controls or they are passing to and fro like yo-yos. No, as long as one mate has got internet access on the phone, titillating pictures can spread like silent wildfire to every desk in 6C before the teacher can say *Penthouse*. Bell notes that the Sex Education Forum found that half of children using the internet are exposed to porn and that almost a third of children receive unwanted sexual comments via email, chat, instant message or text. Some teachers are picking up on it. 'I caught one kid, aged 12, looking at porn in one of my lessons,' says Andrea O'Neale, a secondary-school teacher in Sheffield. 'It wasn't hardcore or anything

– it was a woman lifting her top up and down, with naked boobs, on repetition. His parents were brought in to pick up the phone and he got after-school detention. I mean, kids get all kinds of stuff on their mobiles; a lot of boys are Bluetoothing porn. I think they are quite widely exposed to it; they're not easily shockable. Do I mean just boys? Yes. Girls don't go anywhere near it.'

The internet phone allows a sexualized view of women to be proliferated in a school far more easily than ever before. One of our cousins has a son who got into trouble for selling the odd porn mag at school because he was taller than everyone else and could not only reach the newsagent's uppermost shelves but looked old enough to make such purchases. This sort of activity would reach a small core of boys in a school. With Bluetooth the whole year can share images in seconds. This fuels a distorted, misogynistic view of relationships which feed body-image problems, eating disorders, self-harm, depression, teen pregnancy and pressure to have sex. The UK has the highest rate of teenage pregnancy in Europe and, as we shall see in a later chapter, not insignificant issues with child mental health. None of this is surprising given incidents such as the following. A 16-year-old boy used his phone to film his friend having sex with a 14-year-old and then sent it to five of her classmates. Another two 16-year-old schoolboys were arrested for making a porn video of a 14-year-old girl on a mobile phone and circulating it around their school in Perth, Scotland. Girls, who are the ultimate losers in this sort of activity, are pretty pessimistic about stopping degrading images circulating. 'I don't think quick access of porn on the internet could EVER be stopped, ever,' comments Kera.[55]

This is a serious issue and it is a challenge for handset manufacturers and mobile service providers alike. Currently, these companies don't collect age data when phones are purchased, so it's not easy to know who's actually using internet-enabled phones. If date-of-birth was captured then access could be controlled. Most service providers offer the internet through what's called a 'walled garden' – which limits how information is fed through to the handset. Porn sites could be filtered out as part of this when the handset was known to be owned by a child. When mobile internet begins to be affordable for kids the issue will really take off. Watch this screen.

The big silver screen

Whilst most of the controversy surrounds smaller screens – what of the big screen, the silver screen, the backdrop for the distant dreams of a bygone generation? Back in the days when the only place you could see a film was in the cinema, it used to be the place where the young went to idolize heroes from afar; to look at gods and goddesses which they could admire but never touch. Alan Bennett's semi-autobiography *Untold Stories* includes the most wonderful little chapter about going to the 'pictures' ('seldom the "cinema" and never the "movies"') as he was growing up during the 1940s and 1950s in Leeds and, briefly, Guildford. 'Films,' he observes at one point, 'taught you to be happy that you are ordinary.' The world gilded by Bette

Davis, Richard Burton and Elizabeth Taylor was not accessible to mere mortals and, because films tended to be designed to deliver a strong moral message, the not insubstantial trials and tribulations endured were mostly beyond the reality of mere mortals and 12-year-old Yorkshire lads too. 'I came out into Wortley Road [location of the Leeds Picturedrome] grateful that, unlike Charles Boyer, we were not called on to stand up against the Nazi oppressor or battle like Jennifer Jones against the small-mindedness of nuns or like Cornel Wilde cough blood over the piano keys in order to liberate our country from the foreign yoke.'

In addition to being firmly and considerably larger than life, the film screen introduced children, above all, to stories. Plato, in his *Republic*, took a strong line that stories were central to childhood and that if there was one thing parents should get right, in terms of education, it was to take care about the stories children should hear. Alan Bennett alludes to the same thing, finding comfort that 'where actors stood on the moral scale was as plain as if they were characters in a fairy story. We knew what they would do long before they did it, whatever the plot their roles in it fixed and immutable; they had no need to unpack their belongings: as soon as they showed their faces on the screen one knew what they had brought.'

Children, of course, still watch films in their droves and children still need tales of right and wrong, of good and evil, of trial and tribulation, of intrigue and outcome. However, as films are accessible not only at the local ABC but on DVD, TV and PC, in the back seat of the car and in the pocket, the commercial world has taken hold of film and – in one box-office-busting swoop – stories, with their heroes and villains, too.

High school cash-ical

2008 was the year of *High School Musical 3*, just as 2007 was the year of *High School Musical 2* and 2006 was the year of *High School Musical*. The first singing, leaping, kissing, basketballing glitterama was seen by 160 million people. The second was beamed to 100 countries in a matter of months. And Zac Efron-encrusted duvet covers, curtains, cushions, T-shirts and towels became the must-have Christmas gifts for any self-respecting 9 to 14-year-old girl. Now there's nothing wrong with encouraging a teen yearning to make it as a singer, dancer, basketball player, maths genius or even heart throb – but promoting kids' self-esteem through clean-cut dreams is not really what it's about. Disney spent $4.2 million on the original *High School Musical* but has since earned 100 times that: it has boosted every division of the giant business empire. It has sold more than 6.5 million DVDs and was the best-selling CD of 2006; 4.5 million books about the characters have flown off the shelves; it has sold out a 42-city tour of the USA, and the Disney Channel's revenue has soared. About 300 different licensed products are available through partnering retail outlets like Wal-Mart. When *High School Musical 2* was premiered on the Disney Channel in the USA during the summer of 2007, it ignited a startling set of statistics: most-watched cable TV programme of all time; most-watched cable film of all time;

highest rated television programme ever for 6 to 11-year-olds; and most viewed Friday television telecast, cable or broadcast in the past five years.

'People are looking at this as a franchise,' says Anne Sweeney, president of Disney-ABC Television Group. 'We're looking at the different ways it can branch out.' So, it's not really about the story or the moral message or even the art of film-making – no, it's about 'branching out' or, in other words, 'cashing in'.

High School Musical karaoke games for Sony's PlayStation2 and Nintendo's Wii have been released and it's even made it on to the national dance curriculum in UK schools after Disney sponsored an 'educational' DVD with dance extracts from the movie, choreography notes and lesson plans. Around 2,500 schools use this resource, free from Disney, reaching 500,000 kids.[56] Plans are also underway for feature versions of *High School Musical* for the stage both in English and with local casts in India and Latin America. Perhaps even more indicative of the true mission of *High School Musical* is that sober-suited investment analysts who normally talk in grim tones of 'emerging market hedge funds', or 'crises in sub-prime mortgage lending' are now turning their hushed voices and pinstripes to the pre-teen world. One analyst, Peter Jankovskis, research director at Illinois-based Oakbrook Investments LLC, looked at the business model and concluded, 'Having an ensemble cast of relative newcomers kept costs down and amplified profits. *High School Musical 2* may make even more than the original.' He went on, 'It's Disney at its best, they've rolled it out in different formats for people. They capitalize on their intellectual property.' He should be pleased as his corporation holds 660,000 Disney shares. 'The great thing about having a hit like this,' enthused Michael Cuggino, president of Pacific Heights Asset Management LLC in San Francisco, 'is that there are many different ways of monetizing that hit over and over.'[57]

'Monetizing that hit' – try to imagine those words applied to *The Wizard of Oz*, *Swallows and Amazons* or *The Railway Children*. Hard, isn't it? With the feature film having irreversibly changed address from the larger-than-life cinema screen to the part-of-life, in-pocket mobile screen, and with heroes having morphed from the inaccessible to the downloadable, that security felt by Alan Bennett about the moral baggage of each character has somehow shifted too. If the primary purpose is to monetize rather than educate, where does this leave Plato's concern about children and stories?

Beckham to the rescue

Of course, fairy tales, goodies and baddies, and will-he-won't-he cliff hangers are all still enjoyed by children and still form an important part of their development, despite the commercialization of so much of their growing up. In fact, kids are now using the fabric of their material world to grapple with such age-old battles as doing what you should against doing what you want. In an earlier chapter, we reported on discussions with junior-school children that unearthed deep-seated barbarities towards Barbie dolls.[58] In the same programme of research, we were struck by how so many of the children used the antics of British soccer hero David Beckham to debate and comment on their emerging view of morality and ethics.[59] It was a surprising and spontaneous theme which crossed age groups and gender. We'd asked the children to talk about brands, particularly the ones they were into (or, in Barbie's case, not into). For these 7 to 11-year-olds the world of the brand was enmeshed with the world of celebrity, with Beckham and his wife, Victoria – Posh and Becks – up there with the best. Like brands, celebrities are now served up through commercial spectacles, creating role models and cultural icons which are produced and presented through the mass media and merchandising fests.

David Beckham is one of the most iconic sports personalities and even though his playing career is in its twilight years, it was fascinating to see how children related to him.[60] Significantly, Beckham's celebrity is also driven by the commercial world: he is used in a host of lucrative merchandising initiatives and sponsorship deals from Marks and Spencer's boys' clothing range to Gillette shaving products. This is part of a phenomenon that is widely referred to as 'Brand Beckham' – another case of the power and significance of 'monetization'. The children's conversations around 'Becks' were loud, emotional, argumentative and passionate. Views conflicted fiercely and were strongly expressed, but there was absolute consistency in the topics which children chose to argue about. The screaming and shouting centred on tensions between the real and the superficial. In short, how far can you trust what is around you, if you know it is commercial?

In Katie's view, 'He's had like, goods and bads in his life and when he writes his autobiography so you actually know what he's been through and everything, so I think you should give him a bit of respect for what he does and everything.' She, like others, tries to see who Beckham really is, but she and others were also quick to censure any behaviour which had a whiff of 'going over the top' – i.e. over-doing it, showing off or being inauthentic (tantamount to a criminal offence in a contemporary junior school). David put it like this: 'I don't know, I just sort of feel, I dunno like, he just tries to look, like handsome . . . But he ends up being, looking like he wants to look handsome. Like he's trying too hard.' Some of this condemnation was linked to extravagant and frivolous spending. Here's Ewan: 'Well, I'm, I'm – I don't particularly like him because he's a bit of a – he's always trying, I dunno, diamond earrings on which are worth 2 million pounds which is actually pointless . . . And, he's kind of always shows off and like getting new hairstyles every week isn't – it's very odd . . .'

For 10-year-old Chloe the 'real' Beckham was embodied in his physical status as a metrosexual pin-up: something which her male classmates found disturbing. Sophie starts the discussion, 'I hate David Beckham, he's horrible, he just shows off, every magazine I read, he's in there, he just shows off.' Chloe is quick to defend her hero: 'Do you know why, cause he's actually fit and no one else is fitter than him and that's why he's always in the magazines and adverts.' (We should point out that she is not talking about his training programme here but his sexual attractiveness.) Joe butts in, 'For one advert he must get about five million pounds.' Chloe to the rescue: 'That's cause he's mega fit.' 'Stop saying that,' appeals Joe, 'it's scary!' Chloe is undeterred: 'I'm trying to get round to you that he is F – I – T, that does spell fit!' Good looks justify financial reward for Chloe whilst for Joe this is not a fair exchange.

From celebrity brands beamed through television to film hits, phone porn and internet scams, technology has changed childhood. Across the different screens that children use, commercialized technology offers excitement, challenge and endless fun. The technology, though, puts children in touch with an adult world from which, ironically, the adults closest to them are excluded as parents struggle to keep up with their children in order to understand, communicate and protect.

There are no standards that separate out educational content from the fluff and guff of life online. There is no equivalent of the 'traffic light' food labels we wrote about earlier, to make it clearer to parents and children what sites are about or how the commercial proposition is being made. What is out there – on video-games and films – tends to focus on preventing harm rather than promoting what could be of educational value for children.

Children, meanwhile use the very fabric of the star-studded commercial world which engulfs them in order to fathom out their own moral values. As the fairy tale of David

Beckham, told in so many different ways, suggests, the mediated story world of these children is more morally blurred than the films of the 1950s. Their commercially imbued world is no longer as black and white as it used to be and children seem to be dealing with grey areas from a younger age. However, looking at the sophisticated conversations of today's primary-school children, it's clear that they are adapting, adopting and thinking.

Let's move now to the latest techno-influence on our children – social networking.

6. Networked Child

'On all of my addresses, I'm 20. Games, Bebo. If you want to go on a website, you lie about your age.' Esme, age 13

We have now looked at food, fashion and technology. In this chapter, the last of our four investigations into the consumer lives of children, we look at how the cold hard profit motive, deep at the core of the rapidly evolving social networks and the emerging virtual worlds, are affecting that most precious of things for children – their friendships.

Bebo, MySpace, Facebook and MSN are all ways to keep in touch online. The most active users across the UK are 13-year-old girls.[1] A remarkable 72 per cent of 7 to 16-year-old boys and girls are signed up to a social-networking site and over half have created their own profile. Child users of social-networking sites outnumber adults by two to one[2] and Bebo is not only the most popular social-networking site for kids; it is also the most popular kids' website, full stop. It has now dramatically outstripped fun and games sites like

Miniclip, entertainment sites like YouTube, instant messaging like MSN and search engines like Google.[3] It has 12 million British users at the time of writing.[4]

Most teen time on social-networking sites revolves around friendship. They check out what's on the profiles of people they know to see if they want to get to know them better; they search for people they did know but have lost contact with; they preen and update their own image to make it more enticing; and, most of all, they talk to their mates. Downloading music or videos, playing games or checking out events and information all take a back seat to building relationships. And whilst most children use these sites to talk to their existing friends, one in six is actively seeking out new people to befriend.[5] As friends are the soul and essence of a teenager's life, this has become a consuming and addictive business. As comedian Dara O'Briain quipped at a recent Edinburgh Television Festival, 'If anyone here hasn't heard of Bebo – it's basically heroin for 14-year-olds.'[6]

Bebo suicides

At the beginning of 2008 a seventh young person from South Wales hanged herself in what looked like a kind of suicide pact made on Bebo. Natasha Randall, 17, posted this on her profile page in memory of her friend Liam Clarke, 20, who hanged himself just after Christmas 2007: 'RIP Clarky boy!! gonna miss ya! always remember the gd times! love ya x. Me too!' The rest of her profile was perky and seemingly cheery and the 'Me too!' was lost amongst other comments until two weeks later. She hanged herself and the memorial messages started to flood on to the screen, in turn, for her. Jade Knill writes: 'I saw u tha day before babe I cnt believe you didnt tell me wat was going on . . . I wuldnt have cared wat it was or how long it took . . . I got all the time in the world 4 u . . . and u didnt have to do wat you did I was hear 4 u.'[7] Two more teenagers in the next village attempted suicide the following day.

The short existences of these seven youngsters were spent surrounded by the lush green valleys which in bygone years would have resounded with the noise of the winding wheels bringing thousands of tonnes of coal to the surface, the weekend lilt of male voice choirs and the cheer of the crowds when Welsh rugby was the hallmark of international sporting excellence. 'The Valleys', as the area is known locally, was above all about communities: groups of people with a core and a heart who relied on each other in the face of dangerous, dirty jobs. The selfless bravery of groups of miners during the heart-rending attempted rescue operation at the Aberfan tragedy in 1966, when 144 people (including 116 primary-school children) were killed as a giant slag heap cascaded into a school, was a poignant testament to this community spirit. A strong and supportive social life was based on face-to-face human contact whether in the pub, the social club, the rugby club or the chapel. Since the mines closed in the 1980s, the face of South Wales has changed dramatically. One in three children there now lives in poverty, while 11 per cent are not engaged in education, training or employment. In Rhondda Cynon Taff 26 per cent of boys and 13 per cent of girls between

13 and 16 years of age regularly drink above the safe limit; 40 per cent of boy and girls experiment with drugs and 50 per cent of those are current users. In some Valleys communities unemployment is 50 per cent, 91 per cent of the tenants claim housing benefit and 61 per cent of households have no transport.[8] When we ran research with children in local schools, it seemed as if young people were retreating indoors behind their computers. Perhaps with much of their real-life social network in tatters, Jade could only offer Natasha help and support on a virtual social network after it was too late.

The mother of one of the suicides said this: 'It's like a craze – a stupid sort of fad. They all seem to be copying each other by wanting to die.' She went on to comment about the inadequacies of 'social-network speak' to capture the depth of human emotion: 'I think the problem is they do not know how to speak like adults about serious issues like this. They can speak to each other on the computer but do not know how to express their emotions in other ways.' Yet one of the police involved in the investigation notes that the computer can sometimes make it easier to talk: 'It's often easier for them to disclose their real feelings on a computer rather than face to face with an adult or even their friends, and social networking sites are the ideal way to do that.'[9] Some kids would agree. 'I personally think it develops your social skills by allowing you to meet new people even if you aren't very outgoing in real life';[10] 'I rily love my online friends cuz u sumtimes get 2 tell them more than u can tell ur offline ones, and they'd b able 2 help! . . . no matter wat we shud b careful but not 2 way that we get parinoed and think every1 is lying!'[11]

The bottom line is that we don't really know how social-networking sites are affecting children and impacting on how they express their emotions. However, we do know that adults are a million miles behind their children when it comes to understanding what's going on online and they really need to catch up fast, because the number of children unsupervised in any way by parents in relation to their use of the internet has increased by two-thirds since 2000.[12]

Cyber-predators

One reason for parental vigilance is the shadowy presence of cyber-predators. All the networks seem to have problems with instances of predatory behaviour by adults. Perhaps the most interesting response has been from Bebo, which has signed up one of its own critics to do something about it. Rachel O'Connell was academic director of the cyberspace research unit at the University of Central Lancashire until 2006 when she was recruited by Bebo to head up safety programmes for the site.[14] O'Connell previously had described sites where children can upload pictures and give details of their everyday life as a 'paedophile's dream'. She had found that, while most children from as young as 8 were savvy enough to know the theory that they should not meet up with their cyber friends in real life, in practice the more time children spent online, the less likely they were to stick to the safety guidelines.[15] According to US research, 'fully 32 per cent of online teens have been contacted by someone with no connection to them or any of their friends' but only '7 per cent of online teens say they have felt scared or uncomfortable as a result of contact by an online stranger'.[16]

You will have to watch this space, or rather your children's screen, to know how this story will pan out, but there is a fundamental tension at the heart of how children use social networks to experiment with and learn about relationships. Parents and children know that, online, they should keep personal information private. Indeed, our own research shows that children have received this message loud and clear: don't give out your address, don't give out the name of your school, don't give out your phone number, keep things secret and don't use your real name.[17] However, parents and children also know that the heart of friendship (the core of social networks) is honesty, sincerity and trust. Friendship is about sharing secrets and being your true self. How should children navigate the moral maze when they know that truth is a precious commodity in building valuable relationships but that truth is a social danger when it comes to online safety advice? Children are caught in the middle. Their battle here, as with the moral complexity of David Beckham, is not so much between good and evil but between the real and the inauthentic.

West Side Story?

There are other, different stories that show how bringing people together online is not always about genuine and caring relationship-building. In the Devon town of

Cullompton, in June 2007, around 30 pupils converged on a playing field to kick each other around the park. Coming from three rival secondary schools – Tiverton High School, Cullompton Community College and Uffculme School – they were armed with metal bars, baseball bats and bicycle chains. The fight had been arranged on Bebo. Luckily, though, even if the local constabulary were not Bebo members, someone tipped them off and the police turned up in time to prevent loss of limb or life. Helpfully for this sort of social arrangement, Bebo organizes its users by the school they attend, but this is not *West Side Story* coming to Devon, with its rival teenage gangs the 'American' Jets and the Puerto Rican Sharks, and a love story that wins out. Perhaps like the suicides it is closer to a fad, like the craze for 'fight clubs' named after the 1999 film starring Brad Pitt and Helena Bonham Carter in which men arrange to meet to pummel the living daylights out of each other. The film provoked criticism because it presented violence as a seductive 'lifestyle choice' for young men.

Cyber-bullying

For girls, social networks facilitate another sort of undesirable 'lifestyle choice'. A lot of social-network-related violence is more emotional than physical and this is evident in the rise of cyber-bullying and the new breed of e-thugs that can make children's lives a misery. Over the past five years the number of UK children suffering from internet or text aggression rose from 14.5 per cent to 20.6 per cent and more than a third of 12 to 15-year-olds have faced some kind of cyber-bullying, according to a government study.[18]

Nathalie Noret of York St John University[19] told a British Psychological Society conference that teachers and parents needed to realize that children's computers were not just means of communication, but also ways for bullies to reach their victims 24 hours a day: 'What we have found is, traditional bullying is moving out of the playground and off the school bus and being played out at home.' She added that while common sense dictated that children were safe within their own homes, pupils were increasingly seeing nasty messages appearing on websites such as MySpace and Bebo. The trend was disturbing because it exposed more children to abuse. 'Young people are very good at keeping up with the latest technology and have become very adept at setting up their own websites,' she said. The most commonplace bullying that occurs online is over instant messaging, but it also can occur on any of the other new technologies.

Cyber-bullying encompasses a range of activities. Some-one might delete you from a 'buddy list' to make you feel left out; someone might hack into your profile and write comments pretending they're from you. It might take the form of a threat sent to you or published for everyone else to see. It might be a nasty comment about you on a profile page, or a rumour about things you have (or haven't) done. The bullying could be a totally fake profile set up about you or it could be the mass-mailing of private photos that you really don't want anyone else to see.[20]

And it tends to be a girl thing. The York St John study

confirmed that 'bullying among girls has always centred more on indirect aggression, such as name-calling, and text-messaging and the internet are ideal vehicles for that'. The same findings are coming out of the USA. As Amanda Lenhart of the Pew Internet Project puts it in her 'data memo' on cyber-bullying: 'girls are more likely than boys to say that they have ever experienced cyber-bullying – 38 per cent of online girls report being bullied, compared with 26 per cent of online boys'.

Children agree with the teachers' assessment of the situation. 'Just copy and paste whatever somebody says,' a middle-school girl explains as she describes online bullying tactics. 'You have to watch what you say . . .' counsels another middle-school girl. 'If that person's at their house and if you say something about them and you don't know they're there or if you think that person's your friend and you trust them and you're like, "Oh, well, she's really being annoying," she could copy and paste and send it to [anyone] . . .'[21] Perhaps not surprisingly, some UK schools have moved to ban social-networking sites altogether.[22]

The blame for bullying cannot, of course, be laid squarely at the door of social-networking sites but perhaps these stories show that even though the networked world doesn't change who we are as human beings, it does offer a new social setting which can amplify the best and worst of what we can be.

Brand new brand friends

However, if their friends betray them on Bebo at least children can now have a brand new kind of best friend: a soft drink, a hamburger, a camisole top or even a film. It's the latest corporate craze. It's beyond Customer Relationship Management; it's much, much more personal than that – much more net-age. Youth brands are falling over each other to steal a competitive advantage in the 'friending' game. It may seem bizarre to become a 'friend' of a brand – after all, what did they ever do for you and could you rely on them when the chips are down? But marketers know it works. In a digital world, where what is around you can be shaped like Plasticine to fit what you want, company personal-profile pages are appearing on Facebook and MySpace. When children connect to them, the logo emblazons their own user profiles and further encourages their friends to click on it and visit the company profile page, and so on and so on. The companies that led the way on this range from clothes firms, like the American lingerie company PINK, through to films and entertainment. Al Gore's film on global warming, *An Inconvenient Truth*, has 96,000 friends, but it is a minnow. The movie *X-Men: The Last Stand* has more than 2.6 million MySpace users as friends.

Corporations have been very quick off the mark to understand the cold, hard profit potential of two phenomena which emerge along with 'friending': first, the rapid mass-scale awareness-raising possibilities of parading the brand across multitudinous networks of youth; and, second, the possibility of playing on children's friendship insecurities to inveigle the brand into their hearts and souls. Remember the statistics we flagged up in our chapter on blitz marketing? While only 28 per cent of people believe what the admen say, 68 per cent still trust their friends – so why not use social networks to have your brand endorsed by loyal peers?

In a recent poll for *Advertising Age*, 84 per cent of 12 to 35-year-olds listed web-surfing as a top activity and 76 per cent said spending time with friends.[23] Put the two together and we are talking about a fertile trading ground the size and scope of which has never before been witnessed. Social-networking sites are exploding with corporate-sponsored 'user generated content', propagated like a virus through the myriad of contacts between millions of people (MySpace alone had 77 million members at time of writing). But how do brands do this without turning off and alienating a generation of media cynics? They do it with a technique which the industry calls 'embedded marketing' and they're all catching on to it.

The social-networking sites themselves are keen to be at the forefront. They understand how kids operate on the internet and so they sell on that information to youth-hungry brand managers. They are not just selling space on their sites; they are selling tips, tricks and information by the cyberload. Corporations are offered a dazzling array of customized possibilities.

As we saw above, brands can create their own profile and tout for their own friends. Wendy's and Sprite have just taken on MySpace's mighty marketing know-how to do this. Colin Digiaro, senior vice president of sales at MySpace, is confident that he is streets ahead of major client Wendy's in understanding the embedding game. He explains it like this: 'They [Wendy's] thought we could put up banners and hope someone clicked on it. We said we could create a plat-form that speaks to this audience in a more relevant way.'[24] Wendy's came up with a big idea for engaging kids. They invented a persona for the square hamburger, a kind of char-acter dubbed 'Smart'. It seems that Smart's rather irreverent tone struck a chord with kids and the embedding part of the friending approach started to work. As Smart spread his personality across groups of friends, Wendy's would infiltrate the brand network it had spawned with its own content. It attracted 90,000 friends on launch. 'We call it opt-in brand-ing,' Digiaro says. 'They chose to interact with the brand. There's a deep level of brand engagement and it becomes a great vehicle to spur word-of-mouth marketing.'

We are not sure to what extent children really have 'opted-in' to carry out low-cost marketing on behalf of a junk-food restaurant. And what exactly does 'deep level of brand engagement' actually mean? Perhaps the wise words of Mr Digiaro on the success of the Sprite embedding campaign can enlighten us. According to him, the brand (owned by the Coca-Cola Corporation) 'took interesting content and incorporated it into the overall MySpace experience. It allows the brand to give the community something of value.' He concluded that, 'this generation is all about self-expression and consuming content in its own way'.

Hmm! This sounds like cyber-nonsense but it is intriguing what this 'something of value' might possibly be. And surely this generation of children – far from consuming content in its own way – is consuming content precisely in the way the corporations want them to. It calls to mind a comment made by Ray Krok, the powerful CEO of McDonald's from 1968 until 1984. 'The definition of salesmanship,' he mused over his profits, 'is the gentle art of letting the customer have it your way.' But Colin Digiaro is nothing if not enthusiastic and has yet more to say about how young people are forming deep emotional bonds with brands. Apparently, they interact with brand networks just as they would with their friend network. 'It's a normal communication pattern,' he says.

Well, Colin, you may consider it 'normal' to form an intimate and loving relationship with a piece of beef trapped in a bun or a sugar-rich, carbonized liquid, but we're not that convinced . . . Call us cynical but we tend to think it has more to do with cash. MySpace rival Bebo has just been bought by the giant Time Warner Media empire for $850 million, making Michael and Xochi Birch – who started the company – a very rich couple indeed.[25] Was this deal about helping children and young people to grow and maintain their friendships? Not much. 'What drew us to Bebo,' Randy Falco of Time Warner said, 'was its substantial and fast-growing worldwide user base, its vision of a truly social web.' So far, so much hot air (what is a 'truly social web'?), but the crux of the purchase is contained in his next remark when we come to 'the monetization opportunities': 'this positions us to offer advertisers even greater reach and marketers significant insights into the desires and needs of consumers.'

Indeed, even before Randy got his claws into this teenage market the site had already made clear who it was serving and it certainly wasn't children. Here's an extract from Bebo's communications with potential corporate partners:[26]

The Bebo Open Media Platform is for professional content creators and media companies to create community and distribute content to the 40 million-strong Bebo audience while retaining control over their programming.

- Create and Extend Community – extend content and brand relationships to large, hard-to-reach young audience

- Distribute Content – Access power of viral, word-of-mouth dynamic that is key to shaping media choices

- Control – Brand, Programming, Player, and Advertising

- Monetize – sell and serve your own advertising and keep the revenue.

Here are the words which are behind the social network revolution: Create Community, Distribute, Control and Monetize. It's a marketing mantra for a new age where friendship is for sale.

Sponsor a singer: place a product

Friending is not the only opportunity available to corporations. Sponsorship is another embedding strategy offered by the social networks. A brand can sponsor specific users with particularly high profiles or can sponsor bands, concert tours and films. This can give a not particularly cool brand the social cachet of being associated with a cool band or film along with its fans and ensures wildfire exposure the likes of which it couldn't possibly achieve all alone. Aquafina water, for example, is a prominent advertiser on MySpace's film channel. Brands can also sponsor the 'Top Artists' section, while advertising on the music, movie, film and comedy channels is also popular these days, as is the home page. Going back to Colin Digiaro again for some illumination, we discover that MySpace has 'advertiser representation in nearly every major vertical'. So, what's that in English?

KateModern offers the monetizers something different again. Kate is the eponymous heroine of an online, inter-active drama, screened in two-minute episodes, five days a week on Bebo. Set in Britain, *KateModern* is funded entirely by product placement and aimed at teenagers. And it is a roaring success, with 48 million views by 2008. It's designed, like all product placements, to create brand loyalty without the viewer realizing what's going on. In October 2007, before the AOL purchase, they signed a promotional deal with Warner Music Group's Atlantic Record Division.[27] Atlantic band The Days was 'integrated into selected episodes' of the drama. The three-month promotion was scheduled to coincide with the band's new release and was designed to

include 'embedded purchasing opportunities'. Under the
deal, Bebo also included music from other Warner musicians. No one knows quite how much money changed
hands in this deal.

KateModern has also featured product placements for
Skittles, Orange, MSN, Procter & Gamble and Paramount
Pictures. In one episode, for example, the story turns to
Cadbury's Creme Eggs, with a discussion of how many it
would take to fill a car.[28] It followed the same model as
Lonelygirl15, another site which made its fortune from
product placements for Hershey's sweets and Neutrogena.

The same model of product placement is permeating the
rapidly growing 'virtual worlds'. These are simulated online
environments that allow you to interact and participate in
the guise of an on-screen character you can choose – your
avatar. As they have become more sophisticated, children
seem to have taken to them like ducks to water. Visits to
children's virtual worlds have grown 68 per cent over the
past year.[29] All, except Club Penguin which has a subscription
model, are experimenting with new ways to partner with
advertisers. The advertising spend in virtual worlds is
predicted to increase at the least tenfold by 2012. At the heart
of this marketing push are children's virtual worlds, which
now represent four out of the top five virtual worlds online.[30]
Webkinz.com, clubpenguin.com, stardoll.com and habbo.com
all rate higher than popular, adult-oriented equivalents,
Second Life and World of Warcraft.

The critique of the advertising industry, *The Hidden
Persuaders*,[31] was written over 50 years ago, but technology

today gives its title new meanings. We'll take a look at these in the next chapter. In the meantime, according to commentator Ingrid Lunden, whilst 'the deal underscores Bebo's attempts at pushing new revenue streams into its social network', she does wonder 'if *KateModern*'s viewers will question the integrity of a program that is built on user-generated content that also allows for for-profit product placement'. Given what happened to Facebook at the end of 2007, this is a reasonable concern.

Egg on my Facebook

In a blog entry posted on his site in early December 2007, Mark Zuckerberg, the billionaire founder of Facebook, issued the following rather surprising announcement: 'We've made a lot of mistakes building this feature, but we've made even more with how we've handled them. We simply did a bad job with this release, and I apologise for it.'[32] Not quite what we expect to hear from media moguls. Something must have gone really wrong. Well, to be confronted with a petition from 69,000 users of his social-networking site probably wasn't quite what he'd had in mind when he launched Facebook Ads and Beacon.

In November 2007 a dozen brands, among them Coca-Cola, Blockbusters, Sony Pictures and Crest Whitestripes, signed up to Facebook Ads. Under the deal the Coca-Cola Corporation created a page for Sprite which enticed users with a few bits of fun stuff. They could add the animated character 'Sprite Sips' to their own page and personalize him or her. But, of course, there was a catch. To really have fun you had to buy some of the sugar-rich beverage. A PIN code had been placed under the cap of every 2007 bottle of Sprite which could unlock all sorts of extra features and accessories.[33] Offline meets online meets sales meets profit.

Whilst this was all quite clever, Facebook Ads didn't differ too much from the business models of any of its rivals and that's not what the big fuss was about. Beacon is what really caused the uproar and sparked furious protests about privacy. For Beacon is not just about illumination, as the name would suggest, but also about surveillance and stalking on a scale hitherto unimaginable. This is what gave Beacon simultaneously its competitive advantage and its lambasting from users. For Beacon follows Facebook users around the net, watches what they do, takes notes and plans ways of cashing in on the information. The petition was entitled 'Facebook, stop invading my privacy!' and users accused the site of adopting Big Brother tactics to make money.

Beacon works through a technique known in the trade as 'behavioural targeting' that we came across in our blitz marketing chapter. A network of cookies sucks in and assembles a host of information about what Facebook members are buying through the other websites they visit. Then it passes on all the facts and figures to their friends. So if you have just bought a new Gucci handbag, Beacon will send a message to your best friend letting them know, 'Hey! Agnes has just got a really cool Gucci handbag!' According to Facebook, Beacon is all part of normal net behaviour where friends share the tastes they have in common – after all, we've all bought a book or a CD on a friend's recommendation, haven't we? We disagree. Just as it's not normal to bond with a burger, it's not normal for a profit-hungry third party to barge in and manipulate what one friend chooses to disclose to another.

Perhaps the biggest mistake Facebook made in its rush to monetize its new behavioural targeting application was to set the system up to work automatically: no opt-in, not even any opt-out, just a barrage of messages telling all my friends exactly what I've bought and where. The controversy has been one of the worst in the short life of Facebook, which was established in February 2004 and has rapidly become a global phenomenon. Microsoft recently bought a minority stake in the website in a deal valuing the venture at $15 billion (£7.3 billion), which made Zuckerberg, 23, the youngest billionaire ever.[34]

We don't know where this will end. Can 69,000 petitioners make a difference when the client base of social-networking sites has hit the tens of millions and when two of the companies behind them are owned by the might of Rupert Murdoch and Time Warner? Perhaps Condé Nast's teen site Flip.com offers a way forward to suit both teens and corporations. It asks its users which ads they want to be displayed on their profiles when they register. The good side of this is that they are being upfront about the need for advertising to support a free service and they are allowing users to participate by saying what kinds of advertising they want to receive. It is not perfect but, in giving young people enough respect by being straight with them, it is certainly more intelligent.

One thing we do know is that more change is coming. The younger you are, the more receptive you are to advertising on user-generated content sites and the more resistant you are to traditional media sites.[35] If you are over 35, you may not be aware of the extraordinary boom in online advertising to young people, because your profile shapes what you see, and the marketing spend for you remains directed towards the traditional world of advertising on page, TV and billboard. You pay much less conscious attention to adverts on 'user-generated content': they aren't designed for you and, as we shall see in the next chapter, when the advertising is tugging – even subconsciously – at our emotions the effect is much stronger.

This is, therefore, an age of experimentation. As social networks and virtual worlds become a significant force in young teenage lives, new opportunities and new risks emerge. The technology gives new form to old problems, such as the wave of cyber-bullying. And, in terms of cyber-friendship, it opens up new ways for companies to tap into the power and influence of one child over another. At present, we have no more than a sketchy regulatory framework to respond and it is far from clear whether good practice will rise to the top or sink to the bottom.

Some things, however, perhaps can't wait for the long term. Concerns about the privacy of young people on social-networking sites need to be addressed now. For today's kids, Bebo is like an elaborate Dear Diary entry. It documents in painful detail how you've evolved; it's a digital scrapbook. Many fear that the indelible trail left behind could stop you getting a job; 71 per cent of 14 to 21-year-olds say they would not want colleges or employers to do a web search on them before they had removed some material. 95 per cent were concerned about their details being passed on to advertisers or other websites.[36] They put it like this – Girl, 16, Yorkshire: 'I had a blog a couple of years ago and want to delete it – but I can't, and I had personal details on it!'; Boy, 16, South-east England: 'Really annoying, a search on Google brings up stuff I put online when I was really young and I can't get rid of it'; Girl, 14, Scotland: 'Initial thoughts – who cares? Subsequent thoughts – omg [oh my God]!!!'[37]

We couldn't have put it better ourselves. On the one hand the social network revolution is fun and exciting, but subsequent thoughts – OMG!

7. Who's Messing with My Mind?

'It does my head in . . . buy it, buy it, buy it!' Jordan, age 10

If we live in a world of pervasive marketing, there is a case for saying that the most remarkable thing about it is that children appear as savvy as adults and more in control. There is some truth in this, but there is also growing evidence that there is indeed a genuine difference between the way that children and adults are able to process and respond to marketing. They may be consumer kids, but they are still kids. In this chapter, we look at how marketing works on young minds.

We will start with how children develop. We'll then go on to examine compelling new findings from child psychologists and cognitive neuroscientists which tell us that even when children are old enough and savvy enough to understand what marketers are doing, it doesn't mean they can resist the effects of their messages. What's more, just because they don't remember something, it doesn't mean that they are not strongly influenced. In fact, what they don't remember can actually have the greatest impact on what they do when they get to the shops. This is particularly true for marketing that works with emotions rather than facts, i.e. most children's marketing.

Brain power

Everybody knows about advertising and marketing. Children know. So, surely – despite occasional marketing excesses – they are perfectly capable of deciding what to buy and what not to buy and, with a bit of help from intelligent adults, they can defend themselves against unwanted approaches from profit-hungry business? Catherine Lumby and Duncan Fine, authors of *Why TV is Good for Kids,* certainly think so: indeed, to 'claim that children are entirely helpless and absolutely open to manipulation in such a wholesale way is actually to strip them of agency and, in a sense, to divest them of a level of humanity'.[1] Their book and others on video-games, such as *Don't Bother Me, Mom – I'm Learning,* are among recent publications that try to shift the balance away from the more established, fearful debate – in the latter case to reassure parents that screen life can be a force for good. 'Set your children free' is the moral, or perhaps 'The only thing that children have to fear is fearful parents'. In relation to advertising, for example, Karen Sternheimer, author of *It's not the Media,* decries the 'media fears [that] continue to insist that we view children's minds as blank slates that advertisers easily manipulate'.[2] Along with Lumby and Fine, she reassures parents of the very young that these little ones don't even remember the adverts they have seen and so can't possibly be influenced in any enduring way.

However, a long-established body of work by developmental psychologists is in no doubt that, whatever we might like to believe about children's levels of sophistication, their brains simply aren't developed enough to cope with the art of persuasion when they are very young. Indeed, a recent report by the American Psychological Association has made it quite clear that children are more vulnerable to advertising than adults: 'Because young children lack the cognitive skills and abilities of older children and adults, they do not comprehend commercial messages in the same way as do more mature audiences, and, hence, are uniquely susceptible to advertising influence.'[3]

It has been agreed for decades that the skill of coping with adverts is directly related to a child's ability to understand abstract concepts and how these affect social encounters. This understanding is gradually acquired as the child grows older and, most importantly, as different parts of the brain develop. This means that no matter how intelligent or savvy or sophisticated a 5-year-old is, he/she simply does not have the brain power to grasp some of the basic psychological tactics of advertisers in the way that a 16-year-old does. As established by the developmental psychologist Jean Piaget in the 1960s,[4] children's understanding (cognitive capacity) evolves biologically through a series of pre-determined stages from birth to adulthood which roughly follow the age bands: 0–3, 3–7, 7–11 and 11+. As children slowly progress through these stages they also develop the ability to see the world from the perspective of other people.[5]

Researchers in 'consumer socialization' (or how children learn to operate in a commercial world) have agreed a three-stage process through which children mature, evolve and start to operate like adults: the 'perceptual' stage (age 3–7); the 'analytical' stage (age 7–11) and the 'reflective' stage (age 11–16).[6] In the first stage children understand their universe in terms of what they can easily observe around them and they also tend to focus on a single dimension at a time. Children of this age have difficulty in thinking about their point of view and that of another person simultaneously. Thus 2 and 3-year-olds have difficulty in telling the difference between an advert and a programme and when they learn to do this (at around 4 or 5) they base their decision on the length of the advert or recognition of a jingle rather than understanding intent. The concept of persuasion is not readily understood by the under-7s because they are figuring out how they fit into the world themselves, not how other people are trying to relate to them. The analytical stage (7–11) is a period of huge change for children's development during which they begin to appreciate more abstract concepts such as value for money and start to develop understanding of advertisers' intentions. Children of this age are also called 'cued processors'[7] as, although they may know for example what advertising is for, they need cues (such as clearly labelled adverts) in order to be able to retrieve this information. After the age of 11 children's processing capabilities become much more strategic and they begin to understand

that other people have different perspectives and play different roles in a social group or system (for example, that businesses exist to make money by selling stuff). After entering
secondary school most children start to appreciate complex
notions of a market economy, the social significance of
brands and can also start to develop some scepticism towards
claims made by advertisers (for example, to appreciate that
a celebrity is being paid to endorse a product).

It is often assumed that once children have the cognitive
capacity to be sceptical then they are somehow equipped to
deal with advertising. However, this is not necessarily the
case.[8] One team of researchers put it like this: 'merely having
the concepts in some latent form does little if anything to
prevent children from being led astray by advertising'.[9] So
whilst there is general consensus that below the age of 12
children's cognitive abilities are really not well enough
developed for them to make unaided assessments about
advertising, mounting evidence shows that even after this
age, knowledge and understanding about the role of advertising in society is not enough to protect children because
they still have difficulty in applying what they know.

We have to remember, too, that most of this research is
based on how children relate to TV advertising. When we
apply these psychological concepts to the fast-moving world
of internet advertising it becomes apparent that children
have even less psychological protection from potentially
deceptive practice, for the online environment is fundamentally different to TV. Children's exposure to advertising online
can be prolonged and continuous rather than confined to

30-second slots during the commercial break and it can be interactive, engaging and exciting. The intention behind online advertising can also be fundamentally different from that of TV adverts. Viral marketing implicates the child in becoming an active advocate for a product; advergames create a bond with the brand based on emotions of winning and losing; and the time-gap between viewing an advert and purchasing the product can be seconds or minutes online compared with days or weeks with TV advertising. The basic economic concepts are rather different, too. Children in junior school understand the principle of the exchange of goods and services for money and know what it means if a toy appears on screen with a price tag attached. However, appreciating that a games site is subsidized by selling advertising space to other companies is a fairly abstract concept which is unlikely to be accessible to children under 12. And the machinations of the behavioural-targeting industry, which deals in data obtained from site registration and cookies, requires in-depth industry knowledge as well as an understanding of the marketing value of information. Few children are likely to understand this: indeed, as we saw earlier in the book, many adults also see themselves as 'clueless' about this.

Hidden persuaders

At a time when advertising formats are being revolutionized, new psychological experiments are also beginning to show that when it comes to how advertising changes children's minds and alters how they behave, secondary-school children are just as susceptible as those in primary school.[10] This is rather puzzling as according to what we know from Piaget and earlier consumer-socialization work, older kids are not only more savvy but they also have much more developed brain capacity.

The answer to this puzzle seems to be to do with how our brain is configured: something we have learned a lot more about over the past few years thanks to brain-scan technology and new experimental methods. Jonathan Haidt in *The Happiness Hypothesis*[11] provides us with some useful metaphors to explain some of this. He tells us that our brain has two discrete parts: a 'head brain' which controls our conscious thinking and decision-making and a 'gut brain' which controls how our body reacts emotionally to stimuli. The head brain is stored in the neocortex and is a rather more recent development in *Homo sapiens*. The gut brain is stored in the limbic system and has been part of human evolution for very, very much longer. It is the gut brain that made our ancestors flee from wolves and which today urges kids to stop on the kerb when they hear a car coming. The head brain helped Stone Age man develop tools and helps contemporary children add up numbers in maths homework.

The effects of this brain division have been contemplated by philosophers as diverse as Buddha, Montaigne, Plato and Freud, but the exact location and nature of the two parts have only recently been identified. Jonathan Haidt likens the relationship between the brain sections to that between horse and rider. The rider is the neocortex which tries and often succeeds in controlling the limbic system. However, the horse is capable of sensing things which the rider can't: scents and sounds inaccessible to the person sitting on top. Just as the horse can be very hard to control if it decides to head off on its own course because it is frightened, hungry or tired, so it is with the emotional or gut part of our brain. It often has its own agenda and is perfectly capable of over-riding our reason.

If we are honest about it, a lot of our decisions are made on 'gut feeling' rather than logical thought. And we should not forget that the deep, limbic parts of the brain appeared much earlier, evolutionarily, and so can be much more finely tuned and effective. Children are, of course, much less experienced riders than we are and so the horse gets its own way much more often.

As we saw above, the fact that children's rational processes are much less developed than those of adults makes them much more vulnerable to marketing and this is compounded by the fact that most marketing to kids gets to their gut brain first because it appeals on an emotional level. Behind the adverts which children encounter lies the contemporary corporate emphasis on building brand equity,[12] defined by marketing gurus as 'everything that exists in the minds of the customer with respect to a brand (e.g. thoughts, feelings, experiences, images, perceptions, beliefs and attitudes)'.[13] So getting across a factual message that brand A is better than brand B is not what's at stake. Instead, it's about creating or manipulating 'everything that exists in the mind'. So a big, green, smiling Shrek on the side of a yoghurt carton reminds 7-year-old Sophie of a funny film and all the other cool Shrek things she's seen ever since the film has been out. This emotional reaction hits her long before any rationality can suggest to her that she doesn't need a yoghurt or that this one is more expensive than the own-brand equivalent. Any parent who has tried to appeal to the neocortex of a toddler will know just how fruitless this will prove.

That's advertainment

We are now starting to uncover just how powerful emotional ads which by-pass the brain's rational controls actually are. Let's take a look at advergames and product placements. Advergames are interactive computer games paid for by big brands which heavily feature their product. They are either paid for and placed on general games sites or form part of the content of dedicated brand websites. The most popular children's games site, Miniclip, for example, features an advergame paid for by Starburst sweets. Children have to 'collect' Starbursts as they rush down a giant water slide.

Two researchers from Western Australia looked at how a similar advergame on the Kellogg's Froot Loop site influenced children's attitudes.[14] The game featured Toucan Sam, a central brand character, and involved scoring points by feeding a monster. The game implies that Froot Loops are better than real fruit by rewarding a child with 10 points for throwing a Froot Loop into a monster's mouth but only 5 points for accurately aiming an apple or an orange. Children were split into two groups: Group A who did not play the game and Group B who did. When questioned explicitly, the kids in both Group A and Group B said fruit was healthier than Froot Loops, so the advergame didn't override all the healthy-eating messages they had had from their parents and teachers. Or at least that's what the kids told the researchers. And that's probably what the kids truly believe. However, when it came down to making an actual choice between the sugary cereal and other kinds of food, it turns out that the advergame had a huge influence: 54 per cent of Group B (who had played the game) chose Froot Loops over a fruit salad, a sandwich or a cheeseburger whereas only 32 per cent of Group A (who hadn't played the game) made the same choice. This is what makes advergames so powerful: they can change kids' behaviour even though those same kids don't believe their minds have been changed at all.

A similar experiment has been performed with a movie product placement (where a brand pays to have a main character use their product or for the product just to be in a prominent position on the screen).[15] Take a look at the 2006 James Bond movie, *Casino Royale*, to see this technique in serious action: Smirnoff vodka, Sony Vaio laptop, Seiko watch, Eriksson mobile phone, Ford Mondeo (what?) and of course the Aston Martin can all be seen. You might also have noticed that James Bond drove a BMW in *Goldeneye*. Why? To launch the Z3 Roadster and ensure enough sales to keep a new state-of-the-art BMW factory in the USA in business. The experiment looked at the effects of a product placement for Pepsi in the film *Home Alone* and was similar to the Froot Loop study. This time Group A watched a 2-minute clip from the film which showed the family around a dinner table eating pizza and drinking Pepsi. The drink is mentioned by name by an adult ('Fuller, go easy on the Pepsi'), and in the course of the clip it spills on the table. The bottle is prominent throughout the clip. Group B also saw a 2-minute clip from *Home Alone* featuring a scene with the family eating and drinking, but in this clip Kevin (the hero) puts an unbranded macaroni cheese ready-meal in the microwave and then eats it along with a glass of milk.

After the screenings, both sets of children were invited into an individual interview to talk about the clip. On the way in they were offered a choice of Pepsi or Coke to drink: 62 per cent of Group A (who saw the Pepsi clip) chose the Pepsi compared with 42 per cent of Group B (who saw the non-Pepsi clip). Compare this to national sales figures where only 25 per cent of cola sales are Pepsi versus 75 per cent Coke. Essentially, viewing the Pepsi in a popular film had a significant influence on the children's choice. Importantly, this choice behaviour had little to do with whether or not the children remembered seeing the placement in the clip. In fact, the researchers concluded that 'without being aware of their exposure to commercial messages, they have been affected by the exposure in some preconscious way'. The effect was even stronger upon those children who had seen the film before – they were even more likely to choose Pepsi. The researchers concluded: 'Given the tendency of young children to watch videos of their favorite films over and over again, the findings have ethical implications for the use of product placement in films targeted at young children who have not yet acquired strategic processing skills.'

Findings such as these make it clear that even if children (or indeed their parents) don't want to admit it, they are highly influenced by advertising. What's more, the *Home Alone* study showed that older children (who are presumably more media-savvy) were just as influenced as younger children.

Having published a range of research papers over the past few years not only on ethics of advertising to children but also on the power of emotions in advertising,[16] Agnes got together with Cordelia Fine, author of *A Mind of Its Own*, to draw together an array of evidence from a wide range of quarters: psychology, neuroscience and marketing research.[17] What emerged was clear evidence on the hidden power of contemporary adverts aimed at children. The research all seemed to say the same thing: the stimuli which kids don't really notice and which create emotional associations are the ones which influence them in the most powerful ways.[18] This process is quite unlike the effects of the sights and sounds which we consciously notice and consider in a thoughtful and rational way. Moreover, unconscious emotional connections seem to be much more enduring than conscious cognitive ones. Here are a few of the recent studies which were uncovered, showing that advertising can indeed 'implicitly persuade'.

One group explored the effects on young men of the movie hero Bruce Willis smoking in a film clip.[19] They found that what the young men said about smoking was not affected by whether they saw a clip of Willis smoking or not smoking. However, for those who thought of Willis as a role model, seeing him smoke in the movie resulted in stronger implicit associations between smoking and their own self image. As the authors put it, 'This implicit association seems consequential, given that among smokers it was a significant, unique predictor of increased intention to smoke.' So it's not what you say about smoking to a bunch of researchers – or even to yourself – that influences your tendency to smoke but the associations you make between the habit and your heroes in the secret space inside your head.

Other research has shown that, compared with people who are flashed subliminally with angry faces, people who are surreptitiously shown pictures of happy faces before being offered a fruit-flavoured drink find it tastier, drink more of it and are willing to pay double the price for it.[20] It seems that the really important thing for the formation of powerful emotional connections with a product is that we don't realize that we are being influenced, or think we are immune.[21] For example, using a celebrity voice in an advert can make you like a product more but only if the voice isn't specifically recognized.[22] Presumably, if you realize who it is then you can allow your cynical head brain to kick in and tell you that the celebrity doesn't really like the product but that they are just doing it for the money – as one of the teenagers we interviewed commented in an earlier chapter. Indeed, as EM Forster noted, 'only what is seen sideways sinks deep'.

So the sneaky stuff works when it happens spontaneously and you haven't got time to think about what's going on. A number of studies have shown that, particularly for food choices, when given time to think we make reasoned, balanced, healthy choices but if you put us under time pressure we'll go for the stuff that our primitive urges desire. People will choose fruit over chocolate given the chance to consider the implications but will go straight for the fat, sugar and calories when they're in a rush.[23] The same is true for brand names. With time to choose we are likely to tell researchers that we are not influenced by brands, but put under time pressure we are likely to show we're much more influenced by branding than we might like to think.[24] For example, when a choice of branded versus non-branded gifts was offered to volunteers they chose according to whether or not they said they liked branded goods. However, when the same choice was made under time pressure, approximately two-thirds went against their self-reported preferences and chose in line with their implicit preference.

It has also been shown that when we are mentally tired our implicit attitudes affect how many sweets we eat. A study with M&Ms demonstrated that for a group of people whose brains were fresh and alert, the rational part of their brain could rein in the other part and restrain their eating. However, another group, who had previously been given a demanding thinking task, ate M&Ms at a rate which corresponded to their implicit feelings towards the chocolate rather than how many they thought they should eat.

This new research added important dimensions to what we already knew about children's limited but evolving cognitive capacities. When a brand is linked to positive, fun images and feelings then it acquires an unconscious, emotional appeal for children that can be quite independent of what they may understand about the reality of the product on a rational level or even how marketing works. The way advertising impacts on children can work in two ways. First of all, kids' attitudes to a brand may actually be based on their subconscious feelings, which have in turn been manipulated through subtle emotional appeals which cannot be well controlled by reason. Second, when children are in a rush, or are too young to have developed many advertising literacy skills, then unconscious learning will dominate over conscious.

So, even when children are old enough to be marketing-savvy they may not have the time, brainpower or inclination to make rational choices. More importantly, they, like their parents, have pretty fragile defences against the hidden emotional power of advertising.

The findings outlined above have very considerable implications for marketing to children. However, they really have not yet hit home. In particular, the research suggests that the two central strategies that governments and campaign groups have championed to help children cope in a commercial world – teaching children about adverts and banning adverts from being shown to children in the first place – both emerge as inadequate. We look at this in more detail in the following section.

Legislate or educate?

Critics and defenders of advertising to children have both approached ethics within the same framework of the age-stage evolution of children's cognitive capacities which we reviewed at the beginning of this chapter, but they have come up with different solutions. Critics want to legislate against advertising to kids whilst defenders want to educate kids to cope with it. Critical governments have simply removed advertising that targets kids. The Greeks, for example, have prohibited adverts for children's products on TV between 7 a.m. and 10 p.m. since 1996 and Sweden has banned both TV commercials designed to attract the attention of the under-12s and commercials around children's programmes.[25]

When Sweden took over Presidency of the Council of the European Union in 2001 there were fears from advertisers across Europe that there would be pressure for other EU countries to follow suit. The advertising industry in the UK has always argued for its 'rights' and 'freedom' to advertise to children. The Swedish Consumer Ombudsman, Axel Edling, when speaking to a conference in London in the run up to the presidency, expressed (politely) his impatience with this view:

Sometimes advertisers defend their right to advertise freely by referring to the notion of 'commercial freedom of speech'. This raises the question of the scope and applicability of the European Convention on Human Rights, Article 10. I will not address that question now but merely acknowledge the difference that surely must be acknowledged between the highly respected principle of freedom of expression in political, religious, scientific and artistic matters and the right of a merchant to promote the sale of certain products.

As it turned out the Swedish presidency did not lead to wider advertising bans. When we met Ed's counterpart, the head of the Swedish Consumers' Association he told us one of the reasons why. When a ban is enacted commercial life flows to find a way around it. Companies who wish to advertise to children get round the ban of advertising to children in Sweden by using advertising space on Swedish channels which are broadcast from the UK.

We don't have to go to Sweden to see how the profit motive can creep round regulations. The UK mobile-phone industry, for example, has for years operated a voluntary code not to advertise or market to children. This dates back to when a government commission suggested that children might face a health risk in using mobile phones. The code was never written down, but is a gentlemen's agreement to which companies have kept. Or have they? If they have, their sales have nevertheless done remarkably well given that the average age for a child to have a first mobile phone is now 8 years old.[26] The point is that with phones, as with many products which children care about, the targeting approach is not that of a precisely aimed rifle but the rougher scatter of the shotgun which results in children seeing advertising all around them, and not just in zones specifically for them.

Chocolate is a case in point. At a conference on promoting food to children in London in 2006,[27] Trish Fields, 'Consumer Impact Director' at Cadbury Schweppes, made much of the fact that her corporation bases its children's advertising policy on what she called 'the universal science' whereby the age of 8 represents a crucial cut-off period after which children's savvy 'increases astronomically'. A member of the audience questioned how her company applied this 8-year-old rule. Ms Fields didn't hesitate to answer: 'There's a very simple answer; we only advertise to adults so we don't have to distinguish between the age. The ads that we make are for adults, that's the position that we've taken.'

Interesting, then, that in a recent survey of children's favourite commercials,[28] Cadbury's 'drumming gorilla' advert was spontaneously mentioned by a fifth of all children across the UK. No other advert came anywhere close: the second place was taken by the Skoda cake car which was recognized by a meagre 3 per cent of children. By 'only advertising to adults' Cadbury's have achieved a magnificent marketing success with 5 to 16-year-olds . . .

It is fair to say that some of this concerns the difficulty of putting the genie back in the bottle. Adverts for mobile phones are everywhere and they do pop up in young spaces, such as on Bebo, but by and large the mobile phone networks stick to their promise not to market directly to children as a specific group and, compared to some countries, the UK emerges as relatively responsible on this matter.[29] We are spared, as a result, some of the questionable toddler phones that litter American homes. Equally, though, the self-imposed ban on marketing means that better products, designed for children, are not given a chance to sell. British parents do not get the option, for example, of buying the children's handsets available to Spanish children that go the extra mile in terms of safety and protection.

What is clear is that the focus by industry and regulators

alike on the notion of age-based cognitive defence is not serving our children well. In spite of bans and self-regulating policies, children are seeing adverts not 'intended' for them, whether beamed from other countries or allegedly beamed just to adults in their own countries. Regulating advertising on this basis misses the cumulative effect which commercialism as a whole has on our children and fails to notice the wrap-around nature of commerce in their always-on, always-tuned-in world. So, if legislation is not sufficient, what about education?

Education, education, education

Those who defend the practice of marketing to children argue that being the target of advertising is an important part of how children grow up and socialize.[30] Their solution, if they concede that any is needed to protect children, lies in media-literacy strategies that educate children about the commercial world and its persuasion techniques. One study, for example, showed that 'advertisements do make an impression on children, but the majority of children in this study did not recognize their persuasive intent'.[31] So, rather than banning advertising, their proposal was that 'children need to be better informed about the nature and intent of advertising'.

'Media literacy' is now part of official government strategy. Our children are to acquire the skills both to read (and comprehend) the information which is 'mediated' to them and to write (and create) their own content, particularly for electronic consumption. Not all media literacy is about commercial media (it also includes comparing the presentation of news in different styles of newspaper), but it is all built on the premise that seeing through what is being presented by any form of media is not the same as rejecting it. Professor David Buckingham from the Institute of Education in London has championed this cause and argues that 'the attempt to protect children by restricting their access to media is doomed to fail. On the contrary, we need to pay much closer attention to how we prepare children to deal with these experiences.'[32]

There are some wonderful things going on in classrooms in terms of creating media content – the 'writing' part of this education process. One of our children has just produced an e-card where Father Christmas, with full reindeer troupe, makes a dramatic and musical entrance into a room via the chimney and an equally sparkling and melodic exit through an opened window. Another has just entertained us with his PowerPoint-aided speech on the intricacies of jazz music, accompanied by YouTube-mediated Miles Davis and Herbie Hancock music on demand. The wealth of user-generated content which festoons the web is testament to the creative media literacy of our children.

So far so good. The 'reading' part is rather harder to teach, however. This part of media literacy has tended to be treated as 'inoculation'[33] – giving children the knowledge and cognitive skills to protect themselves by decoding messages designed to persuade them and encouraging them to employ these skills wherever possible. This is a laudable and, on the face of it, sensible aim. In technical speak, what is being taught is 'cognitive defence': erecting a barrage of reasoning and understanding to defeat rogue ideas. However, and it is a very big however, if marketing to children occurs in a wrap-around fashion which fills their screens and infiltrates their friendships, and if marketing to children works beneath the conscious level in an implicit, unseen way, then we do have to question how effective this inoculation can be. Is it like giving the measles vaccine to protect against cancer?

Certainly, early critiques of media-literacy programmes such as Media Smart in the UK[34] and Concerned Children's Advertisers in Canada[35] have shown up both the complete inadequacy of efforts to measure their effectiveness[36] and the biases in the way they are described.[37] A comparison of two very different media-literacy websites, both offered to UK parents, children and teachers, demonstrates how slippery a term media literacy actually is. We compared the Media Smart website (sponsored by the advertising industry) and Chew on This,[38] operated by the consumer charity, the Food Commission. On the Media Smart site children are told that, 'advertising is essential in an economy based on meeting children's needs' and that 'the advertising business has a long track record of responsible advertising to children'. It is clearly designed to give a particular view of the advertising industry and arousing scepticism is definitely not on the agenda. Compare this with the Chew on This website, which tells children, 'food companies have lots of tricks up their sleeves for persuading you to choose their products'. The site goes on to list the tricks: 'catch them young', 'sell it through schools', 'trigger an impulse purchase', 'link it to

footie', 'hire the professionals', 'advertise' and 'use the internet'. In stark contrast to the Media Smart site, the point
here is almost exclusively to arouse scepticism. What are
children (and parents and teachers) to believe? That advertising is a benign force or that advertising can persuade you
against your will? If media literacy is to be an alternative
(or complement) to regulation and bans then we need a
much more coherent approach and much deeper thinking
behind the strategies in place.[39] Media Smart updated some
of its teaching material after the launch of this website in
2003 but this material is not available online at the time of
writing.

Controlling the unconscious

It is quite clear from the evidence we have shown in this
chapter that neither of these approaches to media literacy
is a match for marketing which works on children's emotions
at an unconscious level. This poses a very different sort of
problem from the one currently up for debate. Teachers
know how to teach thinking skills but how do you teach
children to be on their guard against the workings of their
subconscious? It may be possible to do this, but we know
from psychology and neuroscience that this is quite a tall
order. After all, it is one thing to be able to display scepticism
about an advert but it is quite another thing to recognize
that marketing messages can nonetheless influence your
'gut feeling' about a product. Whether or not children trust
the message is, in fact, unimportant. What matters is
whether they realize that their gut feeling about the product

may have been manipulated and that it is this that they can no longer trust.

Unfortunately, this ability is not something which improves gradually with age. Instead, puberty gets in the way. In fact, the onset of puberty is actually associated with an enhanced responsiveness to rewarding stimuli which is why the peer acceptance which can come with cool brands is particularly potent for young teenagers. The ability to understand what's going on and take action to control it doesn't actually come until young adulthood. This means that far from being immune to adverts by 12 years old, teenagers actually have less protection than junior-school children when emotion-based marketing techniques are used.[40]

We need a better public debate on the ethics of marketing to children – one that is informed by new findings from psychology and neuroscience on how advertising does affect children. When this is done, we will be in a better position to decide how to balance legislation with education.[41] The age of children will no doubt be a factor, but what our analysis shows is that policy makers should consider not just the capacities of the people that advertising messages are targeting but also the formats of the messages themselves. Marketing academics have recently argued that stealth marketing techniques which can be shown to be deceptive, exploitative and intrusive should be subject to public scrutiny.[42] Viral marketing, product placement, advergames and recruiting brand pushers (like Sarah) are all techniques which require some combination of responsibility and, we believe, far stricter restrictions on use. Indeed, given that even adults may have difficulty recognizing marketing messages when they are 'embedded' in traditionally non-commercial contexts, the format could prove to be one practical way to decide on what is fair and what is not. The key principles, whether they are applied through legislation or harnessed through education, are that advertising should be recognizable as advertising and commercial persuasion should not jeopardize people's freedom of choice.

The marketing industry puts great store by the principle of self-regulation, so we could start with some suggestions that are for the industry itself rather than the regulators which it tends to fight against. Top of these is to invest time and money in a thorough overhaul of the jungle of advertising and marketing codes.[43] There needs to be, as part of this, better monitoring of advertising online rather than waiting for people to complain. The current approach of the Advertising Standards Authority, which has done a lot over the years to keep advertisers honest, is fine for billboard advertising but is less likely to work when adverts flash up on screen. There is also a need to move from a system which works on an advert by advert basis to one which considers the cumulative effects of marketing in the lives of children. The widespread use of sexual promise and imagery in adverts is something better dealt with across the board rather than advert by advert. Taking marketing agencies that have a poor track record off the roster of companies that can bid for government advertising and marketing would be a start.

At the national level, government is probably the only

body that can consider the volume of marketing to children and whether it believes that this is problematic.

Even if society decides that there is too much commercial exposure, for younger children in particular, we don't pretend that this is an easily changed course of direction. If an outright ban on marketing to all children is ill-conceived, a better way of addressing the number of adverts would be to put a tax on advertising. You might not do this with children in mind alone. A tax on advertising would be economically efficient, and could be of benefit in terms of the environmental challenges ahead.

The advertising industry must also reconsider how it can best approach responsible and ethical children's advertising. When Vance Packard's *Hidden Persuaders* came out in the late 1950s, one response of the advertising industry was to claim 'there are no hidden persuaders. Advertising works openly, in the bare pitiless sunlight.'[44] It is clear that, despite the best intentions of advertisers, much advertising to children does not work like this at all but instead operates darkly, beyond the light of consciousness. It is not that marketers are unaware of what they are doing. Indeed, industry insiders are already reporting how neuroscientists are working on targeting kids. One consultant put it like this: 'Did you know that some marketers have actually "fired up" kids' brains and observed the brain cell firing and response patterns as product and marketing stimuli are presented to them? Or that some electronic games companies are exploring new technology which will allow them to stimulate key emotional centres of the brain as children play their games?'[45]

This agenda is not just about making sure children understand advertising messages – however complex a task that might be. It's about how the commercial world with its all-embracing, wrap-around presence affects how children feel about themselves and others. So, before showing the positive ways in which children are coping with the commercial world in Part Two, it is time to weigh up the full costs . . . how the commercial world affects children's well-being and why, for children, marketing is often about a broken promise of happiness.

8. A Broken Promise of Happiness

'Adverts are good because they give people a chance to enjoy the pleasures in life.'   Denise, age 14

'Promise, large promise is the soul of an advertisement.' So said Samuel Johnson in the 18th century. Behind the tricks and tactics of contemporary marketing, the soul of advertising is no different today. Yet marketing to today's young people seems to be offering one promise above all others: happiness. The promise of happiness is sold as a right or entitlement: 'because you're worth it'. Just as the right to vote or the right to decent working conditions have galvanized the aspirations of other societies, it is the right to happiness which seems to be the mood music of the contemporary younger generation.

Whether commercial culture is responsible in smaller or larger part, happiness is sold as a tick in the box marked 'the meaning of life'. However, the selling of happiness is a promise that is also programmed ultimately to disappoint. After all, the best way to sell happiness in a product is if people are persuaded to feel unhappy if they don't have it.

So how do you feel about yourself? Have a go at the quiz below.

A = Strongly Disagree,
B = Disagree,
C = Agree,
D = Strongly Agree

On the whole I am satisfied with myself
A☐ **B**☐ **C**☐ **D**☐

I feel that I have a number of good qualities
A☐ **B**☐ **C**☐ **D**☐

I am able to do things as well as most other people
A☐ **B**☐ **C**☐ **D**☐

I feel that I'm a person of value, at least as valuable as others
A☐ **B**☐ **C**☐ **D**☐

I feel good about myself
A☐ **B**☐ **C**☐ **D**☐

Scoring:

1 point for strongly disagree

2 points for disagree

3 points for agree

4 points for strongly agree

The closer your score is to 20 the better you feel about yourself and the closer to 5 the worse you feel. More specifically, a high score indicates that you have high self-esteem.[1]

Self-esteem is a basic human need and is part of a wider psychological construct called 'self-concept' – or how we see ourselves. It's used frequently by health psychologists because it has been repeatedly shown that our self-concept and particularly our self-esteem are strongly related to how we cope with what life throws at us. It is a protection mechanism which human beings have developed during evolution and it is an important developmental milestone for children. They need high self-esteem for their psychological stability. When their self-esteem is low they can't handle problems very well.

Ultimately, low self-esteem can lead to clinical depression. If children's self-esteem is low they gradually come to expect failure and assume that they are less capable in all areas of life. These negative thought patterns can become reinforced during adolescence and continue into adult life.

'Oh Lord, won't you buy me a Mercedes Benz?'

Here is another quiz for you to try:

I'd rather spend time buying things than almost anything else
A ☐   B ☐   C ☐   D ☐

I would be happier if I had more money to buy more things
for myself
A ☐   B ☐   C ☐   D ☐

I have fun just thinking of all the things I own
A ☐   B ☐   C ☐   D ☐

I really enjoy going shopping
A ☐   B ☐   C ☐   D ☐

I like to buy the things my friends have
A ☐   B ☐   C ☐   D ☐

When you grow up the more money you have, the happier
you are
A ☐   B ☐   C ☐   D ☐

I'd rather not share my snacks with others if it means I'll
have less for myself
A ☐   B ☐   C ☐   D ☐

I would like to be able to buy things that cost a lot of money
A ☐ **B** ☐ **C** ☐ **D** ☐

I really like the kids that have very special games and clothes
A ☐ **B** ☐ **C** ☐ **D** ☐

The only kind of job that I want when I grow up is one that gets me lots of money
A ☐ **B** ☐ **C** ☐ **D** ☐

Scoring:

1 point for strongly disagree

2 points for disagree

3 points for agree

4 points for strongly agree

This is a materialism questionnaire.[2] The closer your score to 40 the more materialistic you are and the closer to 10 the less materialistic you are.

Materialism is basically a set of personal life values where money and material possessions fulfil three important life functions: centrality, success and happiness. Centrality means that for materialists, buying and owning possessions is a life focus, so going shopping is a main leisure pursuit and planning for a new car, piece of furniture or house occupies a lot of a person's time. Materialists also believe that material wealth symbolizes success, so the point of owning a large house is not to have more room for the family but to show other people that they have achieved something worthwhile. Importantly, a materialistic value-system incorporates the belief that money and possessions bring happiness. So, focusing on things will not only bestow outward signs of success but will also bring inner contentment.

You might be wondering what is the connection between the two questionnaires. What does self-esteem have to do with materialism? Self-esteem is obviously related to the really serious issue of mental health while a bit of a shopaholic tendency doesn't seem like much of a big deal. After all, a lot of people would like a few more things, wouldn't they? And many of us may have enjoyed the effects on the neighbours of parking a spanking new car in the drive, fiddling dextrously and ostentatiously with our latest techno-gadget or stopping the show with a 'wow' outfit. A few dreams and a bit of showing off surely don't do any harm.

Or do they?

Well, our research has shown quite clearly that there is a strong link between materialism and self-esteem in children. A detailed questionnaire completed by almost 560 children aged 9 to 13[3] demonstrated with statistical significance that the more materialistic children are, the lower their self-esteem. The kids who think that they'd be happier if only they had that new PlayStation, the kids that think that all that matters in a job is to make money and the kids who care a lot about their possessions are all much more likely to feel that they are worthless and inferior to their peers.

The children who are looking outwards for satisfaction are the ones who are hurting internally.

Now, we must make it clear that whilst this link exists we can't say whether materialism causes low self-esteem or low self-esteem causes materialism. We can't tell from a survey which one comes first. On the one hand, it is possible that a constant craving for more and more leads children to be less satisfied. On the other hand, it is also possible that when children feel bad about themselves they think that the latest cool object will improve their social status and make them feel better. Currently, we just don't know which way round this works: both explanations are plausible. The truth is unlikely to be straightforward. It is probable that the relationship between happiness and materialism works in a process of feedback loops with children caught in a complex web woven around the emerging development of their own values, their own attitudes and their own identity.

iPod solution to bullying

Whether low self-esteem leads to greater materialism or vice versa, we believe that the link gives cause for concern. If holding materialistic values actively lowers our children's self-esteem then our society needs to tackle, at its roots, a culture which glorifies wealth, celebrity and status at every turn. If children who have low self-esteem are turning to the material world to solve their problems then this is equally alarming. During our research we talked to one mother who said she'd bought her son an iPod because he was being bullied. What she'd really bought was the idea that this purchase could somehow rectify a complex set of social and emotional problems for her 11-year-old boy.

While a new iPod may make a miserable kid the focus of positive attention in the playground for a couple of days, expensive possessions are not, ultimately, going to create a long-lasting feeling of self-worth. Toby and Olivia are at secondary school in the southwest of England and were delegates at a forum we both attended on the subject of a 'Good Childhood'. We'd been discussing the role of marketing and materialism and Toby chipped in, 'Yes. There is always going to be a next best thing around the corner. It is scary – always trying to get the best thing. It's time consuming and it gets into your head. You have got to get it before anyone else to be great. I use my stuff for confidence.' Olivia was sceptical about Toby's approach to life. 'Does it last?' she asked. Toby gave a laugh. 'Until it goes out of fashion, yes.' Olivia thought for a bit and then asked Toby this: 'Wouldn't it be better to get confidence from confidence itself?' Olivia, it should be said, has had a pretty straightforward and secure childhood and has won a place at Cambridge. Toby, on the other hand, has had a tough time with a mother who was a drug addict. He explained, 'I have had a lot of confidence kicked out of me, so I have to have easy and quick ways or else I get depressed.'

If we nurture a culture which suggests that we can buy 'easy and quick ways' out of our misery, where does this really leave the most economically deprived members of our society? Where does it leave young people like Toby who find it scary but who are propelled to buy the next thing to feel okay? The truth is that a materialistic value-system is divisive at its core and marketing helps to fuel it. We will turn to the issue of materialism in the separate worlds of the 'haves' and the 'have-nots' shortly. First, we want to take a look at two key factors in this complex web of wishing, wanting and well-being. The first is the role of media in forming materialistic values and the second is how family relationships suffer when children are strongly attached to a material culture.

Media manufactures our desires

Children who watch loads of TV are much more materialistic: there is a very strong and statistically significant link.[4] Time staring at the computer screen is also correlated with materialism but the link isn't quite as strong. Again, we can't tell if watching TV programmes which are studded with stars, games shows with promises of wealth beyond your imagination and adverts for hip hi-tech gadgets cause children to desire a lifestyle which revolves around wealth and possessions, or whether children who already worship consumer stuff watch endless TV to reinforce their beliefs. We suspect it is the former. We found that a good number of the children in this survey were like Kyle, who we intro-duced in the 'Techno child' chapter. Kyle is a screen-child par excellence who watches TV almost the whole time he is at home: before school, after school, during meals, most of the weekend and in bed at night. With this sort of exposure to (mainly commercial) TV it is not unreasonable to assume that programmes and adverts play a significant role in shaping Kyle's value-system. Children are not born materialists: they acquire their values. It seems to us very likely that children like Kyle who are exposed to many, many hours of TV a day will pick up their values from the screen – where else is there for him to get them from?

Family time

Children who are materialistic also argue more with their parents and are more likely to think that their mum and dad are boring. We believe that this is a really significant finding which could prove to be the lynchpin for the damaging influence of a material culture on the happiness of our children.

Let us take an example of a lucky little girl whose parents can afford to buy her a lot of what she wants. Jade is 6 and at the moment she wants a 'real camera'. Although she can't analyse or express her motives in depth – she is only 6 after all – Jade's gut feeling tells her that if she gets this real camera it will make her happy and she'll be part of the in-crowd at school. According to Jade, all of the other children in her class will be 'getting' a real camera soon. Jade obviously can't afford something which will cost upwards of £50 – so she has to engage pester-power to get her parents to buy her what she wants.

As we have seen in a number of contexts throughout this book, pester-power is a strong force. Adults seem to have less and less time to think about parenting and less and less emotional energy to devote to laying down the ground rules with their children. It's often easier to just say yes than to endure a lengthy and draining psychological battle with a child who claims they are the only one in the class who doesn't have a real camera or whatever else is current at the moment. But all parents' finances are limited and the 'N' word has to be said eventually. 'No' leads to tantrums on the child's part and guilt for the parents. We know from work done in the Netherlands[5] that kids who watch more TV make more purchase requests and we know from our own work that kids who watch more TV value material possessions very highly. A vicious circle emerges. Children see a glittering array of things for sale through TV and internet advertising and at the same time (through popular programmes like *Deal or No Deal, The National Lottery* and *The X Factor*) they are confronted with a world which values money above all else as the measure of success. They want status objects and a celebrity life so they start to nag. Statistically speaking, more nagging is bound to lead ultimately to more refusals. Refusals cause resentment and guilt. The atmosphere in the house becomes bad and children begin to feel sad.

Anti-parent alliance

It is not just the negativity surrounding nagging and pestering that feeds the circle of watching, wanting and family ill-feeling. In her 2004 book, *Born to Buy*, Juliet Schor talks about an 'anti-parent alliance' between advertisers and children. Advertisers present a wonderful brand world which is parent-free. Since her book was published, the internet has created an even more effective way of excluding parents from direct communications with kids. In an attempt to manipulate children's natural desire for freedom as they hit adolescence some unscrupulous advertisers try to get kids onside and in opposition to their parents.

We tested this out with our 560 UK children. We found that the more materialistic children think their parents are uncool, boring and no fun to be around. And when kids think less of their parents, they think less of themselves, too: the children with a low opinion of their parents also had the lowest self-esteem. So, material culture delivers a double whammy: it's not only linked with children's own unhappiness but it implicates the happiness of the whole family.

Children's mental health

How many children are suffering from low self-esteem or depression? Are children any less happy now than in the past? This subject has attracted heated debate over the past few years. It is hard to dismiss the fact that attempted suicides among teenagers have reached 60–70,000 a year. As many as two or three girls in every 100 make a suicide attempt at some time during their teenage years. Suicide is the second most common cause of death in 15 to 34-year-old males and there has been a 75 per cent increase in suicide rates in young men aged 15 to 24 since 1982.[6] Even more alarmingly, over 4,000 children under 14 tried to kill themselves in the past year:[7] 69 children tried to hang or suffocate themselves, two attempted drowning whilst the majority went for the celebrity solutions of overdoses of medicine, drugs or solvents. A further 13 kids jumped off high buildings or bridges and 4 threw themselves in front of moving vehicles. This is causing alarm to teachers and doctors who don't have specialist support services. Children often attempt suicide when they feel that such drastic action is the only solution to their problems and it seems that there is not adequate and appropriate access for children experiencing emotional and mental distress.

Suicide, however, is the extreme. There are many, many more children living and suffering with mental health problems who are not near to suicide. Add to this the estimate from the Mental Health Foundation that nearly half a million teenagers are self-harming[8] and that 159,000 children were counselled by ChildLine last year[9] and the picture looks pretty bleak. Even market research companies have started to pick up on depression as a key issue for their sample of nationally representative kids. Young people think that there is more depression around now among their peers.[10]

But was it ever thus? Will there always be a proportion of our child population who are damaged for a variety of genetic and social reasons or is today's 'shopping generation' the unhappiest in living memory? There are a number of reasons why it is difficult to disentangle the truth. Some claim that the situation seems to have got worse simply because more disorders are reported than ever before. Others argue that different sets of statistics are compiled using totally different data collection methods, which means that we are often comparing apples and pears. However, a study which appeared in the *Journal of Child Psychology and Psychiatry* in 2004 appears to have by far the most robust answer to date.[11] In this study the four authors set about the huge task of comparing data from large-scale studies over the last 25 years of the 20th century. Most importantly, they only considered data gathered from comparable questionnaires. For the first time, the research really does track adolescent mental health in the UK over a long time span. The results are conclusive. Problems characterized by aggression and anti-social behaviour doubled and depression increased by 50 per cent over the 25 years. At the turn of this century 15-year-olds were more than twice as likely to lie, steal and be disobedient, and were 70 per cent more likely to experience emotional problems, such as anxiety and depression, than those who were born in the early 1960s.

Commenting on this research during the Children's Society's 'Good Childhood Inquiry', child psychiatrist Professor Philip Graham noted that 'it is striking that these increases in mental health [problems] occurred during a period of increasing prosperity, sharply rising GNP [Gross National Product] and growing consumption of material goods'.[12] He has a point. Surely we would expect rising GNP to produce a happier nation? After all, radio presenters are always pronouncing doom and gloom if consumer spending is down. The implication is that shopping is an inherently good thing and that if we shop less the nation will be in peril. Yet it seems quite clear that, whether or not the net rate of mental ill-health in children is rising, the net rate of child happiness has certainly not kept pace with economic growth.

Perhaps the time has come to challenge this fundamental

way of looking at society and its welfare. Richard Layard, one of the UK's leading economists, certainly thinks so. Founder-director of the Centre for Economic Performance at the London School of Economics and an international expert on unemployment and inequality, he has been examining the effects of spending power for many years. The intriguing thing about the thesis put forward in his latest book, *Happiness,* is that it contradicts classic economic thinking.[13] Having money and being able to buy things, he claims, isn't a very good benchmark for national well-being at all. His book provides a substantial amount of empirical evidence drawn from a dazzling array of literatures including 18th-century philosophy, neuroscience, psychiatry, consumer research and what he terms 'the new psychology of happiness'. He introduces us to an essential paradox: most people in the West spend their lives striving for more income but while USA, UK and Japanese income has doubled over the past half century, happiness has not increased at all. Once humans have progressed beyond sheer physical poverty, incremental material wealth just does not bring with it a commensurate increase in feelings of well-being.

There is a long history of writers that have argued the same. John Ruskin, in the 19th century, argued that the Industrial Revolution had generated squalor and misery – producing what he called 'illth' rather than wealth. James Robertson, Herman Daly, Hazel Henderson and other contemporary writers update this perspective, which is now termed 'new economics', and have argued since the 1970s that money is the wrong measure of success for society.

Given that today's high-consuming lifestyles are also hurting the planet, they argue that the goal should be to move from a focus on money to a focus on sustainable well-being. The difference, according to Richard Layard, is that only now are we finally in a position to work out what to do, because we can measure happiness in reliable and sophisticated ways.[14]

He shows that material wealth is but a small part of the overall happiness equation. For adults, less time commuting, less time spent with the boss and more time hanging out with mates seem to be more crucial. He also puts forward a range of overarching explanatory theories for our consideration, concentrating quite heavily on social comparison theory – which, in simple terms, explains why coveting your neighbour's ass is not a recipe for sound mental health. From this he concludes that a key component of the happiness of individuals in society is cooperation and working towards a common good. Goals involving benefit to others apart from ourselves are much more fulfilling.

Haves and have-nots

Let's turn back to our discussion of the haves and the have-nots. If it's true that children are less happy in a materialistic culture, what does this mean for those who can see the dazzling world of toys, gadgets and clothes but can't participate in it because of financial hardship? The statistics for mental health and poverty are telling. In households with a gross weekly income of under £100, 16.1 per cent of children have a mental health problem. The equivalent figures are

14.6 per cent in households with £200–£299; 8.6 per cent in families earning £300–£499; and only 5.3 per cent in the wealthiest homes which share £700+. The correlation looks pretty clear. The poorer you are the more miserable you are.[15]

Is this all bound up in the rise of more of a materialist, consumer culture? Or is this consumer culture in itself a symptom of a more divided, unequal society? Professor Hugh Cunningham, author of *The Invention of Childhood*, writes about the history of children in society. He stresses the resilience and creativity of children over time, contrasting this with any notion that children should be seen as passive victims of what the world throws at them. Despite this optimism, however, he believes that 'in a comparative perspective, societies that are more unequal have more stressed children and we are one of the most unequal societies in the developed world'.[16]

Our own research has shown that the use of media such as TV and internet is a class issue.[17] Children in the UK's most deprived households spend far more time in front of TV and internet screens than do their affluent counterparts.[18] Children in disadvantaged areas are six times more likely to watch TV during the evening meal on weekdays; four times more likely to watch TV in bed before going to sleep; four times more likely to watch TV in the morning before school; and nine times more likely to have the TV on during Sunday lunch. They watch more commercial television, too, with around twice as many children watching Sky, MTV, Cartoon Network and Nickelodeon.

The pattern is similar for time spent on the internet.

Contrary to the idea that there is a 'digital divide' in which poorer households lose out, we found the opposite, at least in those homes with children. Children in disadvantaged areas who have computers use them far more than wealthier children. They are nine times more likely, for example, to eat their meal in front of the computer and five times more likely to be on the computer before they go to bed. This is in part down to whether parents allow televisions and computers in children's bedrooms. As we already noted in the 'Techno Child' chapter, 98 per cent of children aged 9–13 in disadvantaged areas have their own TV, whereas only 48 per cent of the better-off kids do. Similarly, 62 per cent of poorer kids have their own computer, almost double the rate for wealthier families. So, commercial influence is not exerted equally across society. Children in the most deprived households spend more time in front of a TV or computer than their affluent counterparts.

We have already seen that screen-kids are the most materialistic. Add to this the factor of social deprivation and the effect is magnified: 69 per cent of children from deprived backgrounds agree that the only job they want when they grow up is one which gets them a lot of money, while only 28 per cent of children from affluent backgrounds think the same; and 34 per cent of deprived kids are impressed by kids with special games and clothes whilst only 19 per cent of affluent kids are. Also, whilst over half of deprived children think that money makes you happy, only a quarter of affluent children do. The pattern is clear: those who have less want more and this is played on by the profit-motivated parties advertising to our kids. And we know that lower-income groups are deliberately targeted. For example, those with the smallest means to repay loans are bombarded with the greatest number of loan offers by direct mail.[19]

Flourishing or languishing

We have looked at what makes children from different backgrounds feel bad, but what about what makes them feel good? During our research for this book we looked at studies which examine what makes kids happy as well as what might make them miserable. We discovered the work of Corey Keyes, who classified the USA youth population into four categories: flourishing; normally mentally healthy; languishing; or suffering from depressive disorders.[20] Interestingly, the people he found to be flourishing (i.e. actively happy rather than simply not depressed) were those who had high self-esteem which was in part a result of being involved in tasks or projects which they thought were worthwhile. Flourishing also, it turns out, comes down to having good relationships with friends and family, and making contributions to the community, which supports Richard Layard's view of the importance of cooperation and participation in a common good, as well as our finding that a healthy relationship with their parents gives children a good start in life. Tim Kasser, a psychologist who has devoted his research career to studying the effects of materialism (especially on young people), concurs.[21] He has found that children who look to money and possessions to bring them happiness are the least fulfilled and have the worst relationships with their families. Thriving children live in families who make time for each other rather than money and have aspirations with a common good in mind.

Children's views of happiness

What about the kids' view? One of the things we were keen to do, having explored the ideas of happiness in this book, was to test them out with young people themselves. One person we interviewed was 16-year-old Liam, from North London. Over MSN, we asked him when he was most happy. 'Well apart from arsenal victories, i would have to say, either spend lots of money on clothes . . . or relaxing with my mates play pro [Pro Evolution Soccer] on the xbox. You get happiness from the stuff you have, because if you didn't, you wouldn't want it any more.' So, we asked a basic question, why do young people want stuff? He responded:

Friends are the biggest influence, because then you are in direct contact with the object, in advertisements u see it, and think that's nice, looks cool etc, but if u know someone who has something and u physically come into contact with it, you see the happiness that the object gives them, then that encourages you to think yes, if i had that, i too would be happy. The most effective marketing to young people is by other young people. i think most of the companies that appeal to me are, i would say, clever like that. i don't think u can advertise to 16+s and get away with being stupid, or ur not gonna sell anything.

For Liam, at least, the wares peddled by marketers are really important and he realizes that the way they are sold is through his peer group. He admires their approach for being clever. However, he also recognizes the inescapable truth that enough is never enough. What Liam from London tells us echoes almost exactly what Toby from the Southwest had to say: 'I think there is soo much you can have these days, so often a better thing, that you are always wanting. Therefore getting the things u want, does bring u happiness for a period of time, until the next best thing comes out then, the wanting begins again.'[22] Children need the objects sold by the child catchers and they do make them happy – but that happiness is fleeting and ultimately unsatisfying. The promise of happiness is broken again and again.

Someone who hears children's voices all the time is Chantelle Horton, assistant features editor of teen magazine *Bliss*, which has a core readership of 15-year-olds. 'Today's 15-year-olds,' she says, 'worry about the same things 15-year-olds have always worried about – boys and sex and spots. But I think they also have other things to worry about – they worry more about being cool, and about cash and material goods . . . I think they feel a bit lost, and worried, particularly about the future.'[23] More than a third of 14 to 15-year-old girls questioned by *Bliss* magazine in one survey said they have felt unhappy or miserable. Top of the list for making them feel stressed was feeling they had to look good. More than one in six said they'd been bullied, mostly because of what they looked like, while other reasons included being too clever and the clothes they wore.[24] The scrapbooks of adverts put together by children in some of our own research confirm that children are encouraged to look good and not to be clever. In a separate *Bliss* survey in January 2005, 40 per cent of teenage girls said they had considered plastic surgery. Two-thirds of the 2,000 girls in the survey, with an average age of 14, said the pressure came from celebrities with perfect bodies and boys.

At an even younger level, girls want to be slimmer. According to a study in the March 2005 *British Journal of Developmental Psychology*, 71.4 per cent of 7-year-olds wanted to be thinner and most thought this would make them more popular.[25] Our research confirmed the *Bliss* analysis, including the way that the use of celebrities and models in advertising can negatively affect older girls' self perceptions.[26] Some liked and appreciated the use of celebrities. 'I liked these [magazine adverts] because it said your hair could look like Beyonce's or your nails like Christina's. I would like to buy [them]', commented one 11 to 13-year-old girl. But more responses pointed to feelings of their own inadequacy in comparison.

Programmed to pin their hopes on material values, our children are also programmed for disappointment. What other values are available to them?

Values

The relationship between children, money and values is a subject of timeless and cross-cultural concern. For children in the UK, there are the 'spoilt brats' like Veruca Salt in Roald Dahl's *Charlie and the Chocolate Factory*. In the Netherlands, there is the equivalent term *'verwend nest'*, although, curiously, it applies to girls alone. In France, there are the '*enfants gâtés*', the post Second World War generation that never had it so good.

How do you, as a parent or a child, find a way through the ups and downs of a materialist culture? The most hopeful answer, perhaps, is that many parents do find a way and we need to learn from their success. We have drawn, from our research and experience, three guiding principles – enterprise, compassion and resilience – that can help families negotiate a positive relationship with the commercial world. These three principles are explored in detail in the second half of the book, in which we describe examples of how parents, teachers and, especially, children themselves have helped control their inter-face with consumer culture. Before we go into detail, it is also interesting to consider these principles in relation to a body of knowledge on values that spans hundreds of years – the great faiths: we find that similar attitudes on how to deal with wealth and commerce have long been embodied within religious perspectives of goodness and happiness.

We can all be 'spoiled'. The fear that any of us might put possessions above people or money before God is something that each of the great faith traditions talks about. None of the faiths provide a blueprint for every human situation, let alone contemporary childhood, but they do offer signposts, warning markers and encouragement. In Christian teaching, Jesus warns us that no one can serve both God and money. The late Pope John Paul II warned of the 'idolatry of the market', where 'having is more important than being'.[27] In Judaism, in contrast, poverty makes it difficult for people to worship God properly. Wealth is a gift from God of which we are simply guardians, not owners. However, the Mishna asks 'who is rich? One who is satisfied with his portion.' In Islam, God has given humanity a role to play as guardians of his creation. Consequently, Islam does not consider that we own anything in this world, but rather that we have it in trust and must care for it. In the Hindu tradition, the Bhagavad Gita advises 'only a person who has given up desire and the sense of ownership can find peace'. Such peace is an inner experience far more valuable than any material wealth. There are echoes here in the Buddhist principle of detachment, which aims to help followers steer a middle way between sensual indulgence and the extremes of asceticism. Teachings on karma suggest that the way that we act shapes not just our present but our future. Buddhist ethics are not at all opposed to material prosperity, but the challenge is how to find a balance.

In consideration of the first of our three guiding concepts, the benefit of enterprise, one can argue that there is nothing in itself wrong with creating or enjoying wealth, but how you go about making money and how you go about using it matters.

The second concept we will discuss is the benefit of compassion. The risk that wealth and pleasure can sully you if you are distracted from the claims and circumstances of others in need is something that each of the faiths talks about. Given the astonishing wealth of today's society, where children receive more new toys each year than the number of possessions an average family would have had 200 years ago, the call for compassion and social justice in some of the writings of the great faiths have a radicalism rarely heard today. The Early Church father, Basil the Great, said, for example:

When a man strips another of his clothes, he is called a thief. Should not a man who has power to clothe the naked man but does not do so be called the same? That bread which you keep belongs to the hungry; that coat which you preserve in your wardrobe belongs to the naked; those shoes which are rotting in your possession belong to the shoeless; that gold which you have hidden in the ground belongs to the needy. There, as often as you were able to help others and refused, so often you did them wrong.

The third concept is the benefit of resilience. For each faith, a sense of perspective comes from prayer or meditation and builds an inner discipline that trains the mind and, as a result, how you think and act. For the celebrated Buddhist peace campaigner, Thich Nhat Hanh, this means having an awareness of the commercial world and that advertising is based on deception and stimulates greed, as it asks us to crave for things we do not have. He writes that:

our six sense organs – eyes, ears, nose, tongue, body and mind – are in constant contact with sense objects, and these contacts become food for our consciousness. When we drive through a city, our eyes see so many billboards, and these images enter our consciousness.

When we pick up a magazine, the articles and advertisements are food for our consciousness. Advertisements that stimulate our craving for possessions, sex and food can be toxic. If after reading the newspaper, hearing the news, or being in conversation, we feel anxious or worn out, we know that we have been in contact with toxins. Movies are food for our eyes, ears, and minds. When we watch TV, the programme is our food. Children who spend five hours a day watching television are ingesting images that water the negative seeds of craving, fear, anger, and violence in them. We are exposed to so many forms, colours, sounds, smells, tastes, objects of touch and ideas that are toxic and rob our body and consciousness of their well-being. When you feel despair, fear, or depression, it may be because you have ingested too many toxins through your sense impressions. Not only children need to be protected from violent and unwholesome films, TV programmes, books, magazines and games. We, too, can be destroyed by these media. If we are mindful, we will know whether we are ingesting the toxins of fear, hatred, and violence, or eating foods that encourage understanding, compassion, and the determination to help others.[28]

King Midas

In the second part of this book we will look at ways in which we can find and build these competences – enterprise, compassion and resilience. For now, let's consider the classic fable of King Midas. In thinking about the relationship between a materialistic lifestyle and happiness, it struck us that this is indeed the story that is playing itself out amongst our children today. They desperately want everything they touch to turn to gold and may not realize the consequences until it's too late.

Andy Croft, a poet we will meet again later, works with children in schools and brings the King Midas story to life. He asks them to imagine winning the lottery and create an imaginary shopping list. He then asks them to imagine that their house is on fire and they only have time to rescue one thing from the flames. What, or who, would they choose? The answers that they give to these questions open up the Midas story. After telling the first part he asks everyone to make a list of words that describe Midas's craving for gold. Putting the list into the first person, they end up with a collaborative poem about Midas, renamed the 'Bling King' that can look something like this:

Bling King: Before

I love it,
I adore it,
Admire it
I want more of it.
It's the best thing in the world.
I worship it
Depend on it,
I eat off it,
I'm addicted to it,

I treasure it,
I need it,
I crave for it,
Long for it.
I plead for it,
I bleed for it.
It's my passion,
It's my life,
It's my wife.
It's my joy, my future,
My past and my present.
It's my idol,
My god,
It's everything I love most in the world.
I live for it,
I would die for it
Do anything
Give anything
Sacrifice everything for it.
In fact I really wish that
Everything I touch could turn to . . .

He then turns this poem on its head by telling the second half of the Midas story, in which the king realizes that, in reality, turning everything he touches into gold will destroy his life – he cannot eat or drink and cannot touch anyone. Andy asks someone to hot-seat the role of Midas and describe their feelings about gold now. From a new list of words that everyone puts together, a second poem emerges.

Bling King: After

I hate it,
I despise it,
Detest it
Want no more of it
It's the worst thing in the world.
I curse it.
Who needs it?
What good is it?
It's my enemy,
It's worthless
I wish it were gone,
It's nothing more than a piece of scrap metal
I wish I could make it disappear.
I dislike it,
It haunts me
It's my undoing.
It's my hell,
It's destroyed my life.
It's my sadness, my future,
My past and my present.
It's evil, my nightmare,
My weakness, my sorrow,
I wish I could escape from it.
It will be the death of me,
In fact I really wish that
All the gold I have could turn to dust . . .

A world of commercialism offers children the idea that 'having' equals happiness, but this turns out to be a broken promise. The Bling King helps to tell, through words and involvement, the same story – passed down in spoken or written form over generations – of the difference between what costs and what counts and of the dangers in losing yourself in your craving for more.

Part Two: Children Set Free

9. Enterprising Child

'Yeah, like PlayStation or the PS3 what's just come out. It's like £240 to buy brand new but next year it will be half-price.'

Ahmed, age 15

Now let the optimism begin! When we ran through the teachings of the great faiths in the last chapter we concluded that there were at least three directions that could hold out the promise of breaking free from the clutches of the child catchers and their instrumental values. These were: to be entrepreneurial; to have compassion; and to develop resilience. In the following three chapters we look at each of these areas, revealing how young people can respond to the commercial world around them in new and hopeful ways, in an attempt to be free. Together, the chapters could offer a vision of a society that is genuinely different and that neither relegates children to the position of someone else's customer nor assumes that they will be passive victims that need to be protected by older generations. It is a vision of children who are active, who show concern for others and who are strong in themselves.

We've talked a lot about what commercialism does to children and how adults who are focused on profits can harm children's lives, so it is only right to look at the other side of the coin. How are kids taking advantage of a culture steeped in commercialism? We've looked at how the boundaries between adults and children are blurring as children watch TV shows meant for grown-ups; mums wear fashions meant for their daughters; 6-year-olds want 'real' cameras for Christmas; and dads elbow their 10-year-old sons off the PlayStation. In a culture like this, what's to stop youngsters with a bit of get up and go from getting up and going into the adult world to make a bit of cash? And what happens when they do?

To start with, then, we talk to some extraordinary young entrepreneurs whose 'can-do' attitude has helped them embrace and change the commercial world around them. Children are not just addicted to spending money. A number of them want to make it, too.

Beat the boss

The innovative capacity of youngsters is clear to anyone who has happened to catch the CBBC programme *Beat The Boss*. Three primary-school children ('the bright sparks') take on three adult entrepreneurs ('the bosses'). The teams are given a formal brief by a company and have to come up with a new product under demanding time pressure. The playing field is even. The adults are desperate to beat the children, while the children are completely unfazed by competing against people who could be their mums and dads. 'Losers!' they shout at the adults. 'We're going to win . . .' And the adults aren't taking any prisoners either as they plot and scheme in their private boardroom. A typical episode had both teams designing a fun swimming aid. They observed behaviour at the local swimming pool, talked to swimming champions and conducted long brainstorming sessions. The adults came up with an underwater game that involved throwing multi-coloured hoops over a vivid inflatable bollard. The bright sparks designed a float which is worn as a belt and which had detachable animal shaped balls for throwing and catching. The products were tested to destruction by children who had no idea whose product was whose. The adults were determined to win . . . but the kids' idea had a huge majority: as far as the judges were concerned the float belt was a practical help for kids who couldn't swim well and could involve lots of friends in the throwing and catching. Plus, the animals were cute. Victory for the primary school entrepreneurs.

Tiny traders

We saw in an earlier chapter that by age 11 or so children have begun to understand the notion of persuasion and are amassing knowledge of how the commercial world works. In his last year at primary school, Patrick (clearly an entre-preneur of the future) has acquired a sophisticated under-standing of business practice including a secure appreciation of commercial pricing strategies and a precocious under-standing of the laws of supply and demand. He was talking to us about Beyblades, the little spinning tops which have come in and out of fashion across Europe. 'And they [marketers] used to sell them at far too expensive 'cause they knew that everyone wanted to buy them so they were like £6 for one thing . . . so they made them extremely expensive 'cause they know it'd go out of fashion soon so if they could quickly sell them now for lots of money then they would get loads.' You can tell that Patrick would have been selling nylons and chocolate on the black market if he'd been born in another era.

Girls in the same school class had similar strategies for their Barbie dolls. Barbie may be deeply uncool as a play object, but as a business proposition she offers great potential. Jasmine filled us in: 'Barbie aren't as cool as Bratz but . . . like in a few . . . years' time they'll probably be worth quite a lot of money.' Children elsewhere were stashing away their train sets for future profit ventures and discussing the relative merits of leaving dolls in their boxes (rather than playing with them) so as to retain their resale value. But the true entrepreneurs weren't all talk: they had actually embarked on playground trading. Some 10-year-old boys in a fee-paying school were deep in discussion about Pokémon. Jonathan was the smooth operator of the group: 'When I was eight . . . people were coming up to me and saying "I'll give you £20 for one piece of card" and I just think . . . it's easy money, it's easy money.'

'Easy money' is something that two highly successful and very rich young business people had lots to say about when we interviewed them for this book.

Youngest CEO ever

Adam Hildreth, a quietly spoken, unassuming young man from the Northwest of England, is the UK's youngest ever recorded CEO. He set up his first business at 14, started working in it full time at 16 and by 18 was reportedly worth £2 million. He fits the classic young entrepreneur stereotype. In primary school he bought sweets at the local shop in the morning and sold them to his mates in the afternoon at a profit. The business principle is not complicated, he says, you buy at one price and sell for more. We asked him if it really is easy these days for kids to put this principle into practice. Is our commercial culture encouraging aspiring new businessmen and women? Adam's answer was 'Yes and no'. One thing Adam really doesn't like is what he calls 'X Factor Mentality', i.e. the notion that success, celebrity and money are the ultimate goals. He firmly believes that if your number one goal is to make money then you will fail. It's not drive for fame and fortune that will lead to success but a good idea, conscientious research, determination and plain hard work. Jonathan, Jasmine and Patrick need to listen to Adam: current popular culture dishes up the idea of 'easy money' to kids, but the people who've really made it know that's not quite how it works.

Adam's own first business idea emerged because he and his friends were fed up. At 14 they could shop on the high street but couldn't buy online because they were too young for credit cards. Things such as CDs were cheaper online and this didn't seem fair. His school in Harrogate was involved with Young Enterprise, a business and enterprise education charity which operates in 5,500 schools and works with almost 40,000 youngsters.[1] Although the scheme was really for 17 and 18-year-olds, he sweet-talked the teachers into letting him take part. He and six friends started working on the idea of an online payment card for under-18s. They operated professionally. Each team member took on a role and they met up each week to plan strategy. The Young Enterprise advisors weren't impressed at first and sent the team off to prove that there really was a demand for this card. The team threw themselves straight into the task and set up a website designed to attract thousands of teenagers, whose opinions they could then canvass through a chat room. Dubit was born. And Dubit spawned rather more than they had bargained for. The chat room, invented and developed in the lads' bedrooms, attracted thousands and thousands of teenagers. They proved the need for the card pretty quickly by doing online surveys with their site members. However, the site offered a lot more than a piece of quick information for a business plan.

Adam started ducking out of lessons to take business calls on his mobile and spent more and more time away from school talking to contacts about how to develop this platform he had spawned. One of the Young Enterprise advisors was quick to see potential, ploughed in some serious finance and joined Adam full-time. School by now was a needless distraction and Adam called it a day. None of his friends took the risk.

Now, the name Dubit may be ringing a bell. This is the company we talked about in the 'Blitz Marketing' chapter which recruits 7-year-old girls to flog Barbie MP3s to their playmates. Adam himself sold all but a small share of Dubit a while ago (to his original Young Enterprise backer), so we guess he's not primarily responsible for what goes on now, but he would lay claim to crafting the business model which is based on selling research and consultancy services to corporations who want to know exactly how kids tick so they can tap into their spending power. He didn't set out to sell children's data but when he was approached by big boys like Coca-Cola and Reebok he was very quick to see the money-spinning opportunity. Does he see a problem in selling children's data? Well, no: the kids get free stuff and the companies get information. For him this is an exercise in empowerment for children as their opinions are listened to and they have a say in the products and services that are marketed to them. He kept coming back to his belief that 'everything has to be paid for'. Should kids' entertainment be free of commercial influence? Well, of course, but it isn't and even the BBC, beyond its spin-off franchises for kids' favourites like *In the Night Garden* and *Doctor Who*, has to be paid for somehow.

And yet Adam certainly doesn't feel that commercialism should engulf children's lives. He believes that volunteering will come back and that scouts and guides will remain part of the child landscape. Does he think that materialistic values are harmful for kids? Well, kids have always wanted stuff and it's up to the parents to say no. He thinks that kids now use iPods and their possessions to show their success, whereas before it was football skills. Adam thinks that kids are much better off outside playing football than sitting inside playing video-games or watching TV. His youth was spent on the pitch rather than the sofa. He'll be heartened to know that the latest survey by ChildWise for *Newsround* reveals that boys still want to be footballers more than anything else.

Essentially, this super successful and highly likeable young entrepreneur is a pragmatist who has no qualms about selling children's opinions and sees commercialism as simply a natural part of children's lives – nothing sneaky, nothing dishonest, just business.

Yet Adam Hildreth's new business claims very specifically to have nothing but children's interests at heart. Crisp Thinking is a quite, quite different venture. It is a software company which has developed a method of identifying online 'groomers'. It claims that its AGE (Anti Grooming Engine) is 99.9 per cent effective in identifying online adults with sexual motivation. Adam came across paedophiles infiltrating the Dubit site, trying to lure young people to meet up or take part in pornographic messaging. He hired moderators to look out for them in the chat rooms. They were blocked from Dubit, but the moderators realized that the groomers moved into non-moderated chat rooms on other parts of the web. He also told us that groomers work together and share notes, tips and tactics. They aren't all middle-aged men in dirty macs, either. They are male and female and come from all walks of life. Adam's aim is for his software to be part of broadband start-up packages so that it will effectively be installed on everyone's computer in the future. For the moment, parents can purchase the software for a monthly subscription. Given Adam's previous success, his sharp eye for a gap in the market and his sheer hard work, you wouldn't bet against him.

Making money is just a benchmark for achievement

Kieran O'Neill from Winchester bucked the young-entrepreneur trend of leaving formal education early by not only staying on at school to get A-Levels but also completing two years of a business degree at Bath University. He had just packed in education for more important things when we talked to him.

Kieran's business also started with the internet. His dad was head of IT for an insurance company so computers had always been part of his family life: 'I was just playing around with technology – to do with my dad – and things took off . . . a bit of an accident.' His mum's a nurse and his dad has always worked in big companies, so the entrepreneurship isn't genetic. He explained that he had a bit of a reputation at school for making funny flash animations. He wanted to share them with lots of friends but at the time email was too slow to cope. His uncle was also sending him lots of videos at the time and through searching around on the web he just came across a way to stream film and animation. He set up a site which he called Holy Lemon where he could lodge his flash animations and video clips for others to view. 'It cost me $5 a year for a domain name but it got expensive fast – £3,000 a month. My dad footed the bill for that.' So, like Adam's, Kieran's business was born out of looking for a solution to a personal problem. And there were set-up costs – the money was certainly not 'easy'.

The lads are in good company. Google, arguably the biggest and most successful business in the world, began when two PhD students, Sergey Brin and Larry Page, decided it would be handy for their research if they could download the whole of the web on to their computers.[2] 'Optimism is important,' says Page. 'You have to be a little silly about the goals you set. Having a healthy disregard for the impossible.'

This is certainly what got Kieran going: 'My motivation for the first year was not for the money because I didn't know you could make money out of this. My motivation was I just wanted to see how far you could take it. I was curious . . .' He joined a forum for other humour webmasters and came across people who were making a few thousand dollars out of their sites, '. . . and I thought I could make money out of this'. The way all of these other 'webmasters' were cashing in was by selling space on their sites to advertisers. So he turned his curiosity and drive to experimenting with how to manipulate advertising formats to maximize the number of people clicking on them. Like the beginnings of Google, this endeavour was a personal challenge rather than a cynical attempt to work out how to make people part with their cash.

Also like the beginnings of Google, plenty of obsessive hard work was involved. Kieran went back to the forum and read everything everyone had ever written on there to find out exactly how it all worked and how he could be the best at what he was doing. Kieran claims that, for him, making money is just a benchmark for his own achievements. He reckons he'll give it all away. Tellingly, however, he feels that money is a 'natural' gauge for success. Like our tiny traders, this 19-year-old is part of a generation immersed in commercial culture since birth. So the leap from 'I was curious' to 'How many people can I get and how much money can I make?' was almost involuntary. The puzzle of how to send his classmates some stuff for a laugh morphed seamlessly into the challenge of maximizing profits.

Online money-spinning

Having scrutinized years of forum knowledge, Kieran quickly realized that no one pays for entertainment online – everyone expects it for free – so there was no straight exchange model available. There were, however, two other options: collect data to sell or sell some space to advertisers who want to reach your site users. Well, he wasn't collecting data so advertising was the only thing that made sense. He quickly found out about 'ad networks': middle men who act as a sort of broker between the companies who want to advertise to a target audience and webmasters who have a loyal following of devotees and need some cash.

Controlling online advertising

Kieran was able to give us a heads-up on how the whole business of selling ad space works. In previous chapters we raised a number of serious issues about inappropriate advertisements and hidden persuasion techniques on children's popular websites. It transpires that most advertising goes through ad networks who find the advertisers, place the ads, track how many people have clicked and/or responded and then put a cheque in the post to the webmaster. All the webmaster does is put a code on the site and then collect between 40 and 60 per cent of the revenue. So, is it these anonymous middle men who are responsible for some of the dodgy ads on children's sites? Interestingly, the answer is 'not at all'. Kieran told us that the webmasters have complete and utter control over the type of ads that are served on their sites. He, for example, stipulated that he would carry no tobacco ads, no annoying blinking and flashing ones and no 'deceptive' ones.

What about the issue of the gambling and intimate dating ads on sites used by children and adults? To match advertisers to sites, the middle men obviously need to know what kind of people use the site, for which they turn to the webmasters. This turns out to be a rather inexact science. 'We make an educated guess,' said Kieran. Webmasters get information from research companies like Comscore[3] who regularly survey representative panels of users and do their own online surveys. So, for the moment, finding out exactly who your users are – and therefore what kind of ads they might like – is a bit of a problem. It may be that tightening up online ads to children is impossible until the methods for gauging the make-up of the audience have been strengthened. Maybe kids are simply being missed off these surveys. What was clear from our conversation with Kieran was that the ethics of marketing to children doesn't come high up the agenda for advertisers trying to profit from them.

Throughout his journey to success, neither industry peers nor mentors had ever discussed with him the rights and wrongs of the business model pursued by everyone in the game.

Exit strategy

If ethics weren't a big topic of conversation, the exit strategy certainly was and so, in the same way that it was 'natural' for Kieran to turn a personal challenge into a money-spinner, it was also inevitable that he would sell his business. 'Dotcom millionaires' don't cash in on offering long-term value to customers, they cash in on selling the whole business. Just as Adam Hildreth was approached by Coca-Cola and Reebok because he had access to an audience they wanted, a range of bigger organizations started to contact Kieran. Demonstrating calm calculation beyond his years, Kieran didn't rush into the first offer he was made. Livevideo.com tried to woo him, but he was not fooled. Run with the involvement of Brad Greenspan (one of the co-founders of MySpace), Livevideo.com had gobbled up a string of lovingly created back-bedroom sites, and redirected the traffic from each community of users to their site. The aim was to set up in competition to YouTube. In Kieran's view, this practice had ruined a lot of little sites for Livevideo's quick profit. He is scathing about this behaviour as a long-term strategy and he certainly wasn't going to be involved in it. He explained why he thinks such short-term strategies fail. People go to the small sites for a particular reason: they like the intimate, quirky home-grown atmosphere. It's like sharing a secret. If you force people to move to a big impersonal site they won't go back. Besides, the Greenspan business wasn't offering him enough money . . .

ZVue, however, were a much more attractive bet. They are a California-based company specializing in 'cross-screen strategy' which isn't about angry film audiences but about serving up advertising packages to a range of media from TV, mobile phone, film, game consoles and – importantly – portable video players. ZVue make portable video players (like mass market, cheap iPods) which are sold in Wal-Mart to a gigantic customer base. Holy Lemon's customer base could be useful across different parts of the business.

We asked him if this involved tracking and targeting individuals as they interact with all the screens in their lives – thinking of a *Minority Report* scenario. Kieran reckoned that both privacy and technology issues made that impossible at the moment. We went on to talk about customer privacy and asked him if he thought internet users understood that ads paid for free games and were happy to accept them. 'If the customer really wanted the advertising they would agree to it in advance,' he said. What about accepting the terms of privacy policies? 'Customers may have agreed legally but not in reality.' ZVue have just bought Ebaumsworld which was one of our worst offenders in displaying unsuitable ads on sites used by children but Kieran is confident that Holy Lemon will keep its own identity and its own integrity, whilst the shared ownership will provide economies of scale behind the scenes.

Like all good entrepreneurs Kieran has his finger in more

than one pie. While still at school he also set up PlayStation Universe, an information site for the PS3, along with a school friend, Sebastian Hayes. This was set up well in advance of the game console launch and the idea was to make this the best and biggest information site when the product finally hit the shelves. By the time of the PS3 launch, he had a million readers a month. They now have 15 free-lancers writing the content: 6 in the USA, 6 in the UK, 1 in China and a couple in the Netherlands. The business model is the same – selling space to advertisers – but because he has such a niche market he is also considering the Dubit research model. By 2012, the video-games industry will be spending $2 billion just on advertising, so to have access to its target audience and to understand what to sell and how to sell it will be gold dust. Kieran has enlisted some extra powers to help him navigate the ad-buying world. He's sold a part of PlayStation Universe to an agency called Gorilla Nation Media. They'll provide a sales team dedicated to sell-ing ad space to big accounts. The audience for this site is older, wealthier and more dedicated to gaming than that of Holy Lemon.

It's an audience which is wonderfully niche, which is why Kieran's next business idea is a social-networking site which will be a bit like Facebook for gamers. This can connect gamers stuck on the same game level, egg-on the most competitive by comparing high scores, provide a super-targeted environment for games developers and bring in serious money in the process.

So, is advertising the only way to make money on the

internet? Well, maybe not. A Korean company, Nexon, is currently making $100 million a year by selling upgrades to gamers' avatars (online characters). For example, on a car-racing game you can pay $1 to have flames coming out of your car. Thinking of an avatar as a persona, we wondered if this could be a bit like virtual cosmetic surgery. Kieran wasn't sure. He thought it was more about display symbolism. You buy cool stuff for your avatar to enhance your social status and you get to feel cool online, 'Just like buying an Armani jacket in the real world.' Given the highly competitive nature of your average gamer, we guess it makes sense that they are competitive about their position in the social hierarchy too. Not surprisingly, this has been big business for several years in the highly status conscious societies of China and South Korea.

This is a different business model than advertising-generation – getting site users to part with their cash – so the most important issue is making it easy to pay. As we noted already, Habbo Hotel has no less than 36 different methods of paying. These include the prepaid cards Wallie, Paysafe and Ukash as well as cheques, home phone, mobile phone and BT click-and-buy.

Easy money

Kieran has obviously learned fast, but he was very keen to point out that starting a business really isn't 'easy money'. His business cost him (or his Dad!) money for the first few years and it's only now that he's got experience that he's earning. He explained his strategy: always find someone who is one step ahead of you and learn everything you can from that person. When he had a few hundred people in his user community he spent time talking to people who had several thousand in theirs. When he had several thousand he sought out owners of even bigger sites. What sustained him through this learning process wasn't a hunger for money and power, but a curiosity about what was possible and a desire to make things work. If you do things because you're interested in them you will learn through fun. You'll take time and try different experiments and one will finally work.

Ad-blockers

However, there are also technologies which would like to put paid to these revenue streams. One intriguing, near-term innovation is Adblock Plus from adblockplus.org. John Naughton, Professor at the Open University, describes it as 'a plug-in' – i.e. a small program that adds some specified capability to an internet browser. Its purpose is to strip-out all the ads that today litter many web pages. It does what it says on the tin. Right-click on a banner ad, and choose 'Adblock' from the contextual menu, and that banner will never be downloaded again. Alternatively, you can subscribe to a filter list devised by someone else – though it should be someone who shares your culture and values. The effect is remarkable. 'It's like going back to the feel of the web in the early Nineties, before it was strip-malled,' wrote one prominent blogger, Nick Carr. Another was reminded of 'when a blizzard hits Times Square and, for a few hours, the streets are quiet and unhurried, until the snowploughs come to clear away all that white space'.

However, John Naughton highlights the drawbacks of ad-blocking:

> What if a simple browser plug-in put paid to all those revenues? It's a prospect fraught with ambiguity. Of course, it's blissful to encounter web pages as they used to be – stripped of hucksterism. It's refreshing to think of giants like Google being humbled by a piece of free software. In that sense, Adblock Plus is the ultimate antidote to corporate hubris. But there is another side to it. The fact that targeted advertising turned out to be the first major revenue-generator after conventional e-commerce has also brought incalculable benefits in its wake. In particular, it has lowered the barriers for innovators. If you have a smart idea for a web service, then you can start a business with very little capital. You can build a user base by offering at least some services for free, and then earn revenue from advertising. Take away the ad revenues and you're left with subscription-only services – something that only large corporations are good at building.[4]

This is a point Kieran built on during our interview. We asked him if he thought new technologies had spurred on an entrepreneurial generation. He put it like this:

> The economics of how you can become an entrepreneur have changed. Before the internet you had to raise money or have money yourself and you had to be doing

it full time and you had to be a specialist. Now with the internet you can make your website for free if you know how to do it yourself. You can do it while you are at university and you can do 10 different websites until one is successful because they are so fast to do and they don't cost anything. So the barriers to entry for being an entrepreneur have dropped. And if the internet was not around I probably wouldn't have sold a company as young as I did and I probably would not be an entrepreneur. But because I was able to do it, I will be an entrepreneur for life now.

To finish our interview we also asked Kieran what makes a good childhood? For him it's friends, sports and independence. What could be done to create good citizens? A balanced education including sport, drama and the arts. Personal finance should be taught at school to avoid another generation of debtors. Kieran's personal goal? 'I'll work the next 10 years, make £100m and find a good part of the world to live.'

Young companies

The satisfying values inherent in the activities of entrepreneurship, rather than the monetary rewards, are being taken on board in some schools. As well as from talking to our school-age entrepreneurs, we also found good examples of schools that are using enterprise to build positive attitudes. Judette Tapper is Head Teacher at Stockwell Park High School in Clapham. She and her secondary school have created an inner-city success story that rests on a belief in children and what they can achieve. It is a simple ingredient and, in a tough, urban environment, easier to state than to stick to. As you walk up to the school off the busy Clapham Road, the school slogan greets you. Borrowed from NASA, the sign reads 'Attitude determines altitude'. And attitude is what she has in plenty.

Judette has, she explains, a spiritual base to her work, as well as 'an unshakeable belief in children that they can succeed'. As part of this, she has forged strong links with business, but with the aim of making business of use to children rather than children of use to business. From across the city, she succeeded in attracting entrepreneurs that she dubbed 'angels' that could help her in the business of fostering children's self-belief. A Chinese-Irish entrepreneur helped teachers break coursework into smaller chunks and trained them in project-management skills to deliver them to the children. The construction firm that was rebuilding part of the school in an upcoming programme of refurbishment agreed to Judette's suggestion that they help some of the children with building skills, so that they could get jobs with the firm when they left. The school's accountants found themselves delivering courses on accountancy as well as balancing the school books.

The business skills that Judette wanted her children to have, alongside their fast-improving education qualifications, are those that 'they need for an urban environment, to learn to negotiate, to innovate, to seek out opportunities and to capitalize on them, to learn to be assertive'. With a little design help from the angels, the school is blooming with entrepreneurial talent. Enterprises set up by the children included one buying and selling memory sticks, a healthy option milk-shake venture and a shoe-shining business that meant that teachers, pupils and parents had 'the cleanest shoes in any school up and down the country'. Not every business succeeded – one that offered customized T-shirts failed because the designs that the children came up with were too intricate – but they learned more from the setback 'than anything else that year'. The most outstanding success was an African peanut business. The peanuts were purchased wholesale and resold. 'It went down a storm,' and the child that led the business, she confidently predicts, will be the 'Bill Gates of Africa for the future'.

In terms of entrepreneurship, over half of 16 to 21-year-olds want to be self-employed when they are older.[5] Whether young people grow up to be a software engineer or a plumber, they will benefit from learning the attitudes and skills of enterprise. They will need to be more adaptable than ever before in their careers and ready more than ever before to learn new skills throughout their lives. Around one in five children (18 per cent) have now participated in an enterprise project at school and around one in eight (13 per cent) have been involved in hands-on, create-a-company schemes such as Young Enterprise.[6]

Drawing on what is now emerging in schools across the UK, we believe that there is scope for an imaginative step by government. We suggest that government should establish a new type of company called 'young companies'. This would be a company that every child leaving school could take up, an off-the-shelf model, registered in their name without hassle. They could use this for trading, or leave it dormant. After three years, this can be converted, online and free, into a registered company or, indeed, a social enterprise or cooperative. Drawing on similar schemes for young entrepreneurs in Belgium, the Netherlands and Norway, the 'young company' would operate over that time with a healthy tax-benefit – with no tax levied on the first tranche of profit.

Encouraging children towards an entrepreneurial future is not without its problems. William, 13, faced expulsion from his school in Towcaster, Northamptonshire, when he set up a snack-food stall to sell to children who wanted a change from the school canteen. Before the school clamped down on William's venture, arguing that he was undermining official efforts to promote healthy eating, he was making more than £50 a day. The schoolboy, whose idol is Virgin's Richard Branson, said, 'I can't believe it; I don't see what I've done wrong, it's not illegal. Even some of the teachers have been buying from me. The food at lunchtime is rubbish. It's all pasta and vegetables . . . I don't mind some healthy stuff but it costs too much money and there's not enough choice. Now they've taken away all my stock.'[7]

Children live in a commercial world and begin to understand the economics of basic trading in the primary-school playground. However, while popular culture presents fame and fortune as easy and open to all, the successful young entrepreneurs we met are driven by curiosity, meticulous research and sheer hard work. Satisfaction for them comes not from money but from making their project work. Many of these are innovative enterprises, combining young people's love of technology with an internet base that provides a relatively low-cost way of starting up.

Every society relies on stories to knit together its past, present and future. We are surrounded by stories of easy money through winning the lottery or becoming a celebrity. However, these fables of coming to fame and fortune in an effortless fashion are just another way for someone else to make money. Those young people who really are shaping the world around them through enterprise are now starting to tell a radically different story. The young people who get up and go are those who follow a dream rather than those who dream of wealth. They are driven by curiosity and do well when supported by adults who believe in them. They will put something back and are never afraid to work hard and learn along the way.

10. Compassionate Child

'I believe in women's rights.'   Mary, age 14

With record winds of 39mph and sweeping sheets of rain, the tropical storm Alice hit the island soon after lunch, causing unprecedented damage and flooding. The disaster story of Alice is one that is becoming more common as time goes by – another page turned in a world affected by climate change. However, there was more to this particular storm, because the circumstances of the island are unique. First off, the island, Whyville, is inhabited only by children, and an astonishing number of them – close to 3 million between the ages of 8 and 15. Although English is the primary language spoken, the children are migrants that hail from all corners of the world. This is no *Lord of the Flies*, because the island works and thrives with children in charge. Indeed, Whyville is a genuine utopia, in the original sense of the word, as, like Sir Thomas More's own 16th-century island, it is 'nowhere'.

Launched in 1999, Whyville was one of the first online virtual worlds for children. Alice was a virtual storm, created to raise awareness of climate change, and the havoc it wrought was limited to the rubbish and debris it strewed across the screens of the site's members. Over the following days, the children left their shelters and joined together in a massive clean-up effort to restore their environment. Whyville has always been big on responsibility. Children must get their parents' permission and also pass a chat-licence test – which helps them to learn chat etiquette and net safety. It has always had a science bent and Whyville citizens (children) earn currency in the form of 'clams' for the educational activities they engage in on the site. Once you have enough 'clams', you can start a business, the most popular of which offer designs for the faces of children's avatars – echoing the success of the Korean company Kieran O'Neill told us about in the previous chapter.

The idea for Alice was the result of collaboration with Penguin, the publisher of Al Gore's adult book, *An Inconvenient Truth: the Crisis of Global Warming*. Alice helped Whyville's inhabitants to learn about climate change through experiencing it and helped them to get involved in making a difference. At the Whyville Climate Centre, children learn about their carbon footprint and are assigned a calculator to assess their individual contribution to rising CO_2 levels in the virtual world. According to the Centre:

The size of their footprint will increase, or decrease, depending on the personal choices they make, such as the number of virtual accessories they produce in Whyville's avatar factory, the number of trips taken around the world in the warp wagon, the number of times they teleport to the moon or Mars, or even which types of foods they choose to eat. Whyvillians who substantially reduce their impact will be recognized with a distinctive green badge for their avatar and will even be able to trade their carbon credits to other Whyville citizens for 'clams'.[1]

Virtual worlds are, by definition, dreamworlds. Even if presidential candidates in adult real-life countries like France and the USA have set up campaign headquarters on Second Life (an adult-orientated virtual world), few avatars engage in political debates, attend rallies or take part in protests. We are not yet in the world imagined by the Bolivian writer, Edmundo Paz Soldán, as the 'near future', in which anti-globalization activists and authoritarian governments and corporations battle it out in parallel on the streets and in virtual worlds – a conflict he imagines to be led by, and only comprehensible to, teenagers and school leavers.

We have seen, so far, the many ways in which young people are caught up in a world of commercial exchange and of function rather than meaning – paying, getting, spending, watching, buying and selling – but it would be a mistake to assume that this is all that they want. 'The youth of today are by no means as careless, irresponsible and risk-seeking as they are often painted,' says the anthropologist Kate Fox. 'In fact, today's 16–24- year-olds are considerably more risk-averse, conservative, cautious, moderate and security-conscious than their parents' generation.'² The key question is this: if young people, through their engagement with initiatives such as Whyville, can act as citizens and not just consumers in virtual worlds, are they more likely to take responsibility in the real world? This is, after all, the flipside of the questions we encountered earlier as to whether sexual imagery in advertising or violence on screen spill over into the real world. It would be wrong to romanticize what is out there, but there are some signs that the answer is yes, just not with citizenship as we know it. As with so many other things, young people are creating new forms of engagement with the world around them.

Compassion is the second of the values to emerge on our agenda of how to set children free from the clutches of a commercial world dominated by instrumental values. In this chapter we learn that for all the pressures of consumer life a concern for others, which is at the heart of citizenship, is far from dead among the young and, again, we meet some remarkable young activists.

Why aren't all girls feminists?

Throughout this book, we have charted a range of trends that get in the way of compassion and appear to make childhood more of a brutal experience – from blitz marketing through to lives lived more indoors than ever before. If these harsh trends were all that defines childhood, then we could simply conclude that young people are far more likely to be victims of environmental loss and social breakdown than ever turn out to be environmental saviours or future good neighbours . . . or indeed successful parents. The truth is more hopeful. This is the world that children inhabit, but some, at least, are finding ways to turn the tools of consumerism, connectivity and technology into a positive force for change.

The starting point is where children ask the question 'why?' – the essence, after all, of Whyville. We told the story earlier of the schoolgirls from Croydon that demonstrated against WH Smith selling Playboy stationery and accessories to primary-school girls. Another group of girls, of the same age but in Allegheny, Pennsylvania, USA, organized a 'girlcott' of one retailer, Abercrombie and Fitch, for stocking T-shirts printed with slogans like 'Who needs a brain when you have these?' Their action drew national attention, landing them on the nationwide *Today* show to talk about the retailer's misogynistic marketing. The T-shirts were quickly pulled from the stores. Both groups of girls had questioned the behaviour of retailers to positive effect.

However, you won't find T-shirts in Topshop or H&M emblazoned with 'equality for girls', 'feminist' or 'what part of no don't you understand?' and Mary, who is bright, tall, 14 and from North London, explains why:

A few days ago, a friend and I were walking down the road, chatting away, when a man more than twice our age leaned impertinently out of his car window and wolf whistled at us. Although this is in no way uncommon, the two of us were outraged. We then had a lengthy discussion about the impertinence, the rudeness and the disrespect of so many men. So when I asked my friend the question, 'Are you a feminist?' I was sure I knew the answer. But to my utter astonishment, she replied, 'No, I think women's situation nowadays is fine' . . . Ask girls and women what they associate with 'feminism' and they will say: hairy legs, hatred of men, dungarees and not a thought to their appearance. Personally, I call myself a feminist but I have hair free legs, I hold a great interest in fashion, I certainly don't hate men (well, not all . . .) and I would never be seen dead in a pair of dungarees! So does that mean I can't be a feminist? Of course not! Why can't females realize that fine isn't enough and we are still not equal.

Mary submitted this for an essay competition for *The Times*, under the title of 'Why aren't all girls feminists?' The winner would be selected, with school friends, to edit Section 2 (T2) of *The Times*. To her amazement, and nervous surprise, she won and in late 2007 found herself on a two-day work experience trip as the editor of T2. With 11 friends from her class, this was a school trip to the citadels of fame and power. Mary talked about her experience to us on MSN.

I was very excited, it seemed so amazing to be having my writing published in a national paper. It was a bit in this really industrial area, and the entrance was a bit fancy, but inside it was just like any big office, with paper everywhere. We decided all the content. The only things that we were made to change was the length of some pieces, and one boy was told by the school to change his piece on gang culture because it made the school look bad or something. [He had to] cut large sections.

Mary and another girl wrote the page on fashion – something she is passionate about. For her, fashion and feminism have 'nothing to do with each other. I believe in women's rights and I don't see how the way I dress could have an effect on that.' The experience of seeing her words laid out on the page was wonderful and it gave her confidence to express her views on the involvement of young people in the world around them:

I really do think young people should have more of a voice. But more importantly, I think they should want a voice. I have loads of friends who don't give a damn about politics, because they think it doesn't affect them, or feminism, because they don't think it's an issue, but young people, on the whole, don't really think about these things enough to realize that they are an issue, or that they affect them in many ways. Lots and lots of things concern me, but the three that concern me most would probably be sexism, especially in religion and middle eastern countries, global warming, and poverty and the completely unfair distribution of wealth. I think as an individual, I can make small differences, that do matter, but I don't think I can make big changes on my own.

Even if many young people are doubtful about their influence on a big world stage (only one in eight are interested in politics) and only one in three feel influential in the local area,[3] they do want a say. Nine out of ten children believe they can influence the decisions that affect their family and six out of ten think they can influence decisions that affect their school.[4]

Young mayor

One young citizen who does feel she can have an effect on a bigger platform is 17-year-old Luziane Tcheque-Nouta, who lives a stone's throw away from Ed's home in Southeast London. She is one of the youngest elected politicians in the country, being a 'Deputy Young Mayor' for Lewisham. The Young Mayor post was started in 2004 by the old Mayor, who wanted to give more of a voice to those who, being under 18, had not elected him. A genuine, carefully designed election takes place for all children aged 11 to 18 in the borough, with ballot boxes in schools and the opportunity for postal votes. Those over 14 can stand for election. With a 43 per cent turnout, higher than that for local elections, proportionately more people vote for the Young Mayor than for the post of Mayor itself.

Luziane was elected by children in Lewisham on a slate of improving the health and well-being of young people. As she sees it, young people were 'not trusted' by GPs and health professionals, who simply did not know how to engage them. She has also campaigned for half-price gym sessions for under-18s and sessions that offer the activities that they would prefer. When we met her, she was addressing an audience of local councillors on what they could learn from young people. With tinted hair and big, round gold earrings, she wins them over, saying at the outset that 'young people are prejudiced about adults and vice-versa'. She was not trying to take their jobs – 'if you put young people in charge of everything, it would be chaos' – but, she argued, 'every decision that affects young people should be opened up to give young people a say'. 'If you invest in us,' she continues, 'you will get more than you bargained for!'

The election is annual. The Young Mayor receives a budget of £25,000 to spend on services for young children and sits on a project group overseeing services for young people with a budget of £250,000. The first Young Mayor put the money towards a cricket tournament and advice to young people on keeping safe on the streets. The second Young Mayor, Wilf Petherbridge, spent his allocation on a facility for young bands to practise and play. By the time the third Young Mayor was elected, the model was already creating waves, not least with politicians keen to learn how to re-engage young people that they saw as disillusioned with society and government. In 2007, Petherbridge was invited to chair a meeting of the Cabinet itself at 10 Downing Street and, along with campaigner Oona King, helped to lead a damning review of youth services across England. The report was launched by music star Lily Allen, who said

'I want to see a new start for teenagers in communities where they have nothing to do, nowhere to go and nowhere to call their own.'[5]

The review endorsed the idea of giving votes to young people: 'at the age of 16 a young person can choose to finish education, leave home, join the armed forces, have sex, and start a family. If a young person is earning enough they can even pay tax – and yet they do not have the right to vote.' It also called for a programme to roll out youth mayors, youth parliaments and youth manifestos everywhere.[6] While this sounds like one committee endorsing the need for more committees, the truth is far more positive and no one who has ever seen a children's parliament would mistake them for the adult counterpart. On the Scottish islands of Uist and Barra in late 2006, for example, a children's parliament came together to complete a giant mural, teeming with colour and life, all designed to express their ideas and experiences. The children's parliament approach has been described as 'life changing' for some of those who have participated.[7]

When Luziane speaks, it is clear that she fuses a concern for getting things done with the instinctive belief that characterizes so many of her generation in the capacity and responsibility of people as individuals. 'There is no use going to school for all of your childhood, if when you leave, you don't know what to do,' she says, while 'schools need to connect with the reality of people's dreams'. On drugs, she hesitates before putting her finger precisely on the issue that has come up time and again through our book: how to build more resilience for young people when the culture around them can spill over and become corrosive. 'Young people know all about drugs . . . ask about Cannabis and I can give you the A–Z about it. But what encourages drugs is the pressure all around, all the time. You can only resist the pressure if you are confident and comfortable in your own skin.'

If asking 'why?' is a first step for some – such as Mary, Wilf and Luziane – towards activism and involvement, the second step is to ask 'why not?' As Bernard Shaw was reputed to have said, 'you see things; and you say "Why?" But I dream things that never were; and I say "Why not?"' Perhaps it is not surprising, then, that the person, alive or dead, that today's young generation point to more often than any other as someone to respect is the dreamer himself – Martin Luther King.[8]

The Chocolate Manifesto

A good example of young citizenship is the participation of kids in a campaign for equality of which Martin Luther King would undoubtedly have approved – the cause of Fairtrade. Ed was involved in helping to set up the Fairtrade Mark around 15 years ago and remembers a supermarket chief saying he wasn't going to stock Fairtrade goods, because 'only vicars would be mad enough to buy them'. He was wrong. Sales of Fairtrade products reached £493 million in 2008 and are now doubling every two years. Young people have been passionate advocates and in the vanguard of change: 50,000 young people, for example, have signed up to 'change the world' through Fairtrade as Dubble Agents.[9] Each spring, Fairtrade Fortnight acts as a focus for supporters and over 1,800 schools have signed up to become a focal point for action.

In 2006, 11 to 12-year-olds David Williams, Samantha Aspinall and Emma Kinley from Liverpool joined up with 400 other school children to develop a Chocolate Manifesto – a set of demands for a fairer deal for the families making chocolate. As one of those involved said, 'I think it is unfair that people aren't paid for the work they do to make chocolate and we just take it for granted' and another, Kyra, commented online later that 'I love chocolate and I think it is unfair for the people that make such yummy sweets to not be paid fairly!!!'[10] Her comments are true in spirit to the roots of chocolate-manufacturing in the UK – more so perhaps than today's multinational chocolate barons. The Quaker families – the Frys and Cadburys of Bristol, the Rowntrees and Terrys of York – that led chocolate manufacturing in the UK started with an ethical interest. Their primary aim was to promote drinking chocolate as a healthy alternative to gin . . .

The Chocolate Manifesto, developed by children, is surely a more sensuous and appealing name for an act of politics than any that adults have come up with since the Boston Tea Party. In terms of content, it covers the issue of fair shares in world trade. In the classic classroom test of 'who gets the money?', an image of a chocolate bar or a banana is sliced up to see how much the taxman takes, the marketing costs and what the growers get . . . and the growers always seem to get a pittance. Comic Relief recently illustrated for the nation what we think this looks like compared to the reality. If you ask a 12-year-old, he or she will typically estimate that, for a £1 chocolate bar, 23 pence goes to the cocoa growers in the country where it was grown. In a fairer world (and a 12-year-old would part with quite a bit more pocket money to make that come about), growers ought to receive three times that.[11] The true answer for the £1 chocolate bar is that growers probably receive around 5 pence and most of that covers their costs rather than representing net income. Turning your school into a fair-trade school is a way of responding to this. The school, to pass muster, has to make a series of commitments such as including issues of trade and poverty in what is taught and trying to use Fairtrade produce, from food to footballs.

In a number of schools, like Thomas Tallis in Kidbrooke, children themselves run a Fairtrade stall. On cold winter mornings before school starts, outside the dilapidated but well-loved Portakabins, the best-seller by far is Fairtrade hot chocolate. Efforts do not stop at food. There's sports stuff and even, in Oxford, the push for a Fairtrade school uniform. As part of a Channel 4 TV documentary, *Teen Traders*, 14-year-old Martha Schofield from Cowley went with friends on the school trip of a lifetime to India. There, she visited factories to see how shirts were made. She came out convinced that there was a huge difference between doing things the commercial way and doing it the Fairtrade way: 'Many of the workers had become ill in the commercial factories from the pesticides used and they were working 12-hour days for tiny amounts – the equivalent of about 35p.'

She decided to make contact with one of the Fairtrade outlets to see whether they could produce shirts that could be sold as the standard uniform for her school, Cheney School in Oxford.[12] Along with school friends, she is now selling them.

Fairtrade is one example, perhaps, of how young people have responded to the commercial culture around them by championing a different kind of commercial culture that they can own. One in four young people do boycott goods they don't like, but they have also moved way beyond this.[13] Their style of citizenship action hijacks the consumer language and tools of branding and marketing for ends that they can believe in. A grassroots example is the McFLY 2015 project, which is a movement to get Nike to make available to consumers the futuristic trainers seen in the 1989 movie *Back to the Future Part II*.[14] On MySpace, there are thousands of profiles for similar campaigns, most serious, some humorous and some that combine the two. YouthNoise, for example, is a fast-growing campaign forum that describes itself as 'a social-networking site for people . . . who like to connect based on deeper interests than Paris Hilton's wardrobe'.[15] Meanwhile, the UK Youth Parliament is campaigning for a national concession card for all under-18s, to give them reduced fares on buses and trains. This would help them get out and about and 'create the same freedom that pensioners enjoy'.[16]

Although young people can be cynical, Fairtrade seems to have earned their trust. As we have seen, companies can bamboozle people with health information and claims but, with the Fairtrade Mark, as with most organic produce, there is no real way for companies to cheat. The label is certified independently against a clear set of rules. For Fairtrade, this includes affirmative action in favour of marginalized small farmers and workers in poor countries, democratic organization of the producers and investing in supply-chain management and support for producer organizations. As well as a guaranteed minimum price, they get an additional premium.

TakingITGlobal

The UK is the largest market in the world for Fairtrade, but it is Canada that has created perhaps the most impressive of young people's initiatives on world justice. TakingITGlobal is an online youth community started by the energetic and impressive Toronto-born Jennifer Corriero at the age of 19. It has signed up 170,000 members worldwide to access information and take action on local and global issues. No doubt, like all such sites, the tally of those who contribute actively is a small fraction of the overall membership numbers, but there is a seriousness and intensity of commitment that only the young can carry off. For example, one member is Cat, who describes herself as a combination of ice-cream lover, baseball girl and computer addict. She writes online:

> I'm very aware of the difference between thinking of changing the world and actually doing it. I know that to want to change the world is not saying 'I want to change the world', and to change the world is not

claiming 'I will change the world.' So, what have I learned? Everybody knows about 'I have a dream' and what it means, but how many people actually know how it feels like? Just two hours ago, I ran into a poster with the familiar face of Martin Luther King, with his familiar and well-known statement. I have a dream. So, what had I realized, you asked? I had realized . . . that when you want to change the world not because you want to be somebody who changes the world, but because you want the world to be changed, maybe one day you can really do it . . . It will be a lie if I say that I strongly believe I will change the world. However, I do believe that I'll never change anything if I don't try. Well, I don't know why I'm writing this at 2 am the day I'm having my English year 1 exam. But I'm feeling really good now . . . and I do believe in myself and our – my and his – desire to make a difference. Thanks for reading.[17]

Cat (Catthu) is 18 and at school in Vietnam. Through the online community, she connects with people with the same concerns the world over. Other initiatives have made use of the way modern technology reduces the entry costs for people to take citizenship action. The Voices of Youth forums of the United Nations Children's Fund (UNICEF) help to build a constituency of support for action on development issues, while Reach Out is a project that has brought together teenagers from the UK and the Middle East. In many ways, global issues like these are a microcosm of the broader diversity of race and ethnicity that young people tend to experience in their own lives – far more, usually, than their parents will have done. Today, the majority of young people (64 per cent) have friends from a different ethnic group.[18] Perhaps as a result, they are more aware of prejudice. Almost every young teenager (94 per cent, aged 12 to 15) believes that there is racial prejudice in the UK today.[19] Online, is it different? Well, at least in virtual worlds like Whyville and Second Life, it is possible not just to have black, white or brown skin, but orange, green and purple as well. As one teenager commented online, 'I do think, though, that Internet is helping bonds between individuals from different nations strengthen, so I guess (and hope) that discrimination will be overcome in the net in a few decades.'[20]

What else upsets children about the world around them? At primary-school age, the issues that bring frowns and disapproval are cruelty to children, followed closely by cruelty to animals and poverty in Africa.[21] At secondary school, poverty still ranks high but the number one concern for the future is climate change, followed by crime and violence, and then terrorism.[22] The gulf between rich and poor is something that a significant minority of children are able to deplore – in the words of one primary-school child, 'America consumes, Africa wants'.[23] That is not a bad description, as four-word summaries go, of the state of the world in relation to environment and development.

Now, the most important question is whether this idea of global citizenship is an optimistic but ultimately unrealistic, dewy-eyed view of children today. It may be that every generation of children finds a way to articulate a concern for the world around them, whether through stories, exploration, debate or, now, online forums. Their ability to do so is one part of what it means to grow up. A more sceptical view, though, could be that this is a 'phase' – a word that we often use as parents even though we know that saying it infuriates children – and it is the casting off of the concerns that you have as a child that are the true measure of coming of age.

When it comes to surveys on climate change, the polls suggest that many young people are quick to express concern. Over three-quarters feel that they can do a little or a lot to slow down climate change.[24] But are today's consumer kids really environmental activists? When Greenpeace named Nintendo as the least green company on the entire planet in the run-up to Christmas 2007, sales of the wildly successful Nintendo Wii games did not appear to falter for a minute.[25] Mary, the 14-year-old school-girl invited to edit *The Times*, says that 'I think a lot more young people take an interest in the environment than adults realize, equally, a lot don't care because they believe that they will be dead before the results kick in so it doesn't matter.'

Are the children that are young ethical consumers and activists persuading their parents or picking it up from them? Perhaps it works both ways. Take the daughter of Jennifer Lance. Jennifer is eco-aware enough not to buy any plastic toys, but after a frustrating trip to the local toy shop her daughter, who wanted a Disney Princess doll, resolved, off her own bat, not to pester her mum but to pester the company.[26] She wrote this letter when she got home:

Dear Disney,

Please make your Disney Princess toys without having lead in them, and please don't make them plastic. If you want to make money, then at least try being eco-friendly. That is how you are going to make more money. The world is getting greener and in the next couple of years, you will not have anyone buying your plastic. The yarn dolls and the wooden jewelry box and the Disney Princess yarn socks and the sleeping bag are pretty much eco-friendly, but you just have to use eco-friendly yarn and paint. All I am asking you is to be eco-friendly. If you don't listen, I am just going to keep sending you more and more emails.

Love,

M

6 years old

Perhaps M in the USA, Cat in Vietnam or Mary in the UK really could change the world. In the course of writing this book, it has often seemed to us that young people just might have a far better idea of how to run a society than the adults in charge, who have a childish capacity either to close their eyes and assume that the big issues have gone away or repeat sullen mantras (such as that 'there is no alternative'). In the context of climate change, and global inequality, the job of adults is surely to stand up as adults – in business life, politics and civil society – and assume responsibility rather than explain away why they can't. The call M makes of large corporations is exactly the type of fundamental shift in economic life that many believe is going to be required. A drastic cut in carbon emissions means that the style of consumption and production that is being lived out by today's adults and fostered among today's children is going to change.

Imagined communities

The extent to which some young people today are involved, active and caring offers signs of hope. To be a citizen, after all, is to have compassion for the world around you. Citizenship, from its roots in the Athenian polity, the ideas of the Treaties of Westphalia in 1648 and the principles that informed American independence over a century later, is not just about where you are born. It is also about what gives you a sense of belonging. Regardless of the differences and inequalities that have characterized countries, the triumph of the nation state is that it has made people feel as if they belong. Over the bloody years of the 20th century, the power of citizenship was, in the words of historian Benedict Anderson, that it made it possible 'for so many millions of people, not so much to kill, as willingly die for such limited imaginings'. According to Anderson, a nation is simply 'an imagined community'.

Today's young generation also want to belong. They are still 'joiners'. In the last two years 35 per cent of young people have signed a petition.[27] Half of 11 to 18-year-olds belong to a youth or community group, with sports, girl guides/scouts and arts being the most common.[28] Research shows that children that are able to take part in 'wild' nature experiences in childhood, like camping and hiking, are more likely to be environmentally concerned when they grow up – much more so than children who pick flowers or help out in the garden. So it is official: girl guide and scout camps are good for the planet.[29]

In terms of what rights they have, which is an essential part of being in a community, children know they have rights, although that doesn't mean that they know what those rights are. Scotland's children stand out as the most informed about their rights, with around half saying that they have heard of the UN Convention on the Rights of the Child.[30] Two out of three children say that they will vote although, like their parents, the proportion that does end up voting is likely to be smaller. The general erosion of trust in politics – people are less loyal to a single party and more sceptical about politicians and political life – has become even more marked among the young. As a result, there is a significant minority who are generally politically inactive and disaffected. Interestingly, this minority tends to be made up of more materialistic children, who focus more on achieving wealth and fame than living a life of public service.[31] However, the decline of party politics does not mean the death of either compassion or social activism for kids.

If young people in the UK today feel they are citizens of any imagined community, it may simply be different in form to what has gone on before – more fractured, certainly, but also more global. Their loyalties are not nailed to a board marked 'citizen of a nation state', but are of a form we might call 'post-it citizens' – adhering to different communities, causes and concerns over time that, with different degrees of ease, can be picked up or put down. Young people are not monogamous, for example, in terms of loyalty to one place. They are open to more than one affiliation, to places they may have visited, lived in or have family in, across different countries. They are aware of issues of power, such as those around gender and race, even if they express them in new ways. They are less likely to set consumer action apart from citizenship. This is a generation that has internalized branding as if it were their first language and they can use consumerism or indeed anti-consumerism as a form of self-expression and protest. They are concerned about global issues, in many ways acting as global citizens well in advance of any structures of global democracy. But whether a flight away from formal politics is ultimately self-defeating and whether their insulation from nature hampers the extent to which tomorrow's world will embrace a sustainable future remains something that only their generation can tell and can only be answered in time.

11. Resilient Child

'I'd make sure I want it first.'   Rhonda, age 11

There is an old story about a man and a horse. The horse is galloping quickly across the land, and it seems to all the world that the rider and his horse are going somewhere urgent and important. However, when another man, standing along the way, calls out, 'Where are you going?', the rider replies, 'I don't know! Ask the horse!' For parents today, it seems like the take-over of childhood by marketing and commercial values has a momentum and direction of its own, but we are given little idea of where it will all end, of what the limits are, or indeed whether there are limits. We race along and it is easy to feel that we are powerless to stop. We have lost control.

For the parents that we surveyed with Care for the Family, commercial pressures are a fact of life.[1] While they feel, as parents, as if they are constantly having to trade their values for those of a commercial world around their children, they also know that young shopping, life online and mobile contact are not going to go away. They want to understand what they can do, rather than what they can't. In short, most parents are trying to navigate the world they find and to change it where they can. In a runaway world, in which everyone has a view on what is good or bad parenting, they simply want to be more in control.

This chapter is the third on setting children free and outlines the experiments and innovations that are proving successful in helping young people to take control. By equipping children to be more resilient and more proactive, these approaches build the resources and skills they need to be able to deal with the excesses of commercial pressures and some of the harmful side-effects of commercial values. However, they all depend, as an essential prerequisite, on children having loving and supportive adults and open and supportive schools around them. The first technique we look at, and the one that we spend most time on, is financial acumen. The commercial world, after all, is about money. Being in control of money, rather than money being in control of you, is an essential first step.

Pocket-money power

It is supposed to be British not to talk about money. Well, that attitude has to go, particularly when it comes to conversations within the family. In the course of researching this book, we've found one particularly powerful tool for developing resilience which parents have in their arsenal, and that is pocket money. Pocket money is not universal but, for most children, it is the norm. Somewhere between 70 per cent and 80 per cent of children aged 6 to 16 receive pocket money.[2] By the time they are 21, children will have been given on average £5,518 in pocket money.[3] Pocket money, or an allowance when they are a teenager, is when real and symbolic commercial power passes from parent to child. It is also an exchange where most children are pretty open to ideas and rules that parents set down in return for the money they give. It is a unique interaction between parent and child around the subject of money – how they can control it and make good use of it on the one hand and how it can dance to the tune of the commercial world on the other. It also provides a regular space and opportunity for touching on issues that matter. Pocket money discussions allow a valuable opportunity to teach children not just about budgeting but other life lessons such as just reward, generosity and patience.

Earn it

In our research, parents shared more tips on pocket money than on anything else.[4] Over 200 tips in all, probably a book in itself, demonstrated just how imaginative and creative parents can be when it comes to bringing up children in a commercial world. You want to know how to do it? Well, here is some of what they have tested and found works for them.

Nearly half of those we talked to agreed that pocket money should be earned in some way. James, the father of a 7-year-old, told us, 'Junior knows that I have to work to earn my income. He is rewarded for good behaviour and helping around the house with small but positive tasks. He is aware that pocket money is not a right.' Mary's children are a bit older and for her, pocket money is also more about the relationship between work and money than the relationship between money and spending: 'I hope by encouraging my 12 and 14-year-old boys to earn their pocket money I am instilling into them the fact that you only get paid for the effort and commitment you make to an employer, i.e. no work-no pay.' She also notes that her children seem to feel a satisfaction from working towards a common good within the family. 'They also enjoy the feel good factor of helping, teamwork and achieving the amount of pocket money they have earned.' From other research, we know that younger children are more likely to have to work in order to get their pocket money, with 69 per cent of 7 to 11-year-olds, compared to 50 per cent of 12 to 16-year-olds, doing jobs around their house in exchange for pocket money.[5] In most cases, this is still tied to a flat level of pocket money rather than being a fee for service and increases in pocket money tend to happen on an ad hoc basis, or annually on a birthday, rather than being tied to specific achievements.

Budget it

Over a third of parents have found that pocket money is a great way for kids to learn budgeting skills – even if it's the hard way. Miriam put it like this: 'Give them little enough when they are young to let them spend it on what THEY want – they will learn that some things are a waste of money early on.' Josiah agrees: 'Don't give in and give more money if they have spent it all. But allow freedom to use their own money how they want to – if they waste it, it will teach them to budget more carefully the next week/month.' Giving kids freedom to spend also allows them to reject overpriced brands for themselves. Mike let us in on his tip: 'If my teenager wants new trainers I look around at what I think are reasonable trainers and find the average price, say £25. Then I give that as a budget and if they want a £50 pair that is fine but they have to make up the shortfall out of their pocket money – it tends to make the cheaper trainers much more attractive!'

However, budgets over breakfast are not necessarily the norm across the country. At present, a good 29 per cent of young people over 16 say they would not know how to prepare and manage a weekly budget.[6] It seems from our research that it's likely they'll take it on board more readily from their parents at a young age than from school as a teenager, particularly if they learn by watching and sharing in the household budgeting process. Explaining to children different ways of budgeting can actually be quite engaging, from showing them how to keep track of your bank account and cash withdrawals to keeping tabs on your spending on a weekly or monthly basis. Kids will see that it's a habit and they can come to understand that sometimes you have to step back from the frontline of marketing and consumption to work out priorities. It encourages feelings of being in control: that habits and values are aligned.

Just as Mary found that her kids enjoyed actually doing the tasks which earned them their pocket money, another mother, Li, found that teaching kids to budget and save really does affect their values and behaviour. As she put it, 'children appreciate things that they have saved for much more than things which are freely given to them'. Lloyds Bank launched their Access card in 1972 with the slogan 'Takes the Waiting out of Wanting'. It seems that our children might actually be a lot happier if – 37 years later – we teach them to put the waiting back in again.

Putting the waiting back in wanting

Given that UK personal debt rose to an all time, staggering high of £1.4 trillion at the end of 2007, and the calamitous situation in world banking at the end of 2008, if more parents were to teach their children the waiting game it might benefit us all.[7] Research by the government together with Martin Lewis, the journalist who runs the leading consumer website moneysavingexpert.com, shows that one in three parents do not discuss debt and credit at home despite the vast majority (83 per cent) having worries that their children will run up debts. It seems that many parents are put off because they don't know what to do if their children find it boring or unimportant and they are worried, above all, about looking 'like a nag'. As a result, around a quarter of 16 to 21-year-olds will not tell their parents about their money situation, even if they are in debt. Meanwhile, 40 per cent of young people over 16 do not know what APR is.[8]

Other interested adults can also help kids wise up about money. Martin Lewis was invited by a school to do just this. Having built a formidable reputation for helping people find their way through the financial services jungle, he turned up at St Simon Stock Catholic secondary school in Maidstone, Kent, to see what he could do to teach a dozen 15-year-olds about the commercial pressures and opportunities in the world around them. He warned them that 'companies spend billions of pounds a year on marketing, advertising and teaching their staff to sell, yet we don't get any buyer's training . . . [or a] practical survival guide to living in one of the most competitive consumer economies in the world'. A company, he said, is not your friend. They are there to make money out of you and you are the only person who is really bothered about you.

Over the course of three lessons, he took the students through companies, credit and debt and why loyalty doesn't pay. At the end they set to work to see how much they could save in their family bills, with the biggest saving being made by the headmaster's son, Tom. The 12 teenagers saved, between them, over £5,000 by getting a better deal on credit cards ('Debt isn't bad,' explains Lewis, 'bad debt is bad'), changing car and pet insurance companies, switching gas and electricity providers and getting a better deal on mobile phones. Their teacher, Caroline, also joined in, saving hundreds of pounds on her digital TV bill. *Teen Cash Class* was broadcast on ITV in the summer of 2007 and has gone on to spawn a book and free guide under the same name.[9]

Poetry pays off

A rather different character, Andy Croft, the writer and poet we introduced in Chapter 8, was also asked to help children learn more creatively about money at the Fens primary school near Hartlepool. Andy passed a coin around the classroom and, when everyone had handled it, asked them to think about how many other people might have handled it in the past. Who were they? What were they like? If the coin could talk, what would it tell us about its past life? He used this to make a poem from the suggestions that the children made:[10]

Money Talks

I was born in a furnace,
Brought up in a bank,
I learned my trade
In an ATM.
I've been wet and cold,
New and old,
I've been dropped down a drain,
I've travelled to Spain.
I've paid the bill,
Been stuck in a till,
Lost in France,
Washed with pants.
Been borrowed and stolen,
Nicked by a crook,
Licked by a dog,
Given as change,
Lost and found.
Buried underground.
I've lived in a wallet,

In pockets and purses,
I've been withdrawn,
Been in dark places,
Been spun, tossed,
Won and lost.
I've been involved in crime.
And I've served my time.
Been on a bus,
Flown by plane,
I was thrown on the line
Of a railway train.
Crushed in gutters,
Hung out with nutters.
I've been thrown in a fountain,
I've swum in the sea,
Dropped and ripped,
And flopped and flipped.
Sometimes tails
And sometimes heads.
I've rolled in the gutter,
Been stuck under beds,
I've done my time
In a magpie's nest.
North and south,
East and west,
Cold hands, hot hands,
Large and small,
Hard and sweaty –
I've seen them all.

Continuing the theme, the children then brought in foreign currency and toy money, along with some real notes. They talked about: why are some pieces of paper worth more than others? Why are some currencies worth more than others? What would happen if the streets really were paved with gold, or if money really did grow on trees? The next poem came when the children invented some funny currencies, like carrots and polar-bears and thought what would happen if they started using them for money.[11]

Funny Money

If carrots were money
We would all start digging.

If smiles could buy things
We would all be jolly.

If soap was money
We'd be filthy rich.

If water was money
We'd be swimming in it.

If friends were precious
We'd all be rich.

If time was money
We'd spend it more carefully.

If chocolate was healthy
We'd all be wealthy.

If cheese was money
We'd be stinking rich.

If life was cheap
Somebody would make a killing . . .

A third poem, 'The Money Tree', showed the children's imagination fired up. 'The bark is as wrinkled and scrunchy as Scrooge's face' is a description of the money tree in spring and, in autumn, 'The bark is as hard as a miser's heart'. Through exercises like these, the project explored the difference between what people want and what they need, what has commercial value, what is precious and the kinds of monetary terms that children come up against in their daily lives. The pupils also developed a Monopoly-like trading game which showed them how different commodities have different values according to what is happening in the world and in different markets. However, it was the poetry that really engaged the pupils and helped them understand money and how it works. As one of the children remarked, 'All of us learnt new things about money that we can use.' The children with special educational needs, in particular, got a lot out of it, said the head teacher: 'They didn't have to think about maths and their ideas were really valued. You could see those children blossoming.'[12]

3S – a framework for mini money managers

So, short of becoming a financial journalist or soulful poet, how can a parent or relative start to develop and deepen a conversation with children about financial values in a commercialized world? It can be awkward given that most of us would actually rather talk about sex and drugs with our children than money. Perhaps the simplest and best framework is that constructed by Nathan Dungan, who sets it out in his book *Prodigal Sons and Material Girls*, which has the wry subtitle *How Not To Be Your Child's ATM*.[13] He encourages us to illustrate and explain the differences between the three primary ways of using money and the three priorities that make up a framework for financial values.

The first is to 'share' – how to give money away to someone or something that is important to you. We teach children from an early age that sharing is good when it comes to toys, games and playing with their friends, but there is much less said about sharing when it comes to money! And how many adverts can you recall that encourage you to share?

The second is to 'save' – how to put money away in reserve for when you need it. When it comes to 12 to 14-year-olds, a savings habit is a rare phenomenon and, according to market research agency BMRB, now an endangered one. Despite having more money in their pocket, children are saving less than ten years ago. Today's children are more likely to see themselves as 'not good at saving money', more likely to believe that they 'spend money without thinking' and that 'young people should enjoy their money not save it', and they are more likely to believe that, anyway, their parents will buy them 'everything they want'.[14]

Finally, 'spend' – how to pay money for something you want. This is something that many children do feel they are good at. 'I think it's pretty normal for kids to be "shopaholics", especially GIRLS! Girls, like myself, love to shop, and if there weren't shopaholics shops would have no business!' says Suzie, 14, from Sussex. But, as we have seen, it is not just girls. Mark, who's 12 and from Shrewsbury, told us, 'I think shopping is great. It's a fab socializing activity with friends or family and it's great to find a bargain.' Equally, children recognize the phenomenon of impulse buying. You buy something because you just have to have it, and then eventually the thrill wears off, sometimes even within a week, as Natasha (13) recounted rather wistfully: 'I love shopping. But I just spend it on things that I don't need.'[15]

We will call this the 3S model: share, save and spend. It underpins the core of what parents have told us about using pocket money as a way to keep children grounded in human values whilst educating them in how to keep tabs on financial values within the great commercial circus which surrounds them. Dungan has a few other practical tips, like the 'three jar' system – labelling one Sharing, one Saving and one Spending. When we tried this out in practice, it became evident that jars were not a high status way of keeping money for Year 6 girls, when friends might come to visit or even stay overnight, and that Hello Kitty purses served a little better. An alternative is to place a sharing jar in the kitchen and fill it up with loose change. When it is full, your children can count it up and help decide, as a family, how the total is going to be shared or given to charity.

Passing the finance test

One of the key tests of 'financial capability' that the Financial Services Authority uses is whether you can read the balance out correctly from a bank statement and whether you can tell if there is enough money in the account to cover a payment that is due. It also asks 'If the inflation rate is 5 per cent and the interest rate you get on your savings is 3 per cent, will your savings have at least as much buying power in a year's time?' and 'Is a cash discount of £30 better than a ten per cent discount on a television with an original price of £250?' If you can do these, then they start to ask about different types of mortgage and what you are saving for retirement.[16] This is more for an adult audience, although there are pressures to bring property investment and retirement funding knowledge to the under-18s. Long-term savings for children now have a strong tax-incentive, something that led Abbey National, mistakenly, to write to babies offering them loans, as good credit risks, of up to £20,000.[17] And while there is no market yet for children's mortgages, with house prices even now at historically high levels we have seen the launch in the UK of 'inter-generational mortgages'. These allow parents to pay only the interest on the sum borrowed and to pass the mortgage on to their children, so that it is paid over generations rather than within the working life of one person.

Alongside budgeting, the Financial Services Authority

now defines the key competences of 'financial capability' as the ability to make ends meet; keep track of personal finances; plan ahead; stay informed about financial matters; and choose financial products. Not surprisingly, given how much is spent for children and by children, if you are a family with children you tend to be less able to make ends meet, but that does not mean that parents lack financial skills. Lone parents, for example, are the most effective consumers in the country when it comes to keeping track of money.[18]

In some ways, this concept of financial capability is a polite way of saying that the powers-that-be believe that too many of us are in debt, are sold the wrong financial product or are failing to save for our retirement. It does make sense to teach children life skills like these. Thankfully, there is now some excellent work underway in many areas. Organizations like the Personal Finance Education Group (Pfeg), the Scottish Centre for Financial Education and the Consumer Council in Northern Ireland are building financial education into schools, while in Wales every secondary-school child will soon have the chance to join a credit union (cooperatives for saving and borrowing). There is also a burgeoning movement experimenting with alternative and ethical investment, all based on the idea that money can be your servant rather than your master. David Boyle, an associate of the New Economics Foundation, writes about the history of these ideas in his book, *The Money Changers*, and contemporary experiments in his pocket guide, *The Little Book of Money*.[19]

Grandparent power

When it comes to teaching children financial values at home, Nathan Dungan in particular encourages grandparents to get involved. It is easy for grandparents, or indeed for friends with no children of their own, to enjoy giving to children. Spoiling children with big ticket gifts is known in the language of marketing as 'compensatory consumption' and you are encouraged to do it. Yet, as Dungan puts it rather earnestly, while it is fun and easy to lavish stuff on your grandchildren, wouldn't you do better to teach them financial skills that could benefit them for decades . . . ? One of his practical suggestions is to hand over a cheque with everything filled out but the name of who to pay it to, and ask your grandchildren to fill it out in the name of a club or charitable organization. An alternative is to ask them how they would use their money if they won the lottery, and use this as a basis for talking about what matters most.

Giving children a framework for financial values alongside their pocket money is the most effective way of equipping them for the choices they will face in today's commercial world. It can also be a way of dealing with everyday pester-power in the sense that, as they grow older, parents can escape the trap of being seen as a walking wallet for children by responding 'if you want it, and it is in your budget, you buy it'. All of this probably does depend on parents setting a good example and 'walking the walk' themselves. Children take more of their spending cues from watching the way that their parents act in relation to money rather than what they say. There is a lot that you can do when you are making decisions to illustrate the financial values that you are demonstrating – 'teachable moments' about being money-wise.

Here are a few everyday teachable moments from parents:

CASH MACHINE When you take money out, you can use the receipt to discuss how much money you've got left in the hole in the wall, when you'll get your next pay cheque and how long the money has to last.

SHOPPING One mum uses this simple way to demonstrate budgeting when she goes shopping with her children: she puts the money she thinks she'll spend in an envelope and gets her children to estimate how much they'll spend on what. Then the kids take out the money each time they pay. The kids are often surprised at the results.

SUPERMARKET CHECK-OUT Other parents explain the financial transaction to their kids as they fill up the bags at the check-out. The food may be paid for with plastic but it's just the same as the coins and notes in a purse and disappears as the same rate. Parents also explain how interest charges work on credit cards and how quickly they can add up.

EATING OUT Look at what you're eating and compare what it costs in a restaurant and, perhaps, what it might have cost to make at home.

HOLIDAYS Families often save up all year for the family holiday. Some parents have found that helping their kids to save their holiday money at the same time helps them see that saving is an important part of life for everyone.

Life at school

So what about school? What should schools of the future do if they are to equip children to survive and thrive in a hyper-commercial world? The focus of education is all too often on how to pass on knowledge better and how to ensure that more of what is taught is in fact learned. This does well enough if the yardstick of success – such as IQ or exams – is intellectual achievement, but if the yardstick is a wider conception of capability and life skills, then schools overall appear to do less well.

The educationalist Howard Gardner offers one such yardstick. He suggests that there are eight or nine key intelligences that we are born with and that help us to get by. These include being smart in terms of spatial awareness or musical ability or being smart in terms of self-awareness or an understanding of others. Schooling, Gardner says, can cultivate these intelligences and it can also sometimes crush them. The idea that these matter in terms of how you get on is borne out by Nobel Prize-winning economist James Heckman, who points to their importance in explaining who gets a job and who doesn't and how much people are paid. He shows that having a high IQ does not make you successful. What counts are factors such as self-discipline, persistence and reliability. Thinking back to our two young entrepreneurs, Adam Hildreth and Kieran O'Neill, these are exactly the skills that they had cultivated in themselves.

Daniel Goleman builds upon Gardner's work, talking about emotional intelligence and developing a set of 20 competences for life that revolve around four key skills: self-awareness, social awareness, self-management and relationship management. In an area once thought hippy or intangible, this kind of work does a welcome job of beginning to fill in the gaps of language and theory.

Even if these ideas help to explain how children can flourish and succeed later in life, they are categorically not on the national curriculum at present. The disciplines of ethics, respect and working with others, aspects that Howard Gardner points to, are far less well understood than the disciplines of reading, writing, history or maths. Arguably, though, they are just as important. So, how can they be taught . . . or, rather, how can they be learned?

Studio schools

One man with an answer is Geoff Mulgan, someone we have worked with closely over the years. He runs the energetic and eclectic charity, the Young Foundation, in the East End of London and is piloting a series of entirely new schools – studio schools – across the UK. He explains:

> Eastern civilizations have a rather richer tradition of thinking about social learning and the cultivation of inner disciplines than the west, which has tended to assume that education is about the transmission of bodies of

knowledge to freestanding individuals. What they offer is a less unitary self than the western view of a coherent ego consciously making judgements according to a calculus of rules. Instead they see the self as made up of processes of which we are unaware, indeed of which we cannot be aware. Our mind creates structures, including ethical dispositions and social skills, out of experience as well as out of conscious choices. Experience and action are inseparable.[20]

That's a rather abstract way of saying something quite fundamental: that we become what we do. The implication is that children can learn a wider range of skills if they can practise them and reflect on them, especially in a setting that is shared with others – either though an apprenticeship or being in a team. The studio schools that the Young Foundation is developing will be unlike any other. The central feature is that the schools are organized around a series of operating businesses run by the students themselves. Each school contains no more than 300 young people, from age 14 to 19. Each is connected to a different industry cluster, such as construction, fashion or food services. Its ethos aims to excite and motivate young people who are disengaged from learning.

The young people are participants and contributors as much as students. The staff comprises a mix of teachers and people with business expertise. With a combination of enterprise projects and tutorials, students can work for qualifications that also enable them to pick up key social skills such as teamwork, communication and entrepreneurship that are often neglected in other schools. The field trials for the first studio school began in Luton in late 2007 and there are hopes for more pioneers from Barking and Barnsley to Sheffield and South Tyneside.

Giving young teenagers responsibility is a key to their flourishing. The psychiatrist Professor Philip Graham, who we came across in an earlier chapter, believes that empowering young people is central to helping them cope in a world which is often after their money.[21] Young people agree. When we talked to Harry, age 14, from the Southwest, who fits the profile for a studio school if one started locally, he said, 'I'd love to go to a school like that. It sounds like a great idea. I don't like sitting down, I like getting up and doing things. I learn quicker like that.'

At present, two-thirds of employers do not think that school is equipping young people entering work with skills like teamwork and communication.[22] And while most companies used to hire people on the basis of 90 per cent experience and 10 per cent attitude, now it is something like 40 per cent 'attitude' – in other words, work ethic, teamwork and other soft skills. As Geoff Mulgan sees it, 'we want teaching and learning which encourages tacit knowledge, creativity, uncertainty, oral communications, teamwork and the conversion of new ideas into reality – rather than internalizing a body of received knowledge.'[23]

Happiness lessons

Apart from distance learning, there have been few big innovations in the institutional building blocks of education over the last 50 years, so studio schools are a brave experiment and have their work cut out for them. The Young Foundation also has its eye on influencing the operations of all schools through a pilot programme it is running with economist Richard Layard on how to promote well-being. We talked about Richard earlier. His take on economic reality is that striving for greater material wealth does not result in greater happiness, but working on team projects for the common good brings about contentment.

In summer 2008, 2,000 12-year-olds from across 21 schools in Manchester, South Tyneside and Hertfordshire completed the first year of 'resilience' training under this new pilot scheme. The training is part of a three-year trial, with rigorous evaluation. The content was developed in the USA by psychologist Martin Seligman. After years of studying depression and the way in which people learn habits that trap them into helplessness, Seligman's eureka moment was to realize that if people could learn to be depressed, then some of them could be taught to be happy. He called it 'positive psychology', focusing on this key characteristic of optimism as the factor that makes a difference.

The Young Foundation's Geoff Mulgan explains. 'The primary goal of the programme is to build resilience and promote optimistic thinking in children to help them respond better to daily challenges and problems. Children are encouraged to identify and challenge negative beliefs, to employ evidence to make more accurate appraisals of situations and events, and to use effective coping mechanisms when faced with adversity. They also learn techniques for positive social behaviour, assertiveness, negotiation, decision making, and relaxation.'[24] In short, the very children that everyone knows are most vulnerable and sensitive – in the transition from childhood to adolescence and having just transferred from primary school to secondary school – could be trained to be the happiest of all.

Children in charge

No doubt this feels like a busy agenda for schools, but so it should. It is a changing world out there. The role of schools is to open minds and equip children for life – to set them free – and schooling has never been more important, while teachers that can support children have never been more needed. The happiness trial is designed to promote more can-do, optimistic children. The studio school is designed to celebrate entrepreneurship. Parents are using pocket money to help children build a healthy attitude to money, while more schools are now starting to teach children money management skills. Some families are even finding it financially rewarding to involve children in the household budget. All these approaches converge on one, central concern that runs through the evidence on marketing to children that we have set out from such a wide range of sources over the course of this book. Children are rather passive in the face of commercial pressures. Currently, if they are being encouraged to participate in economic life (as agent, informer or brand friend), it is not on terms that they have set.

With parents and schools behind them, children can take more control of the opportunities around them. As they develop, they will have the inner resources and outer skills to be able to engage in a more commercial world. Projects like these help to put children in charge of the hopes, dreams and insecurities which the marketing machine currently plays on. They help to put children more firmly in charge of the money they spend and the desires which marketing awakes in them. They turn children from passive commercial fodder to active economic participants. In short, rather than children who have been caught, they become children set free.

12. The Children's Marketing Manifesto

'Make it simple and straightforward and don't lie or make promises you can't keep.' Tanya, age 14

Enterprise, compassion and resilience can all make a difference for children and families, but there is a need for a national debate and a programme of wider system change, too. The evidence from this book shows clearly that commercial pressures and values in the lives of children are now running fast, out of control and unchecked. Children aged 7 should not be working for multinationals. Marketing practices should not intrude on or interrupt children's relationships with their peers or their parents. Junk food should not be sold as health food. Children should not be sold porno bunnies and suggestive lingerie. Corporations should not be allowed to turn a profit whilst turning a blind eye to ethics.

If advertisements can be creative and fun – at their best

somewhat like public art – it's time to acknowledge that wider marketing and the sheer volume of commercial exposure from an early age creates a cumulative effect. Children are beginning to feel overloaded, ripped off and failed.

This is not working for young people now, and it is also not fit for the future. We face the challenge of adapting our carbon-wasteful lifestyles, particularly in countries like the UK, in the context of climate change. This is not a good time to be raising a generation hooked on high consumption. At the same time, this cannot mean turning the clock back to an age when children were supposed to be seen and not heard (nor seen out shopping). The call for respect that we have reported from young people is not a passing cry, but one component of a genuine shift in paradigm that is coming in relation to children's needs. It is all too easy to treat children in the same way that the Victorian world treated women – as delicate, vulnerable and needing to be kept at home – instead of giving children themselves a leading role in the rules that are designed to protect and promote their interests.[1]

The one overriding need, we conclude, is to be able to harness technology for children's freedom, development and well-being. The forces of scientific know-how and technological invention are accelerating so fast, argues Ray Kurzweil, the breathy and optimistic technology forecaster,[2] that over the course of a single year we now see as much change as would have taken 200 years at any other point in human history. What we have seen in this book is that the pace of change is driven more by technology than by companies, even if companies are first to adapt and find ways to mainstream and commercialize that technology.

With new technology there inevitably come new opportunities for interaction, new tools for marketing and new models for doing business. This is why the dramatic growth of marketing to children is a new and urgent issue, and not simply a conundrum as old as advertising. In an open, competitive and more and more lucrative market, companies will try anything because the boundaries of responsibility, by and large, are not yet set.

The business models for the children's market online, for example, are something entirely new. In many ways, they are a remarkable mix – they are flavoured, ironically for this point in history, with the extremes of communism, anarchism and capitalism. The online world is communist in that it tends to be free at the point of access. It is anarchist in that its underlying structure favours a 'creative commons' of online communities and collaboration.[3] But, above all, for children, it is also capitalist in tooth and claw. Once they have used the infrastructure of the internet, put up content for free access and learned how to tap into children's yearning for friendships and community, then companies seem to operate a no-holds-barred strategy to recoup costs through influence, advertising and marketing. It is highly innovative. It is always pushing boundaries. Sometimes, as we have seen, it is deeply irresponsible.

This generation is more consumer-savvy than any before, but it is also touched by the uncaring values of the commercial world around it. It is also a brutal world for those that fail in the consumer society. Trends in children's mental health are of real concern: this is not the promise of happiness that we were sold.

The simple truth is that the more children are exposed to commercialism, the more materialistic they are encouraged to become. Yet if anything has been learned about the nature of happiness, from the days of the Greek philosophers through to the work of positive psychologists and neuroscientists today, it is that children need inner strength and understanding to flourish – not materialism. They need warm bonds of friendship with their peers – not competitive consumption. They need strong relationships with their parents – not the alienation that can be encouraged by marketing. They need to be occupied in projects which work for the common good of a community. In a commercial world, the odds are stacked against achieving this.

The warning bells are sounding out loud and clear. The technology-fuelled world of marketing is moving faster than society has been able to catch up. Many or most children today are indeed consumer kids but, as such, they surely have at least one more consumer right than we do as adults, which is their fundamental right to development and well-being. It is time for us all to slow down, look around and collectively decide how to move on. It is time to plan an agenda for what to do next.

The Children's Manifesto

To start with, how do children themselves respond to the world which has their pockets in its sight? We asked small groups of children, aged between 11 and 16 and from different socio-economic backgrounds, to develop guidelines for marketing to children. After a discussion about how companies sell to younger people, the groups filled out post-cards with the advice they have for the world around them. The agenda that was put forward by these children, we believe, is as sophisticated, balanced and meaningful as anything that adults or marketing and policy experts might have designed. They said three things:

1. Please be honest and upfront with us about products and services.

2. Please treat us with respect and take us seriously.

3. Please protect us from inappropriate marketing and control advertising for products that are bad for us.

We couldn't agree more. Drawing on what we have found and what you have read in this book, we now take these three calls as the basis for a children's manifesto:

Honesty
- Label advertising very clearly in every medium (not just TV)
- Ensure that peer marketing is openly declared as such

- Disclose and declare marketing techniques that can easily be overlooked, such as embedded marketing
- Don't sell junk food as health food
- Tell us how much you spend on marketing to children like us
- Enter into a public debate on the hidden power of emotional advertising
- Enter into a public debate about the desirability of stealth marketing techniques such as advergames, product placements, celebrity endorsement and brand ambassadors

Respect
- Don't pressurize us into buying
- Leave our friendships alone
- Don't encourage us to pester our parents
- Don't tell us our parents aren't cool
- Don't make us feel bad for not having stuff
- Don't promise that we'll be happy if we buy stuff
- Make provision for us all to register a company when we leave school

Protection
- If a site's audience is more than 25 per cent kids ban adverts for dating, gambling, credit, violent games, cosmetic surgery and age-restricted products and services
- Tell us very clearly if a game or a website is unsuitable for us

- Don't let shops sell us sexualized clothes, dolls, under-wear and stationery
- Set up children's panels to comment on what you do
- Help develop standards for educational value
- Get the internet regulations in line across the world
- Provide us with some entertainment which isn't dependent on commerce

The Parents' Manifesto

This is new terrain for parents. Like salmon caught up the wrong tributary, we are trying to find our way back to our own childhoods, swimming against the tide, fearing that we are failing. As parents, we want our children to be happy, but we are not sure whether what we learned from our childhood is sufficient to disentangle the consumer promise of pre-packaged, purchased happiness from the well-being which comes, unbidden, from personal fulfilment.

Many of the ideas in this book come from parents who are finding ways to support and nurture children success-fully in a commercial world. They teach us that the context is new, and some of the conversation is new, within families or between them, but the instincts of parents to care for their children are the same. So, it seems only appropriate to close with suggestions for parents that we have drawn from our research and found of particular use in our personal lives with our own families, helping children by nurturing enterprise, compassion and resilience.

Enterprise
- Encourage children to work for their pocket money
- Use pocket money to teach the skills of budgeting and self-control.
- Encourage curiosity
- Encourage enjoyment
- Discourage making money as a goal in itself
- Discourage fame as a goal in itself

Compassion
- Encourage children to give away some of their pocket money
- Encourage volunteering
- Praise them when they help out
- Talk about what might go on behind low-priced products

Resilience
- Teach children to manage money
- Catch up on what's happening on the internet
- Ask your children to teach you
- Teach children about marketing tactics and tricks
- Find out what the latest regulations about marketing to children are
- Find teachable moments
- Watch TV, surf the net and read magazines together to discuss how food, fashion and success are sold to us.

These are the suggestions we make, following the directions set by the young people and parents that we talked to. They may or may not turn out to be the right ones or sufficient to the task, but they are a start and we do need that start. Above all, as a significant influence on children's lives, we need the world of marketing to turn its efforts from catching children to setting them free.

As one of the UK's most inspiring marketers told us, 'Rather than one or another advert shaping how children behave, it is the whole wider commercial world of celebrities, music and film that is far more powerful. You could say that advertising is supposed to offer a mirror to the world, but the truth is that we probably help to create the commercial world and now have to take some responsibility for that.'[4]

Helpful Organizations

This book does not just represent two lone voices. The impact of commercial values on our children's lives is the issue of our day and there is a host of organizations that have sprung up or turned their attention to this debate. What the future looks like in relation to children's experience, both as citizens and as young consumers, depends in no small part on the activism and energy of these organizations. We've listed here those we know best.

4Children (formerly Kids' Club Network) www.4children.org.uk

11 Million (Children's Commissioner for England) www.11million. org.uk

Advisory Centre for Education www.ace-ed.org.uk

Alliance for Childhood www.allianceforchildhood.org.uk

Barnardo's www.barnardos.org.uk

British Youth Council www.byc.org.uk

Campaign for State Education www.campaignforstateeducation. org.uk

Care for the Family www.careforthefamily.org.uk

Child Poverty Action Group www.cpag.org.uk

ChildNet International www.childnet-int.org

Children's Commissioner for Wales www.childcom.org.uk

Children's Rights Alliance www.crae.org.uk

Children's Society www.childrenssociety.org.uk

Citizenship Foundation www.citizenshipfoundation.org.uk

Compass www.compassonline.org.uk

Contact a Family www.cafamily.org.uk

Daycare Trust www.daycaretrust.org.uk

English Secondary Students' Association www.studentvoice. co.uk

Envision www.envision.org.uk

Fairtrade Foundation www.fairtrade.org.uk

Family and Parenting Institute www.familyandparenting.org

Family Rights Group www.frg.org.uk

Fatherhood Institute www.fatherhoodinstitute.org

Forest Schools www.forestschools.com

Funky Dragon www.funkydragon.org

Gingerbread www.gingerbread.org.uk

Media Watch www.mediawatchuk.org

Mumsnet www.mumsnet.com

National Children's Bureau www.ncb.org.uk

National Confederation of Parent Teacher Associations www.ncpta. org.uk

National Governors Association www.nga.org.uk

National Union of Teachers www.teachers.org.uk

National Children's Home www.nch.org.uk

Netmums www.netmums.com

New Economics Foundation www.neweconomics.org

Northern Ireland Commissioner for Children and Young People www.niccy.org

Northern Ireland Youth Forum www.niyf.org

NSPCC www.nspcc.org.uk

Parenting UK www.parentinguk.org

Parentline Plus www.parentlineplus.org.uk

Personal Finance Education Group www.pfeg.org

Save the Children www.savethechildren.org.uk

Scotland's Commissioner for Children and Young People www.sccyp.org.uk

Small Schools www.smallschools.org.uk

Sustain www.sustainweb.org

UNICEF www.unicef.org.uk

Which? www.which.co.uk

Young Enterprise www.young-enterprise.org.uk

Young Foundation www.youngfoundation.org.uk

Young Minds www.youngminds.org.uk

YouthNet www.youthnet.org

Youth Parliament www.ukyouthparliament.org.uk and www.scottishyouthparliament.org.uk

Youth Voice: Peer Power www.yvpp.co.uk

Notes

Introduction

1   Closely based on a 'job advert' posted on www.dubitinsider.com and accessed on 14 November 2007. Whilst fictitious, Sarah precisely meets all the criteria for a successful applicant.

Chapter 1

1   Phil Sumner, Postwatch, personal correspondence, 10 March 2008

2   21 per cent of 7–10 year-olds read the *Beano* in the past seven days, www.bmrb-tgi.co.uk/main.asp?p=440&finfo=381&r=3850 .298, accessed 18 September 2007

3   www.tgisurveys.com/tgi/Youth2006.PDF, accessed 7 January 2008

4   *ChildWise, The Monitor Report 2007–2008*, SMRC ChildWise, Norwich

5   Access Asia, 'Kids in China 2007: child consumers and lifestyle trends – Generation Zhang', www.accessasia.co.uk/show report.asp?RptId=561, accessed 8 January 2008. See also Pearl

Research, 'The Phoenix Generation: A Report on Chinese Youth Spending, Culture and Behaviour', www.pearlresearch.com/products/CYP07.html, accessed 11 October 2007

6 Presentation by Ben Page, Ipsos MORI Social Research Institute, 'What Young People Think About Public Services', 2007

7 Eric Clark, *The Real Toy Story: Inside the ruthless battle for Britain's youngest consumers*, Black Swan, London, 2007, p172

8 The research described in this section is set out in detail in Agnes Nairn, Christine Griffin, Patricia Gaya Wicks, *The Simpsons are Cool but Barbie's a Minger: The role of brands in the everyday lives of Junior School Children*, University of Bath, Bath, 2005

9 http://en.wikipedia.org/wiki/Barbie, accessed 1 July 2007

10 'Vintage Barbie struts her stuff', 22 September 2006, http://news.bbc.co.uk/1/hi/business/5370398.stm, accessed 1 July 2007

11 'Girls often "torture" Barbies, researchers say', CBC News, www.cbc.ca/world/story/2005/12/19/barbie-study-051219.html, accessed 1 July 2007

12 Sarah Womack, 'The generation of "damaged" girls', *Daily Telegraph*, 21 February 2007

13 Eric Clark, op. cit. pp. 132–3

14 ChildWise, op. cit.

15 Ed Mayo, *Shopping Generation*, National Consumer Council, London, 2005

16 CBBC, 'Are you a shopaholic?', 29 November 2004,http://news.bbc.co.uk/go/pr/fr/-/cbbcnews/hi/newsid_4040000/newsid_4045400/4045427.stm, accessed 18 March 2005

17 Quote posted by her mother Kathy Sierra:
http://headrush.typepad.com/creating_passionate_users/200
6/03/ultrafast_relea.html, accessed 2 March 2008

18 Jules Shropshire and Sue Middleton, *Small Expectations; Learning to be poor*, York Publishing Services for Joseph Rowntree Foundation, York, 1999

19 On their UK website the company heralds the appreciation of one parent who told them, 'My son is nine months old and has been enjoying your videos from three weeks of age.' www.babyeinstein.com/uk/OurProducts.shtml, accessed 7 January 2008

20 Sarah Womack, 'Helicopter parents hinder children's learning', *Daily Telegraph*, 27 December 2007 www.telegraph.co.uk/news/main.jhtml?xml=/news/2007/12/26/nparents126.xml, accessed 3 January 2008

21 For example, 'Active Kids' is Sainsbury's redemption scheme, which combines free educational resources with print advertising, PR and in-store promotion. 'Playground Partnerships' is an initiative developed by Woolworths Kids First, the high-street retailer's charitable foundation. Here, primary-school pupils compete for grants to redevelop their playgrounds. Those who get involved are estimated to be 30 per cent more likely to shop at Woolworths as a result

22 30 per cent of parents worldwide ask their children for advice on car purchases. Juliet B Schor, *Born to Buy: The commercialized child and the new consumer culture*, Scribner, New York, 2004, p.131

23 Elizabeth Gotze, Christiane Prange and Iveta Uhrovska, 'Children's impact on innovative decision-making – A diary study', *European Journal of Marketing*, 2009

24 A poll by the publishers for children's author, Jacqueline Wilson, suggests that over half of parents believe that childhood is over by the age of 11. 'Childhood now ends at 11 parents say', *Daily Telegraph*, 18 April 2000, www.telegraph.co.uk/news/uknews/1580540/Childhood-now-ends-at-11,-parents-say.html, accessed 14 June 2008. For a view of the effect on adults, see Benjamin R Barber, *Consumed: How Markets Corrupt Children, Infantilize Adults and Swallow Citizens Whole*, WW Norton, New York, 2007

25 This includes all purchases related directly to the upbringing of children, but not additional family purchases influenced by children. The average cost of bringing up children, according to Liverpool Victoria, is now £186,032 from birth to the age of 21 – an annualized cost of £8,859. From birth to 16, the average annual cost is slightly lower at £8,545 which for 11.6 million children 16 or under, according to the Office of National Statistics, equals an overall annual expenditure of £99.122 billion. Sources: authors' own calculations from Liverpool Victoria, 'Cost of a Child' survey, www.lv.com/media_centre/press_releases/cost, accessed 8 January 2008 and ONS, 'Social Trends 37', www.statistics.gov.uk/downloads/theme_social/Social_Trends37/Social_Trends_37.pdf, accessed 8 January 2008, Table 1.2, p.2, 2005 (boys and girls figures added and rounded). A previous estimate of the children's market, in 2002, was £30 billion. Liz Hollis, 'We know what she wants', *Guardian*, 6 November 2002, www.guardian.co.uk/parents/story/0,,834350,00.html, accessed 25 March 2005

26 Annual and five-year market growth, authors' own calculations from Liverpool Victoria, 'Cost of a Child' survey,

www.lv.com/media_centre/press_releases/cost, accessed 8 January 2008

27 Agnes Nairn, Christine Griffin, Patricia Gaya Wicks, op. cit.

28 www.thisnext.com/item/B4II86D2/Hello-Kitty-Assault-Rifle, accessed 29 December 2007. This is a USA product and, according to the makers, 'A perfect gift for the young lady of the house'. www.glamguns.com/hk47.html, accessed 8 January 2008. You can also buy a Kalashnikov AK47 Transparent Mini Rifle from Amazon UK,
www.amazon.co.uk/Kalashnikov-AK47-Transparent-Mini-Rifle/dp/B000ZYMKUY, accessed 8 January 2008. Brightly coloured or translucent ball bearing (bb) guns are not considered imitation firearms and so can be sold as toys

29 Lily Allen, 'Everything's Just Wonderful' from *Alright Still*, EMI, 2006

30 S Middleton, K Ashworth and R Walker, *Family Fortunes: Pressures on parents and children in the 1990s*, Child Poverty Action Group, London, 1994

31 Richard Elliott and Claire Leonard, 'Peer Pressures and Poverty', *Journal of Consumer Behaviour*, 3 (4), 2004

32 'Up Front, This much I know', interview with Camilla Batmanghelidjh by Hilly James, OM Magazine, *Observer*, 10 August 2003, p.8

33 'Children's Pocket Money Creates Over £70m Spending Power', 'Halifax Pocket Money Survey 2004', www.hbosplc.com/media/pressreleases/articles/halifax/2004-07-24-00.asp, accessed 18 May 2005

34 ChildWise, op. cit.

35 Agnes Nairn and Jo Ormrod, with Paul Bottomley, *Watching,*

Wanting and Wellbeing, National Consumer Council, London, 2007

36 Ibid.

37 ChildWise, op. cit.

38 Ibid.

39 'Consumer Issues & Youth: A Research Report into Best Practice in Consumer Education Targeting Young Australians' www.consumersonline.gov.au/downloads/youth_jul2002.pdf, accessed 18 May 2005. At the same time, mobile phones are also the products that children rank as the greatest rip-offs in terms of price – see 'Halifax Pocket Money Survey 2007', www.hbosplc.com/media/includes/15_%2004_%2006_%20 Pocket_%20Money_%20Survey_%202006%20_%20National .doc, accessed July 19 2007

40 'Generation M: Media in the Lives of 8 –18 Year-olds', Kaiser Foundation, www.kff.org/entmedia/upload/Generation-M-Media-in-the-Lives-of-8-18-Year-olds-Report.pdf, accessed 25 May 2007

41 ChildWise, op. cit.

42 Children spend 890 hours in class at age 7/8 and 933 hours at age 12/14. OECD Education at a Glance 2007 http://www.oecd.org/dataoecd/35/8/39287251.xls accessed January 12 2008. In terms of multi-tasking, estimates from the USA are that 8.5 hours of media consumption is packed into 6.5 hours of time. We are not aware of comparable data that is definitive for UK children on this point. Generation M: Media in the Lives of 8–18 Year-olds, Kaiser Foundation, http://www.kff.org/entmedia/upload/Generation-M-Media-in-the-Lives-of-8-18-Year-olds-Report.pdf, accessed 25 May 2007

43 Jon Savage, Teenage: The Creation of Youth 1875 – 1945, Chatto & Windus, London, 2007, www.medialifemagazine.com/cgi-bin/artman/exec/view.cgi?archive=513&num=11898, accessed 14 May 2007

44 Agnes Nairn, Christine Griffin, Patricia Gaya Wicks, op. cit.

Chapter 2

1   Niccolò Machiavelli, *The Prince*, Bantam Classics, London, 1984

2   Sun Tzu, *The Art of War*, El Paso Norte Press, El Paso, 2005

3   'Youth TGI: the definitive marketing data source for 7–19-year-olds in Great Britain'. TGI, London, 2006, downloadable from www.tgisurveys.com/tgi/Youth2006.PDF, accessed 18 September 2007

4   'Notes of Guidance', 2007, www.bacc.org.uk/NR/rdonlyres/ 71A7BDBD-22FF-4C94-8FAD-A3557145B3D2/0/ NotesofGuidancepdf.pdf, accessed 9 November 2007

5   Marketing Week Conference, 29–30 October 2007, London

6   Creating Loyal Brand Advocates And Positive Brand Buzz Through Measurable Peer-To-Peer Marketing. Haymarket Conference, 27 September 2007

7   Create Positive and Measurable Buzz Through Your Loyal Brand Advocates For Powerful Peer-To-Peer Marketing: A One Day Conference, 27 November 2007, The Selfridge, London

8   http://blogs.mediapost.com/spin/, accessed 9 November 2007

9   Agnes Nairn and Dowsiri Monkgol, 'Children and Online Privacy', *Journal of Direct, Data and Digital Marketing Practice*, Vol 8. No 4, 2007

10 Boy, age 10. Anna Fielder, Will Gardner, Agnes Nairn and Jillian Pitt, *Fair Game? Assessing commercial activity on children's*

favourite websites and online environments, National Consumer Council, London, 2007

11 Ibid.

12 92 per cent of the 40 sites we researched in one piece of work had a clearly labelled privacy policy.

13 www.miniclip.com/games/en/privacy-policy.php, accessed 9 June 2008

14 http://shop.orange.co.uk/shop/terms#privacy, accessed 9 June 2008

15 Agnes Nairn and Dowsiri Monkgol, op. cit.

16 Sonia Livingstone and Monica Bober, *UK Children Go Online: Final Report of Key Project Findings*, London School of Economics and Political Science, London, 2005

17 www.dubit.co.uk, accessed 14 November 2007. Dubit is one of the 'largest and trendiest interactive communities' for youth

18 Ibid.

19 Agnes Nairn, Christine Griffin, Patricia Gaya-Wicks, op. cit.

20 www.dubit.com, accessed 12 July 2008

21 Cited in Cordelia Fine, 'Marketers with a Licence to Manipulate', www.brisbanetimes.com.au/articles/2007/08/17/1186857765o, accessed 4 March 2008

22 David Kisilevsky, Vice President of Marketing, EMEA, Burger King in a presentation to the Haymarket Conference 'Engage Children, Attract Parents', 26 June 2008, London

23 www.partypoker.com, accessed 10 December 2007

24 www.gangstermind.com, accessed 1 December 2008

25 Kathryn Braun La Tour, Michael La Tour and George Zinkhan, 'Using Childhood Memories to Gain Insight into Brand Meaning', *Journal of Marketing*, Vol 71, April 2007

26 www.euromonitor.com/Tweens_empowered_and_with_money
    _to_burn, accessed 5 January 2008

Chapter 3

1   Pitti Immagine Bimbo is a fashion show for children's
    gear, with displays from over 400 brands. Dates on www.
    eventseye. com/fairs/trade_fair_event_9991.html, accessed
    14 May 2007

2   A controversial French/UK website for girls of 9–16 years old
    perhaps captures the spirit of what 'bimbo' means by encour-
    aging girls to compete against other children to earn 'bimbo
    dollars' to buy plastic surgery, diet pills, facelifts, lingerie and
    fashionable nightclub outfits. See www.missbimbo.com,
    accessed 14 June 2008. The Wikipedia definition of 'bimbo' is
    a female who is 'attractive but stupid'

3   www.spiegel.de/international/spiegel/0,1518,443145,00.html,
    accessed 14 May 2007

4   This description is widely echoed by retailers. See, for example,
    http://shopproducts.howstuffworks.com/Burberry-Baby-
    Touch-Perfume-by-Burberry-6-6-oz-Gentle-Baby-Balm-for-
    Kids/SF-1/PID-32495488, accessed 27 July 2007

5   Karin Caifa, 'Perfume makers look to infants for new market',
    http://jscms.jrn.columbia.edu/cns/2006-02-28/caifa-
    babyperfume, accessed 30 April 2007

6   Eric Clark, op. cit. p.134

7   Sarah Mahoney, 'Mattel's Barbie And Bonne Bell To Push
    Makeup For Little Girls', 12 June 2007, http://publications.
    mediapost.com/index.cfm?fuseaction=Articles.showArticle-
    HomePage&art_aid=62166, accessed 24 June 2007

8   Russell Budden, 'The guide to 11 to 14-year-olds', *Media Week*, 6 October 2004

9   http://news.bbc.co.uk/1/hi/england/london/4125356.stm, accessed 16 February 2007

10 Rachel Bell, 'It's porn, innit?', 15 August 2005, www.guardian. co.uk/gender/story/0,,1812,1549273,00.html, accessed 20 July 2007

11 Ibid.

12 www.johnlewis.com/Nursery/Baby+Travel/Baby+Travel/ Buggies/2121/230406849/Product.aspx, accessed 27 July 2007

13 German Textiles Retailers Association, www.tmcnet.com/usub- mit/2007/05/12/2609854.htm, accessed 14 May 2007

14 'The Cost of Kids', BBC *Money Programme*, broadcast Friday 2 March 2007 at 7 p.m. on BBC2

15 Comment from parent, Central London, www.dailymail.co.uk/ pages/live/femail/article.html?in_article_id=476409&in_page _id=1879, accessed 26 November 2007

16 Roger Cohen, 'Twixt 8 and 12, the Tween', *New York Times*, 12 July 2007

17 There is an eminent school of historical analysis that claims that you are only a child if you wear the right clothes. The high point of this view was the historical study by Philippe Aries, *Centuries of Childhood*, which claimed that childhood 'did not exist' in European medieval societies, in part because there was no apparent distinction between the clothing worn by adults and children over the age of 5. Modern childhood, Aries argued, only really emerged in the 17th century when children could boast 'an outfit reserved for his own age group, which set him apart from adults'. Perhaps future historians will decide that childhood only really arrived on the scene when children had

learned how to accessorize. See P. Aries, *Centuries of Childhood*, Jonathan Cape, London, 1962, p.48

18 'Mini Me: The birth of kids' fashion in the boutique era', Pollock's Toy Museum, London, 2007

19 Ibid.

20 www.juniormagazine.co.uk/news/article.asp?UAN=37, accessed 26 November 2007

21 David Hayes, 'The real designer babies: As more top labels launch children's ranges, is it much too young?', *Daily Mail*, 19 August 2007, www.dailymail.co.uk/pages/live/femail/article.html?in_article_id=476409&in_page_id=1879, accessed 26 November 2007

22 Lucie Greene, 'London Calling Little Luxury Shoppers', *Women's Wear Daily*, 10 September 2007, p.34

23 Russell Budden, 'The little people with big pockets', *Marketing Week*, 28 October 2004

24 For example, Gorgeous Girls Parties, set up in 2000, runs beauty make-over birthday parties for girls aged 4–14 across Berkshire, Surrey and Hampshire. An all-inclusive two-hour Party Package for children includes trying temporary hair extensions which the girls keep at the end of the party, glitter spray, make-up with fun colours, temporary body art, nail painting and nail art. A party starts at £130 for eight girls. www.gorgeousgirlsparty.com/1389/frames.php, accessed 20 December 2007

25 'Advertising For Kids: Are They Ready?', www.worldsinmotion.biz/2007/10advertising_for_kids_are_they.php, accessed 8 January 2008. Despite this, children are aware that brands can prove to be a rip-off. 74 per cent of children, for example, say that designer clothes are overpriced. 'Children In

London Are 2006's Pocket Money Winners', 'Halifax Pocket Money Survey 2007'

26 Sharon Boden, Christopher Pole, Jane Pilcher, Tim Edwards, 'New Consumers? The Social and Cultural Significance of Children's Fashion Consumption', Department of Sociology, University of Leicester, 2004

27 In our survey, 10 to 12-year-olds are evenly split over the importance of brand names when they buy something (46 per cent agree, 42 per cent disagree). By the time they reach teenhood, the majority are keen on brands (57 per cent of 13 to 15-year-olds and 56 per cent of 16 to 17-year-olds). These findings tally with Mintel research that the younger age-groups (5 to 9) go more for 'character-led merchandising' but by the time they're reaching the upper end of the 10 to 14-year-old bracket, fashion-led clothing brands take precedence 'as image assumes greater importance'. Mintel, 'What really matters to children aged 11–14', for Chartered Institute of Marketing www.cim.co.uk/mediastore/research_mintel_whatmatters.pdf, accessed 7 June 2005

28 Study done by Iconkids & Youth for the Bauer Media Group, cited in www.tdctrade.com/imn/04070802/clothing139.htm, accessed 14 May 2007

29 Quotations taken from Sharon Boden, Christopher Pole, Jane Pilcher, Tim Edwards, op. cit. and Jane Pilcher, Christopher Pole, Sharon Boden, 'New Consumers? Children, Fashion and Consumption' paper presented at 'Knowing Consumers: Actors, Images, Identities in Modern History' conference, Universitat Bielefeld, Germany. 27–28 February 2004 https://lra.le.ac.uk/bitstream/2381/46/1/Pole1.doc, accessed 21 July 2007

30 S Middleton, K Ashworth, R Walker, op. cit.

31 Helene Conrady, 'The flighty world of German teenage fashion', *International Market News*, 8 July 2004, www.tdctrade.com/ imn/04070802/clothing139.htm, accessed 8 January 2008

32 Office of Fair Trading, 'Supply of school uniforms review, Report of GfK NOP findings', September 2006

33 7–14 year-olds, cited in presentation by Ben Page, Ipsos MORI Social Research Institute, 'What Young People Think About Public Services', 2007

34 Vanessa O'Connell, 'Fashion Bullies Attack – In Middle School As More Designers Target Kids, Label-Consciousness Grows', *Wall Street Journal*, 25 October 2007, http://online.wsj.com public/article/SB119326834963770540-n57Ra8x8FUa9uUdD- kpdfTuEtoXA_20071123.html?mod=tff_main_tff_top, accessed 9 November 2007

35 www.commonsensemedia.org/news/daily-news.php?id=326, accessed 14 May 2007

36 Russell Budden, op. cit.

37 www.campaignforrealbeauty.co.uk/dsef07/t5.aspx?id=8137, accessed 9 January 2007

38 These include *Daughters*, *Onslaught*, *Amy* and *Evolution*, which won two Grand Prix awards at Cannes

39 www.youtube.com/watch?v=SwDEF-w4rJk, accessed 15 March 2008

40 'Steroid use "on par with heroin"', BBC News, 20 May 2007, http://news.bbc.co.uk/1/hi/health/6673449.stm, accessed 9 January 2008

41 Dove, cited in Stephen Hull, 'Mum, please can I have some Botox?', *Metro*, 11 August 2006, p.13

42 JJ Brumberg, *The Body Project: An intimate history of American girls*, Vintage, New York, 1997

43 Libby Brooks, 'A tide of bland imagery tells girls that sexy is everything', *Guardian*, 20 December 2007, p.32

44 Ages 15–17. N Etcoff, S Orbach, J Scott, H D'Agostino, 'Beyond Stereotypes: Rebuilding the Foundation of Beauty Beliefs: findings of the 2005', Dove Global Study, February 2006, www.campaignforrealbeauty.co.uk/DoveBeyondStereotypesWhitePaper.pdf, accessed 9 January 2008

45 Ed Mayo, op. cit.

46 Judith Woods, 'Girls just need to be young', *Daily Telegraph*, 20 February 2007, www.telegraph.co.uk/portal/main.jhtml; jsessionid=MT4C45R5ZD5KXQFIQMFCFF4AVCBQYIVo?xml =/portal/2007/02/20/nosplit/ftbritney20.xml, accessed 9 January 2008

47 'How can any mother buy her child a thong?', www.mirror. co.uk, 29 May 2003

48 Ibid

49 T Reichert and C Carpenter, 'An update on sex in magazine advertising: 1983 to 2003', *Journalism and Mass Communication Quarterly*, 81, 2004, pp. 823–37. This and other research on the portrayal of women and girls in the media is summarized in American Psychological Association, Report of the 'APA Task Force on the Sexualization of Girls, 2007', www.apa.org/pi/wpo/ sexualizationrep.pdf, accessed 23 July 2007

50 T Reichert, 'The prevalence of sexual imagery in ads targeted to young adults', *Journal of Consumer Affairs*, December 2003

51 J Kelly and SL Smith, 'Where the girls aren't: Gender disparity saturates G-rated films', 2006 www.thriveoncreative.com/

clients/seejane/pdfs/where.the.girls.arent.pdf, accessed 9 January 2008. They found similar biases in terms of a focus on race and diversity and an exclusion of homosexuality. See Jane seeks to engage professionals and parents in a call to dramatically increase the percentages of female characters, and to reduce gender stereotyping, in media made for children 11 and under. See Jane founder, actor Geena Davis, says, 'By making it common for our youngest children to see everywhere a balance of active and complex male and female characters, girls and boys will grow up to empathize with and care more about each other's stories'

52 Researchers coded the content of 164 songs from 16 artists popular with teens. Overall, 15 per cent of songs contained sexually degrading lyrics

53 Ziauddin Sardar, 'Walt Disney and the Double Victimisation of Pocahontas', in *Islam, Postmodernism and Other Futures: A Ziauddin Sardar Reader*, edited by Sohail Inayatullah and Gail Boxwell, Pluto Press, London, 2003, pp. 127–56

54 Quoted in Ziauddin Sardar, op. cit.

55 According to the writings of the contemporary William Strachey, at Jamestown, the first permanent English settlement in North America, the young Pocahontas, full of spirit but innocent, would 'get the boys forth with her into the market place and make them wheel, falling on their hands, turning their heels upwards; whom she would follow, and wheel herself, naked as she was, all the Fort over.' William Strachey, *The History of Travel into Virginia Britannia*, edited by LB Wright and V Freund, Hakluyt Society, London, 1953, originally published in 1612. Cited in Ziauddin Sardar, op. cit.

56 'Care for the Family', *Family*, Autumn 2007, p.1

57 Presentation by Peter Hutton and Annabelle Phillips, MORI, 'Understanding the Next Generation of Consumer', 7 February 2002

58 When the UNICEF report came out, we learned that civil servants got to work behind the scenes to try to unpick it. The method had a disproportionate focus on adolescents, they argued, because it relied on a World Health Organisation survey of 11–15-year-olds. The data wasn't up to date enough, as some things, like the rate of teenage pregnancies and the risk of accidental injury, had now improved. It didn't cover housing, where the UK has lower levels of overcrowding for children than other countries. It looked at relative rather than absolute poverty. The weight given to the different indicators chosen could have been done differently. None of this has really made a dent in the findings, though. The bottom line is that the UNICEF report was a fair rendition of much of the best data that exists across countries about children's well-being. Of industrialized countries, in short, the UK is one of the worst places in the world to bring up children.

59 Judith Woods, op. cit.

60 Libby Brooks, *The Story of Childhood: Growing up in Modern Britain*, Bloomsbury, London, 2006, p.320

61 Ibid.

62 American Psychological Association, 'Report of the APA Task Force on the Sexualization of Girls', 2007, www.apa.org/pi wpo/sexualizationrep.pdf, accessed 23 July 2007

Chapter 4

1   Yale Rudd Center, www.yaleruddcenter.org/home.aspx, accessed 9 September 2007

2   BBC, 'Children's diet better in 1950s', 30 November 1999, http://news.bbc.co.uk/1/hi/health/542205.stm, accessed 19 September 2007

3   In other countries of Europe, who have promoted road safety better over recent years, it is lower still

4   Department of Health, 'Forecasting obesity to 2010', 2006

5   International Obesity Taskforce, 'Obesity and overweight rates have risen dramatically among English schoolchildren', http://www.iotf.org/popout.asp?linkto=http://www.iotf.org/media/iotfchildhoodUK.pdf, accessed 19 September 2007

6   'Foresight, Tackling Obesity: future choices – project report', Government Office for Science, Department of Innovation, Universities and Skills, 2007

7   'Hide the salt pots, says minister', BBC News, 28 February 2008, http://news.bbc.co.uk/1/hi/uk_politics/7269595.stm, accessed 8 March 2008

8   Cancer Research, 'UK failing to eat 5 a day', 21 September 2007, http://info.cancerresearchuk.org/news/pressreleases/2007/september/365860, accessed 26 September 2007. The Food Standards Agency Low-Income Diet Survey carried out in 2007 suggests that inequalities in diet are not as pronounced as the agency had feared, but that there are aspects of poorer diet that remain of concern and, in any case, diets across income groups fall short of healthy living guidelines. www.food.gov.uk/science/dietarysurveys/lidnsbranch/#h_3, accessed 26 September 2007

9   Department of Health, 'Health Survey for England 2004: updating of trend tables to include childhood obesity data', London, 2006

10   MORI, 2001, 'Eating and Today's Lifestyle', *Nestlé Family Monitor*, 13

11   Ofcom, 'Child obesity – food advertising in context. Children's food choices, parents' understanding and influence, and the role of food promotions',
www.ofcom.org.uk/research/tv/reports/food_ads/report.pdf, accessed 16 September 2007

12   Food Standards Agency, 'Publication of national diet and nutrition survey of young people aged 4–18', 1 June 2000, http://www.food.gov.uk/news/pressreleases/2000/jun/nationaldiet, accessed 26 September 2007

13   Christine Gilbert, Chief Inspector, Ofsted, personal communication, 13 September 2007

14   www.vegsoc.org/info/statveg-youth.html, accessed 26 September 2007

15   Food Standards Agency, op. cit., and www.eatwell.gov.uk/healthydiet/nutritionessentials/fruitandveg/, accessed 26 September 2007

16   Youth TGI: the definitive marketing data source for 7–19-year-olds in Great Britain', TGI, downloadable from www.tgisurveys.com/tgi/Youth2006.PDF, accessed 18 September 2007

17   Datamonitor, cited in *Daily Mail*, 'British children top EU sweet poll', 26 January 2007, www.dailymail.co.uk/pages/live/articles/news/news.html?in_article_id=431509&in_page_id=1770, accessed 20 June 2007

18 'Sodexho School Meals Survey', cited in Ofcom, 'Child obesity', op cit.

19 John Balding, *Young People into 2007: the Health Related Behaviour Questionnaire for 68,495 young people between the ages of 10 and 15*, Schools Health Education Unit, Exeter, 2007

20 Ofcom, 'Child obesity', op. cit.

21 Aged 15–18. Food Standards Agency, 'Publication of national diet and nutrition survey of young people aged 4–18', op. cit.

22 Vasanti S Malik, Matthias B Schulze, Frank B Hu, 'Intake of sugar-sweetened beverages and weight gain: a systematic review', in *American Journal of Clinical Nutrition*, Vol 84, No 2, 274–88, August 2006

23 www.bbc.co.uk/radio1/news/newsbeat/061102_teenagers. shtml, accessed 5 October 2007

24 This is a tally that includes more girls than boys, in part because girls' bodies are more sensitive to the effects of alcohol. Jonathan Owen, 'The Rehab generation', *Independent on Sunday*, 4 November 2007, pp.8–9

25 Cally Matthews, 'Does TV encourage teenage drinking?', *Food Magazine*, 76, 10 March 2007

26 Our calculations, from figures cited by Dame Deirdre Hutton, 'Diet and Health for the Future', speech at the Future of Foods conference, 8 April 2004

27 Comments by Bob Eagle, www.fau.org.uk/091298_proceedings. pdf, accessed 29 September 2007

28 'TV food adverts increase obese children's appetite by 134 per cent', www.liv.ac.uk/newsroom/press_releases/2007/04/ obesity _ads.htm, accessed 3 September 2007

29 *Food Fables*, Which?, London, 2006

30 Ofcom, Regulating TV advertising of food and drink to children, conducted by Opinion Leader Research, September 2006

31 A Which? survey of 815 parents of 0–16- year-olds in Great Britain between 9 February and 7 March 2006. Cited in *Food Fables*, op. cit.

32 www.fau.org.uk/html/2003_conference.html, accessed 29 September 2007

33 Chris Holmes, National Centre for Social Marketing, National Consumer Council, personal correspondence, March 2008

34 So, in reality, multibuy promotions are not true value promotions in that if you have been given 100 per cent more for free and yet you return to your normal spending habits in only 10 per cent more time, then you only benefit from 10 per cent of the apparent value – 10p in the £1. The old adage 'there is no such thing as a free lunch' remains true

35 Ibid.

36 It is interesting that some food manufacturers would be happy to get off these promotions, as they see that these train people to shop on price rather than encouraging an emotional relationship with the brand.

37 www.fau.org.uk/211100_proceedings.pdf, accessed 29 September 2007

38 On similar grounds, we could also say that, although international cooperation is far from easy, the international reach of marketing calls for a response at the same level. It is encouraging that in 2009 the World Health Assembly, for example, is due to consider proposals drawn up by Consumers International and health groups for an overarching, international Code of Conduct on the marketing of food to children

39 The Advertising Standards Authority also found in favour of the advertising strapline for Nestlé's Cheerios, 'good eating habits are easy to pick up', despite evidence from the indomitable Food Commission that the cereal was high in both salt and sugar

40 *Food Fables*, op. cit.

41 Advertising Association, 'Interim Review of the Media Landscape Food Advertising Changes in Context', 2007

42 Ofcom, 'Child obesity', op. cit.

43 One recent research project compared Subway, which positions itself as a healthy, positive option for food on the go, with McDonald's, with surprising findings that touch on this idea of a halo of health. See Miranda Hitti, 'Calorie Catch in Healthy Fast Food: People Tend to Underestimate Calories in "Healthy" Fast Food, Study Shows', WebMD Medical, www.webmd.com/diet/news/20070831/calorie-catch-in-healthy-fast-food?src=rss_psychtoday, accessed 18 September 2007

44 From 'Mend Participant Testimonials', presented at Sainsburys Healthy Eating event, October 2007, see www.mendprogramme.org/, accessed 21 November 2007. For more on social marketing and how it is being taken out across the NHS, see www.nsms.org.uk/public/default.aspx

45 '2CV, Insight and Action to Help Stem the Rise of Childhood Obesity: full report of qualitative findings', prepared for COI on behalf of Department of Health and the Obesity Social Marketing Research Programme, 2007

46 Ellie Lewis, 'Children's Views on Non-broadcast food and drink advertising, report for the Office of the Children's Commissioner', National Children's Bureau, 2006

47 *Food Fables*, op. cit.

48 Ofcom, 'Child obesity', op. cit.

Chapter 5

1 Quoted in 'Ypulse Daily Update', Ypulse.com, 6 July 2007, accessed 5 January 2008

2 Sherry Turkle, *The Second Self. Computers and the Human Spirit*, Twentieth Anniversary Edition, Simon and Schuster, London, 2004

3 Marshall MacLuhan, *Understanding Media*, Mentor, New York, 1964, p.5

4 See for example www.cheatplanet.com, accessed 15 March 2008

5 Rhiannon Edward, 'Computer games "may be good for children"', *Scotsman*, 2 July 2007, http://news.scotsman.com/ scitech. cfm?id=1028652007, accessed 15 July 2007

6 http://uk.reuters.com/article/internetNews/idUKL22848 10620070622, accessed 15 July 2007

7 Overall, 30 per cent of children get just 4 to 7 hours' sleep as opposed to the recommended 8 or 9 hours. The Council also found that 40 per cent of children feel tired each day, with girls aged 15 to 16 faring the worst. Reuters, '"Junk sleep" damaging teenagers' health', 28 August 2007, www.reuters.com/article/ technologyNews/idUSL2854227920070828, accessed 1 September 2007

8 Dr Aric Sigman, 'Agricultural Literacy: giving concrete children food for thought', www.wfu.org.uk/downloads/Agricultural per cent20Literacy.pdf, accessed 27 November 2007

9 RM Pyle, *Thunder Tree: Lessons from a Secondhand Landscape*, Houghton Mifflin, New York, 1993

10 Andrew Balmford, Lizzie Clegg, Tim Coulson, Jennie Taylor, Department of Zoology, University of Cambridge, 'Why Conservationists Should Heed Pokémon', letter to *Science*, vol 295, 29 March 2002

11 See www.lhhl.uiuc.edu, accessed 29 November 2007

12 See Ken Worpole, *No particular place to go? Children, young people and public space*, Groundwork, 2003 www.groundwork. org.uk/upload/publications/publication6.pdf, accessed 15 July 2007

13 Cited in Ken Worpole, op. cit.

14 James Crabtree, personal correspondence, November 2007

15 Cited in David Nicholson-Lord, *Green Cities – and why we need them*, New Economics Foundation, Pocketbook 9, London, 2003

16 'Make Space Youth Review: transforming the offer for young people in the UK', 4Children, 2007, www.makespace.org.uk/ documents/Youth per cent20Review per cent20Full per cent20Report.pdf, accessed 3 December 2007

17 Howard League for Penal Reform, 'Survey reveals that 95 per cent of children are victims of crime', 10 October 2007, www.howardleague.org/fileadmin/howard_league/user/pdf/pr ess_2007/Children_as_victims_survey_10_October_2007.pdf, accessed 3 December 2007

18 David Simpson DJ (MC), 'An Introduction to Sentencing in the Youth Court', lecture, King's College London, October 2004

19 Research with teenagers in the UK shows that one-fifth claim to have taken drugs to make themselves look cool, but, and this will come as a relief to parents, in reality many do nothing

of the kind. See Alexandra Frean, 'Tribal teens and a big lie about drugs, Parents reassured that youngsters' boasts are often just talk to win friends', *The Times*, 23 August 2004

20 David Mason, 'ASBOs – use and abuse', *New Law Journal*, 28 January 2005

21 Jaap Doek, Chairman of the UN Committee on the Rights of the Child, cited in John Carvel, 'Britain violates rights of child say UN', *Guardian*, 29 November 2004,

22 'Make Space Youth Review, School Holiday Misery Looms For Millions Of Teenagers', 11 July 2007, www.makespace.org.uk/documents/MSYouthReview_press_release_11-7-07.doc, accessed 3 December 2007

23 Gillian Thomas and Gina Hocking, *Other People's Children*, Demos, 2003

24 Decca Aitkenhead, 'Why we need to set our kids free', *Guardian*, 3 November 2007

25 A third of secondary school pupils surf the web from the sanctuary of their bedroom and one in ten 5 to 10-year-olds can do the same. ChildWise, op. cit.

26 Anna Fielder, Will Gardner, Agnes Nairn, Jillian Pitt, op. cit.

27 Ofcom Consumer Panel, 'Children and the Internet', 2007

28 Data from Agnes Nairn, Jo Ormrod, Paul Bottomley, op. cit.

29 Andrew Clarke, *Guardian*, 18 May 2007

30 Agnes Nairn, Jo Ormrod, Paul Bottomley, op. cit.

31 Anna Fielder, Will Gardner, Agnes Nairn, Jillian Pitt, op. cit.

32 Andrew Gregory, 'Cards that let kids of 14 buy alcohol, knives and porn', *People*, 26 August 2007

33 Emma Smith, 29 April 2007, *The Times*

34 JP Benway, DM Lane, 'Banner Blindness: Web Searchers

Often Miss "Obvious" Links', Internet Technical Group, Rice University, 1998

35 So, for example, in the ICC Code of Advertising Practice that governs industry rules, one fundamental principle should be reasserted, that advertising should easily be identified as such

36 Anna Fielder, Will Gardner, Agnes Nairn, Jillian Pitt, op. cit.

37 www.purevideonetworks.com/advertise.html, accessed 4 April 2008

38 Save Kids' TV, 'Response to Ofcom Consultation: "The future of children's television programming"', 17 December 2007, www.savekidstv.org.uk/wp-content/d/SKTVofcomresponse. pdf, accessed 9 January 2008. To date, public service broadcasting has tended to be fairly nationalistic, seeing its role in part as one of supporting the values of the nation it stems from or, indeed, as one of protecting domestic producers. This misses the point, perhaps, for children. Instead, the aim should be to support a better balance of content for children online and indeed it would be good to see governments and companies come together at an international level to support something like this

39 Agnes Nairn and Jon Mattias, 'Pester Power: Families Surviving the Consumer Society, a joint initiative by Care for the Family, Ed Mayo and Agnes Nairn', Care for the Family, 2007

40 www.monitoringsoftwarereviews.org/?gclid=CKjCpqKFqYw CFRWOEgodoCMCSg, accessed 25 January 2008

41 Frank 'Candarelli' Multari, online review of GTA3 at www.gta3.com/index.php?zone=review1, accessed 25 May 2007

42 See for example Craig A Anderson, Leonard Berkowitz, Edward Donnerstein, L Rowell Huesmann, James D Johnson, Daniel

Linz, Neil M Malamuth and Ellen Wartella, 'The Influence of Media Violence on Youth', *Journal Of Psychological Science*, Vol 4, No 3, December 2003, pp 81–110

43 David Buckingham, *After the Death of Childhood*, Polity, Cambridge, 2000, p.16

44 Tanya Byron, *Safer Children in a Digital World. The Report of the Byron Review*. DCSF, London, March 2008, www.dcsf.gov.uk/byronreview

45 Shelley Pasnik, 'Focus: Teen Voices On Digital Media And Society – A Global Kids Online Dialogue', report to the Macarthur Foundation, 2007, www.globalkids.org/olp/focus/focusreport.pdf, accessed 7 September 2007

46 See http://champagnefortheladies.com/cgis.htm and http://kukanstudio.com/games_coolest_girl_in_school.html, both accessed 3 December 2007

47 Carly Shuler, *D is for Digital: An Analysis of the Children's Interactive Media Environment With a Focus on Mass Marketed Products that Promote Learning*, Joan Ganz Cooney Center, New York, 2007, www.joanganzcooneycenter.org/pdf/DisforDigital.pdf, accessed 9 January 2008

48 David Stewart, Competition Policy Director, Ofcom, personal communication, 27 June 2008

49 ChildWise, op. cit.

50 Ibid.

51 Richard Wray, *Guardian*, 26 March 2007

52 www.blyk.co.uk/about/tour, accessed 15 February 2008

53 Ibid.

54 Rachel Bell, 'Love in the time of phone porn', *Guardian*, 30 January 2007

55   Shelley Pasnik, op. cit.

56   www.schoolpartnershipmarketing.co.uk/case_studies/
hsm.html, accessed 3 July 2008. Essentially this is the commercialization of the curriculum. Companies give money for the
development of curriculum materials for schools that enter
into partnership and of course their brand is promoted with
the materials

57   Andy Fixmer and Katie Hoffmann, Bloomberg, 16 August 2007,
http://www.bloomberg.com/apps/news?pid=20601109&sid=a
WAWq4DtVtb8&refer=home, accessed 28 January 2008

58   Agnes Nairn, Christine Griffin, Patricia Gaya Wicks, op. cit.

59   Patricia Gaya Wicks, Agnes Nairn, Christine Griffin, 'The Role
of Consumption Culture in Children's Moral Development: the
Case of David Beckham', *Consumption, Markets and Culture*,
Vol 10, No 4, December 2006

60   David Beckham is an English soccer player (for those readers
who know neither soccer nor England) who has achieved fame
and recognition worldwide both on and off the pitch. With his
wife Victoria, part of the pop band Spice Girls, the couple have
been in the media limelight since the start of their relationship
in 1997

Chapter 6

1   Charlene Li, 'How Consumers Use Social Networks', Forrester,
www.forrester.com/Research/Document/0,7211,41626,00.html,
accessed 15 July 2007

2   ChildWise, op. cit.

3   Ibid.

4   Jemima Kiss, 'Record users for Bebo and Facebook', *Guardian*,

19 May 2008, www.guardian.co.uk/technology/2008/may/19/
facebook.bebo?gusrc=rss&feed=networkfront, accessed 9 June
2008

5   ChildWise, op. cit.

6   Dominic White, 'The story so far . . . millions are hooked by
online soap', 27 August 2007, http://www.telegraph.co.uk/
money/main.jhtml?xml=/money/2007/08/27/cnsoap127.xml,
accessed 1 September 2007

7   Sarah Philips, 'How friends paid tribute online to dead youngsters', *Guardian*, 23 January 2008

8   www.valleyskids.org/why.htm, accessed 28 January 2008

9   Nick Britten and Richard Savill, 'Police fear internet cult
inspires teen suicides', *Daily Telegraph*, 24 January 2008,
www.telegraph.co.uk/news/main.jhtml?xml=/news/2008/01/2
3/nsuicide123.xml, accessed 29 January 2008

10 Shelley Pasnik, op. cit.

11 Ibid.

12 John Balding, *Young People into 2007*, op. cit.

13 'Protecting your kids from cyber predators', www.business-
week.com/magazine/content/05_50/b3963015.htm, accessed
12 June 2007

14 http://news.bbc.co.uk/1/hi/scotland/4209801.stm, accessed 12
June 2007

15 http://society.guardian.co.uk/children/comment/0,,1142463,00.
html, accessed 12 June 2007

16 Aaron Smith, 'Teens and Online Stranger Contact, Data Memo',
14 October 2007, www.pewinternet.org/pdfs/PIP_Stranger_
Contact_Data_Memo.pdf, accessed 6 January 2008

17 Anna Fielder, Will Gardner, Agnes Nairn, Jillian Pitt, op. cit.

18 BBC News, 21 September 2007, http://news.bbc.co.uk/1/hi/
    education/7005389.stm, accessed 3 October 2007

19 Ibid.

20 Source www.cyberbully411.com/, accessed 15 March 2008

21 Amanda Lenhart, 'Cyberbullying and Online Teens, Data
    Memo', 27 June 2007, Pew Internet and American Life Project,
    www.pewinternet.org/pdfs/PIP%20Cyberbullying%20Memo.
    pdf, accessed 13 July 2007

22 http://education.guardian.co.uk/schools/story/0,,1873404,00.
    html, accessed 12 June 2007

23 Tobi Elkin, 'Just An Online Minute . . . My Media, MySpace',
    Media Insider, 18 May 2006

24 Ibid.

25 Mark Sweeney, 'AOL to buy Bebo for $850m', www.guardian.
    co.uk/media/2008/mar/13/bebo.digitalmedia/print accessed 13
    March 2008

26 www.bebo.com/OpenMedia.jsp, accessed 14 March 2008

27 www.hollywoodreporter.com/hr/content_display/film/market
    ing/e3i771ec849d7b7f8a9168fbac90b2b8576

28 Chantelle Fiddy, 'Drama.com', *London Paper*, 25 June 2008, p.10

29 LeeAnn Prescott, 'Virtual worlds ranking — Runescape #1',
    Hitwise,   http://weblogs.hitwise.com/leeann-prescott/2007/
    04/virtual_worlds_ranking_runesca.html, accessed 7 September
    2007

30 Hitwise, June 2007, ranking of virtual worlds, and Parks
    Associates, advertising projection, both cited in Carly Shuler,
    D is for Digital, op. cit.

31 Vance Packard, *The Hidden Persuaders*, Pocket Books, New York,
    1957

32 Andrew Clark, 'Facebook apologises for mistakes over adver-
    tising', *Guardian*, 6 December 2007

33 *Media Post's Marketing Daily*, 7 November 2007

34 www.nydailynews.com/money/2008/03/06/2008-03-
    06_facebook_founder_on_elite_list.html, accessed 13 March 2008

35 www.comscore.com/blog/2007/05/younger_consumers
    _receptive_to.html, accessed 25 May 2007

36 '4.5 million young Brits' futures could be compromised by
    their electronic footprint', Information Commissioner's Office,
    press release, 23 November 2007

37 Ibid.

Chapter 7

1   Catherine Lumby and Duncan Fine, *Why TV is Good for Kids*,
    Macmillan, Sydney, 2006

2   Karen Sternheimer, 'It's not the media: the truth about pop
    culture's influence on children', Westview Press, Boulder,
    Colorado, 2003

3   D Kunkel, BL Wilcox, J Cantor, E Palmer, S Linn, P Dowrick,
    'American Psychological Association (2004) Report of the APA
    Task Force on Advertising and Children'. Section: Psychological
    issues in the increasing commercialization of childhood

4   Jean Piaget, *General Problems of the Psychological Development
    of the Child, in Discussions on Child Development: Proceedings of
    the World Health Organisation Study Group on Psychological
    Development of the Child IV*, Edited by JM Tanner and B Elders,
    NY International Universities Press, New York, 1960

5   RL Selman, *The Growth of Interpersonal Understanding*, Academic
    Press, New York, 1980

6   Deborah Roedder John, 'Consumer Socialization of Children: A Retrospective Look at Twenty-Five Years of Research', *Journal of Consumer Research*, 26, 1999, pp. 183–213

7   Deborah Roedder John, 'Age differences in children's responses to television advertising: An information-processing approach', *Journal of Consumer Research*, 8, 1981, pp. 144–53

8   M Brucks, GM Armstrong and ME Goldberg, 'Children's Uses of Cognitive Defenses against Television Advertising: A Cognitive Response Approach', *Journal of Consumer Research*, 14 March 1988, pp. 471–82

9   LJ Moses and DA Baldwin, 'What Can the Study of Cognitive Development Reveal About Children's Ability to Appreciate and Cope with Advertising?', *Journal of Public Policy and Marketing*, 24(2), 2005, pp. 186–201

10 S Livingstone and EJ Helsper, 'Does advertising literacy mediate the effects of advertising on children? A critical examination of two linked research literatures in relation to obesity and food choice', *Journal of Communication*, 56, 2006, pp. 560–84

11 Jonathan Haidt, *The Happiness Hypothesis*, Basic Books, New York, 2006

12 Paul Feldwick, 'What is brand equity anyway?', WARC, Henley-on-Thames, 2002

13 Kevin Lane Keller and D Lehmann, 'How do brands create value?', *Marketing Management*, July/August 2003, p.28

14 Victoria Mallinckrodt and Dick Mizerski, 'The Effects of Playing an Advergame on Young Children's Perceptions, Preferences and Requests', *Journal of Advertising*, Vol 36, No 2, Summer 2007

15 Susan Auty and Charlie Lewis, 'Exploring Children's Choice:

The Reminder Effect of Product Placements', *Psychology and Marketing*, Vol 21, No 9, September 2004

16 See for example: Robert Heath and Agnes Nairn, 'Measuring Affective Advertising: Implications of Low Attention Processing on Recall', *Journal of Advertising Research*, Vol 45, No 2, pp. 269–81; Robert Heath, David Brandt, Agnes Nairn, 'Brand Relationships: Strengthened by Emotion, Weakened by Attention', *Journal of Advertising Research*, Vol 46, No 4, 2006; Agnes Nairn and Pierre Berthon, 'Affecting Adolescence: Scrutinizing the Link between Segmentation and Advertising', *Business and Society*, Vol 44, No 3, September 2003, pp. 318–45; Agnes Nairn and Pierre Berthon, 'Creating the Consumer: The Influence of Advertising on Consumer Market Segments – Evidence and Ethics', *Journal of Business Ethics*, Vol 42, No 1, January 2005, pp. 83–99

17 Agnes Nairn and Cordelia Fine, 'Who's Messing with My Mind?, The Implications of Dual Process Models for the Ethics of Advertising to Children', *International Journal of Advertising*. Special Issue on Brain Sciences, August, 2009

18 Much of this work stems from pioneering work by leading figures such as Daniel Schachter, Professor of Psychology at Harvard University (see, for example, *Searching for Memory*, Basic Books, New York, 1996); Antonio Damasio, Professor of Neuroscience at University of Southern California (see, for example, *Descartes Error: Emotion, Reason and the Human Brain*, Putnam, New York, 1994 and *The Feeling of What Happens: Body and Emotion in the Making of Consciousness*, Heinemann, London, 1999)

19 S Dal Cin, B Gibson, MP Zanna, R Shumate, GT Fong,

'Smoking in movies, implicit associations of smoking with the self, and intentions to smoke', *Psychological Science*, Vol 18, No 7, pp. 559–63

20 KC Berridge and P Winkielman, 'What is an unconscious emotion: The case for unconscious "liking"', *Cognition and Emotion*, 17, 2003, pp. 181–211

21 J Bargh, 'Losing Consciousness: Automatic influences on consumer judgment, behavior, and motivation', *Journal of Consumer Research*, 29, 2002, pp. 280–85

22 MR Forehand and A Perkins, 'Implicit Assimilation and Explicit Contrast: A set/reset model of response to celebrity voice-overs', *Journal of Consumer Research*, 32, 2005, pp 435–44

23 M Perugini, 'Predictive models of implicit and explicit attitudes', *British Journal of Social Psychology*, Vol 44, No 1, 2005, pp. 29–45; B Shiv and A Fedorikhin, 'Spontaneous versus controlled influences of stimulus-based effect on choice behaviour', *Organizational Behavior and Human Decision Processes*, Vol 87, No 2, 2002, pp. 342–70

24 M Friese, M Wänke, H Plessner, 'Implicit consumer preferences and their influence on product choice', *Psychology & Marketing*, 23, 2006, pp. 727–40

25 L Olsen, 'Children and dangerous advertising', Proceedings of Child and Teen Consumption Conference, Trondheim, 24–25 April 2008

26 David Derbyshire, 'The average age for a child to have a first mobile is now 8', *Daily Telegraph*, 20 April 2005, www.telegraph. co.uk/news/main.jhtml?xml=/news/2005/04/20/nmob20.xm l&sSheet=/news/2005/04/20/ixhome.html, accessed 2 March 2008

27 Westminster Diet and Health Forum, Food Promotion to Children, London, July 2006

28 ChildWise, op. cit.

29 In part, this is due also to the vigilance and efforts of charities such as NCH, the Children's Charities' Coalition for Internet Safety and ChildWise. However, the industry does have more to do. The commitments of mobile phone companies are not systematically brought together into a consumer code nor openly reviewed on a regular basis and they apply very different rules on marketing to children from country to country, even within the EU

30 A Furnham, 'Children and advertising: Politics and research in consumer socialization', in *Children: Consumption, advertising and media*, (Ed.) F Hansen, J Rasmusser, A Martensen, B Tufte, Samfundslitteratur Press, Fredericksberg, Denmark, 2002, pp. 125–48

31 C Oates, M Blades, B Gunter, 'Children and television advertising: When do they understand persuasive intent?', *Journal of Consumer Behaviour*, Vol 1, No 3, 2001, pp. 238–45

32 David Buckingham, *After the Death of Childhood*, op. cit.

33 See Stephanie O'Donohoe and Agnes Nairn, 'Inoculation or Indoctrination? An ideological perspective on children's media literacy websites', Child and Teen Consumption Conference, Trondheim, Norway, April 2008

34 www.mediasmart.org.uk, accessed 13 June 2008

35 www.cca-kids.ca, accessed 13 June 2008

36 L Eagle, 'Commercial Media Literacy: What Does it Do, to Whom – and Does it Matter?', *Journal of Advertising*, Summer 2007, pp. 101–110

37 T O'Sullivan, 'Get MediaSmart®: A critical discourse analysis of controversy around advertising to children in the UK', *Consumption, Markets and Culture*, Vol 10, No 3, September 2007, pp. 293–314

38 http://chewonthis.org.uk, accessed 13 June 2008

39 For example, the government approach to media literacy needs to be better resourced and more joined up. Curriculum for the classroom must do more than simply providing information about how the advertising industry operates. It must specifically educate children (and their parents) about advertising formats which can persuade without them even noticing. Media literacy programmes should educate our children about the non-conscious routes by which advertising can affect consumer preferences and behaviour. More widely, there is a case for bringing together, inside and outside of schools, a more coherent approach to consumer skills

40 L Steinberg, 'Risk taking in adolescence: What changes, and why?', *Annals of New York Academy of Sciences*, 1021, 2004, pp. 51–8; L Steinberg, 'A social neuroscience perspective on adolescent risk-taking', *Developmental Review*, 28, 2008, pp. 78–106; L Steinberg, 'Risk taking in adolescence: New perspectives from brain and behavioral science', *Current Directions in Psychological Science*, Vol 16, No 2, 2007, pp. 55–9

41 One proposal, for example, to help such a debate is the call by the Family and Parenting Institute for companies to find ways to disclose what they spend on marketing to children

42 KD Martin and NC Smith, 'Commercialising Social Interaction: The Ethics of Stealth Marketing', *Journal of Public Policy and Marketing*, Vol 27, No 1, 2008, pp. 45–56

43 Once the overhaul is done, we believe that there needs to be a far more energetic and inclusive process for updating and internationalizing codes – not least for internet marketing which will have spawned yet more unrestricted tactics and techniques by the time this book is in print

44 R Reeves, *Reality in Advertising*, Knopf, New York, 1961

45 Dan Acuff, 'Taking the guesswork out of responsible marketing', *Young Consumers*, 3, 2004

Chapter 8

1 Short form of the Self-esteem Scale in Morris Rosenberg, *Society and the Adolescent Self-Image*, Princeton University Press, Princeton, 1965

2 Marvin Goldberg, Gerald Gorn, Laura Peracchio and Gary Bamossy 'Understanding Materialism among Youth,' *Journal of Consumer Psychology*, no 13, 2003, pp. 278–288

3 Agnes Nairn, Jo Ormrod, Paul Bottomley, 2007, op. cit.

4 Ibid.

5 Moniek Buijzen and Patti Valkenburg, 'The effects of television advertising on materialism, parent-child conflict and unhappiness: a review of research', *Applied Developmental Psychology*, No 24, 2003, pp. 437–56

6 Statistics taken from the Mind website, www.mind.org.uk, accessed 20 May 2005

7 NHS figures quoted in Jo Revill and John Lawless, 'Child suicide bids rise to 4,000', *Guardian*, 6 December 2007

8 www.mentalhealth.org.uk, accessed 20 May 2005

9 www.childline.org.uk, accessed 8 January 2008

10 www.bmrb-tgi.co.uk/main.asp?p=389&finfo=381&r=9734.24, accessed 18 September 2007

11 Stephan Collishaw, Barbara Maughan, Robert Goodman, Andrew Pickles, 'Time trend in adolescent mental health', *Journal of Child Psychology and Psychiatry*, Vol 45, No 8, 2004, pp. 1350–62

12 Philip Graham, 'Mental Health, Consumerism and a Good Childhood', Good Childhood Enquiry, October 2007

13 Richard Layard, *Happiness: Lessons from a New Science*, Penguin Books, London, 2005

14 Ibid., p.19

15 This has not always seemed to be the case. In 1976 the eminent child psychiatrist Professor Michael Rutter noted, 'In children, the associations between social class and mental disorder are variable and inconsistent . . . it seems very probably that social class as such is not very important in the genesis of child psychiatric disorders.' Michael Rutter and Nicola Madge, *Cycles of Disadvantage*, Heinemann, London, 1976

16 BBC *Today Programme*, 18 September 2007

17 Agnes Nairn, Jo Ormrod, Paul Bottomley, op. cit.

18 Ibid.

19 Jon Ronson, 'You've Got Mail!', *Guardian*, 10 February 2007

20 Corey Keyes, 'The Mental Health Continuum from Languishing to Flourishing in Life', *Journal of Health and Social Behaviour*, 43, pp. 207–22; Corey Keyes, 'Mental Health in Adolescence: Is America's Youth Flourishing?', *American Journal of Orthopsychiatry*, Vol 76, No 3, pp. 395–402

21 Tim Kasser, *The High Price of Materialism*, MIT Press, Cambridge, 2005

22 Liam also said, 'Good luck with writing your book!'

23 Quoted in Laura Barton, 'Girls, boys, gangs, drink, exams, sex, clubs, drugs, texting . . .', *Guardian*, 16 March 2005

24 Teenage girls 'depressed by modern life', www2.netdoctor. co.uk/news/index.asp?id=117900&D=24&M=2&Y=2005 and http: //news.bbc.co.uk/1/hi/health/4147961.stm, both accessed 18 May 2005

25 Hayley K Dohnt, Marika Tiggemann, 'Peer influences on body dissatisfaction and dieting awareness in young girls', *British Journal of Developmental Psychology*, Vol 23, No 1, March 2005, pp. 103–116

26 Ed Mayo, op. cit.

27 *Brave New Economy*, New Economics Foundation, London, 1999

28 Thich Nhat Hanh, *The Heart of the Buddha's Teaching: Transforming suffering into peace, joy and liberation*, Rider, London, 1998, pp. 32–3

Chapter 9

1 www.young-enterprise.org.uk, accessed 5 December 2007

2 David Vise, *The Google Story*, Bantam Dell, New York, 2005

3 www.comscore.com, accessed 13 June 2008

4 John Naughton, 'Blocking ads can be fun – and also downright dangerous', *Observer*, 23 September 2007

5 'Children want to be self-employed', 14 March 2006, www.easier. com/view/News/Business/article-43210.html, accessed 20 December 2007

6 'Department for Children, Families and Schools, Young People and Enterprise, Survey of Attitudes', Research Study Conducted for Howard Davies Review Team http://www.dfes.gov.uk/ ebnet/download/AnnexB2.pdf, accessed 7 January 2008

7   John Higginson, 'School ban on boy's grub-dealing empire', *Metro*, 4 July 2006, p.13

Chapter 10

1   www.prweb.com/releases/whyville/virtual/prweb536018.htm, accessed 15 July 2007

2   Cited in *Persuader*, p.21, date uncertain; see also Kate Fox, *Coming of age in the eBay generation: life-shopping and the new life skills in the age of eBay*, Social Issues Research Centre, Oxford, 2005, www.sirc.org/publik/Yeppies.pdf, accessed 27 November 2007

3   Christine Farmer, Office for National Statistics, '2003 Home Office Citizenship Survey: Top-level findings from the Children's and Young People's Survey', www.communities.gov.uk/documents/communities/pdf/452490, accessed 22 November 2007

4   *On the Right Track: what matters to young people in the UK?*, Save the Children, London, 2004

5   'Make Space Youth Review', op. cit.

6   Ibid.

7   University of Glasgow, Faculty of Education, 'Evaluation of the Children's Parliament', February 2007, www.childrensparliament.org.uk/assets/cpevaluation.pdf, accessed 14 May 2007

8   *On the Right Track*, op. cit.

9   'Young Fairtraders from UK and Ghana present "Chocolate Challenge" to International Development Secretary', Department for International Development press release, 13 June 2006

10 www.dubbleagents.org/community/missions/entries.php, accessed 27 November 2007

11 *The Comic Relief Fair Trade Chocolate Education Project, Key Stage 2 & 3 Pupils Questionnaire Report*, Educational Communications, London, 1999

12 'Pupils go to India for TV challenge', *Oxford Mail*, 22 October 2007, www.oxfordmail.net/search/display.var.1778001.0.pupils_go_to_india_for_tv_challenge.php, accessed 28 November 2007

13 Helen Haste, 'My Voice, My Community: a study of young people's civic action and inaction', Nestlé Social Research Programme, report no 4, 2005

14 www.mcfly2015.com, accessed 27 November 2007

15 www.youthnoise.com, accessed 27 November 2007

16 www.ukyp.org.uk/faresfair, accessed 27 November 2007

17 http://catthu.tigblog.org/post/203577?setlangcookie=true, accessed 27 November 2007

18 Christine Farmer, op. cit.

19 Ibid.

20 Shelley Pasnik, op. cit.

21 'BMRB/Mintel, Special Report, Marketing to Children Aged 7–10, 2001/2002', Youth TGI

22 'Climate change "worries children"', BBC News, 23 June 2005 http://news.bbc.co.uk/1/hi/education/4123884.stm, accessed 28 November 2007

23 'The Primary Review, Community Soundings: the Primary Review regional witness sessions', www.primaryreview.org.uk/ Publications/Interimreports.html, accessed 28 November 2007

24 '11–17-year-olds, Attitudes to Climate Change: youth sample', Department for Environment, Food and Rural Affairs, 2006

25 www.greenpeace.org.uk/blog/toxics/gaming-giants-fail-toxic-exam-20071128, accessed 8 January 2008

26 http://ecochildsplay.com/2007/10/18/empowering-children-my-daughters-letter-to-disney/, accessed 5 January 2008

27 Helen Haste, op. cit.

28 *On the Right Track*, op. cit.

29 NM Wells and KS Lekies, 'Nature and the life course: pathways from childhood nature experiences to adult environmentalism', *Children, Youth and Environments*, 16, 2006, pp. 1–24, cited in N Steuer, S Thompson and N Marks, *Review of the environmental dimension of children and young people's well-being*, New Economics Foundation, London, 2006

30 *On the Right Track*, op. cit.

31 Helen Haste, op. cit.

Chapter 11

1 Agnes Nairn and Jon Mattias, op. cit.

2 According to the Halifax, 79 per cent of children receive regular pocket money from their mums and dads (in 2005, they estimated it was higher than this, at 85 per cent): 'Children In London Are 2006's Pocket Money Winners', 'Halifax Pocket Money Survey 2007'. Surveys for an older age range, of 10 to 15, suggest that up to 90 per cent receive pocket money: John Balding, *Young People into 2007*, op. cit. Other research points to similar figures – such as 84 per cent 11 to 14-year-olds receiving pocket money or an allowance, in Russell Budden, 'The guide to 11 to 14-year-olds', *Media Week*, 6 October 2004. The ChildWise 2007 survey estimated that 69 per cent of 5 to 16-year-olds received pocket money

3 Liverpool Victoria, Cost of a Child survey, www.lv.com /media_centre/press_releases/cost, accessed 5 October 2007

4 Agnes Nairn and Jon Mattias, op. cit.

5 'Children In London Are 2006's Pocket Money Winners', 'Halifax Pocket Money Survey 2007', www.hbosplc.com /media/includes/15_ per cent2004_ per cent2006_ per cent20 Pocket_ per cent20Money_ per cent20Survey_ per cent202006 per cent20_ per cent20National.doc, accessed 19 July 2007

6 16–24- year-olds, Barclays, cited in *Helping Young Adults Make Sense of Money: findings and recommendations on financial capability from the Young Adults Working Group*, Financial Authority, March 2006, London

7 www.mortgagestrategy.co.uk/cgi-bin/item.cgi?id= 156189&d=4 04&h=401&f=402, accessed 6 February 2008

8 'Money Taboos Hit Home', www.dfes.gov.uk/pns/Display PN.cgi?pn_id=2007_0053, accessed 14 May 2007

9 'Teen Cash Class. What you didn't see', 30 July 2007, http://blog.moneysavingexpert.com/2007/07/30/teen-cash-class-what-you-didn per centE2 per cent80 per cent99t-see/ and www.moneysavingexpert.com/attachment/teen_cash_guide .pdf, both accessed 20 November 2007

10 Andy Croft, 'Turning Money into Poetry', personal correspondence, 2 January 2008. This project was written up for the charity, the Personal Finance Education Group

11 Ibid.

12 Personal Finance Education Group Annual Report 2007, London

13 Nathan Dungan, *Prodigal Sons and Material Girls: How Not to Be Your Child's ATM*, Wiley, Chichester, 2003. The section below draws extensively on Dungan's suggestions.

14 Russell Budden, 'Small change – income size and source of 12–14-year-olds', *Financial Marketing*, 15 April 2005

15 'Are you a shopaholic?', CBBC, 29 November 2004, http://news.bbc.co.uk/go/pr/fr/- /cbbcnews/hi/newsid_404 0000/ newsid_4045400/4045427.stm, accessed 18 March 2005

16 Adele Atkinson, Stephen McKay, Elaine Kempson, Sharon Collard, 'Levels of Financial Capability in the UK: Results of a baseline survey', *Financial Services Authority, Consumer Research* 47, 2006, prepared by the Personal Finance Research Centre, University of Bristol

17 Jane Croft, 'Abbey "sorry" for baby loan blunder', *Financial Times*, http://news.ft.com/cms/s/6ec8a97e-92c8-11da-a8ff-0000779e2340.html, accessed 10 February 2006

18 Adele Atkinson, Stephen McKay, Elaine Kempson, Sharon Collard, op. cit.

19 For more information, see www.neweconomics.org

20 Geoff Mulgan, 'Learning to Serve', Learning Skills and Development Agency Annual Lecture, 2006

21 Philip Graham, *The End of Adolescence*, Oxford University Press, Oxford, 2004

22 Edge Foundation, cited in Geoff Mulgan, op. cit.

23 This is close to a vision of education long championed by the Royal Society of Arts (RSA), which in its 1985 report Education for Capability argued that 'a well-balanced education should, of course, embrace analysis and acquisition of knowledge. But it must also include the exercise of creative skills, the competence to undertake and complete tasks and the ability to cope with everyday life; and also doing all of these things in co-operation with others.' However, in his

review of progress 20 years later, the RSA's project champion Professor Sir Graham Hills concluded that little had been achieved to move closer to this ideal. Sir Graham Hills, 'In from the Cold – the rise of vocational education', *RSA Journal*, November 2004, pp. 22–5

24 See www.youngfoundation.org.uk/work/local_innovation/ consortiums/wellbeing/emotional_resilience, accessed 21 November 2007. Other experiments in the UK in relation to building social and interpersonal skills in the course of education include the RSA's Opening Minds programme, the Prince's Trust Excel Programme for 14–16- year-olds and SEAL (Social and Emotional Aspects of Learning)

Chapter 12

1 We owe this suggestion to Rod Parker-Rees, co-editor of *Early Years*, the international journal of research and development.

2 Ray Kurzweil, *The Singularity is Near: When Humans Transcend Biology*, Duckworth, London, 2006

3 See, in particular, Yochai Benkler, *The Wealth of Networks: How Social Production Transforms Markets and Freedom*, Yale University Press, Yale, 2006

4 Jez Frampton, Group Chief Executive, Interbrand. Conversation at National Consumer Council, 6 September 2007

Index

Lightning Source UK Ltd.
Milton Keynes UK
UKOW03f1802200314

228540UK00001B/1/P